DERRIDA AND THE WRITING OF THE BODY

For Melissa

Derrida and the Writing of the Body

JONES IRWIN
St. Patrick's College, Dublin City University, Ireland

LONDON AND NEW YORK

First published 2010 by Ashgate Publishing

Published 2016 by Routledge
2 Park Square, Milton Park, Abingdon, Oxfordshire OX14 4RN
711 Third Avenue, New York, NY 10017, USA

First issued in paperback 2016

Routledge is an imprint of the Taylor & Francis Group, an informa business

British Library Cataloguing in Publication Data
Irwin, Jones.
    Derrida and the writing of the body.
    1. Derrida, Jacques. 2. Deconstruction. 3. Literature--
    Philosophy.
    I. Title
    194-dc22

Library of Congress Cataloging-in-Publication Data
Irwin, Jones.
    Derrida and the writing of the body / by Jones Irwin.
        p. cm.
    Includes bibliographical references and index.
    ISBN 978-0-7546-7865-6 (hardback)
        1. Derrida, Jacques. 2. Derrida, Jacques. Icriture et la diffirence. I. Title.

    B2430.D484I57 2010
    194--dc22
                                                                    2010005636

    ISBN 13: 978-1-138-27857-8 (pbk)
    ISBN 13: 978-0-7546-7865-6 (hbk)

Contents

Acknowledgements

A Staff Research Fellowship in the academic year 2008–2009 from St. Patrick's College, Drumcondra, made the writing of this book possible. At St. Pat's, I am lucky to have a supportive and inspiring set of colleagues and friends and I would especially like to thank Andrew O'Shea, Joe Dunne, Maeve O'Brien, Eileen Brennan, Ann Louise Gilligan, Philomena Donnelly, Paula Murphy, Therese Dooley, Ben-Staunton Collins, Deirdre Pearson, Margaruete Kirwan, Mark Morgan and Mary Shine-Thompson. At the previous Philosophy departments where I have taught and studied, I would like to thank the late Fr. Fergal O'Connor, Richard Kearney, Tim Mooney, Mark Dooley and Brendan Purcell at UCD, Martin Warner, Angie Hobbs, Miguel de Beistegui, Stephen Houlgate, Keith Ansell-Pearson, Peter Poellner and Lynda Hemsley at Warwick and Stephen Thornton, John Hayes, David Blake, John Eustace and Roland Tormey at MIC, Limerick. A Visiting Fellowship to the Centre for Philosophy, Literature and the Arts, at the University of Warwick, has been a spur to engage with the most recent Continentalist work, Helena Motoh in Ljubljana and Laima Pačekajutė in Vilnius University made my trips there productive and enjoyable and Rob Fisher generously helped me to get started on the publishing and conference front with ID.Net.

I would also like to thank Ashgate for their support and especially my editor Neil Jordan for patience and insight and Sarah Wardill for editorial help. Deena Des Rioux has been very generous to me in relation to the employment of her work and I look forward to working together on future projects. I would also like to thank Malahide library staff for their help during my work there and Asta Vilkaite for keeping me sane with the chai lattes. Finally, I would like to pay respects to the late Jacques Derrida himself. I first encountered his work as an undergraduate and, although my passion for his work has ebbed and flowed through the years, I am constantly brought back to his immense brilliance as a philosopher and writer.

I have acknowledgments to make to Rodopi publishers in terms of permission to publish from three previous essays of mine. Parts of Chapter 1 have been developed from 'Philosophy as a Theatre of Cruelty: Making Derrida Perform Through Artaud', in *Ethical Encounters: Boundaries of Theatre, Performance and Philosophy*, edited by Daniel Watt and Daniel Meyer-Dinkgrafe (Rodopi, 2010), parts of Chapter 3 have developed from 'Deconstructing God: Defending Derrida Against Radical Orthodoxy', in *Exploring Contemporary Continental Philosophy of Religion*, edited by Peter-Deane Baker and Patrick Maxwell (Rodopi, 2004) and I have developed elements of Chapter 7 from my 'Diogenes, St. Paul, Habermas and Beyond – Derrida on Cosmopolitanism', in *Interculturalism: Between Culture and Politics*, edited by Jones Irwin and Nancy Billias (Rodopi, 2010).

Throughout the writing of this book, my family have been a source of joy and sustenance. Eloïse, Jeremy and Gregory have been fantastic kids and will be delighted to know that Daddy's book is finally finished! I would also like to thank my parents, Leslie and Úna, and sister Judy, and Patrick, Mary and Zoë in Spain, for all their support and kindness. I dedicate this book to Melissa, for being such a wonderful person to share my life with.

Jones Irwin
Dublin
November 2009

Introduction

Opening

'In every reading', Derrida tells us, 'there is a *corps-à-corps* between reader and text' (Derrida 1986c: 126). *Corps-à-corps*, body to body, is not a notion which one readily associates with the work of Jacques Derrida. As he is the first to admit, it is rather as an 'arid intellectualism' (Derrida 1986c: 126) that deconstruction is often pictured, at least by its opponents. Before his eventual *rapprochement* with Derrida, this is the vision which Jürgen Habermas influentially portrays of deconstruction (Habermas 1990): as idealist, self-indulgent and apolitical. While this view of Derrida undoubtedly represents an extreme perspective within the discourse surrounding his work, it is undeniable that even more moderate viewpoints often contain a residual element from this picture. That is, we can say, deconstruction is widely perceived as having little or nothing to say about embodiment, existence, desire, politics or sexuality.

Against these manifest appearances, I will argue for an understanding of Derrida's work which connects it powerfully to the very themes which many commentators wish to deny to it, precisely such themes as embodiment, existence, desire, politics or sexuality. As always with Derrida, the consideration of these themes is nuanced and patient in his work, but close reading of his texts demonstrates the significance of this trajectory from his early work onwards. Here, my guiding notion will be a Derridean 'writing of the body' ('l'écriture du corps', Derrida 1967h: 287) as an exploratory theme for looking at deconstruction. I will trace this conception of a 'writing of the body' successively through Derrida's readings of the work of the *avant-garde*,[1] most notably of Antonin Artaud (where

---

1   I will employ the term 'avant-garde', throughout this book, as what I consider to be the most appropriate collective noun for the disparate group of intellectual and artistic figures who populate Derrida's texts: Artaud, Bataille, Mallarmé, Klossowski, Leiris, etc. This term, first, allows me to distinguish these latter thinkers from more mainstream philosophical movements and corresponds, more or less, to their own self-understanding. Second, it foregrounds their allegiance (and Derrida's) to specific art movements, most especially surrealism. Derrida's relation to surrealism is not as readily apparent in comparison with the other figures and his own early preoccupation with philosophical and phenomenological meaning (via Husserl) distinguishes his work from theirs. Nonetheless, as we shall see, despite the disaffinities, there is also a surprising level of affinity and congruence, which Derrida brings out powerfully in his interpretations of their work. Third, it highlights a certain 'revolutionary' or subversive tendency within the work of this collective group. Although I make clear that I do not wish to reduce Derrida's oeuvre to *avant-gardism*, I am

a 'l'écriture du corps' first emerges) and Georges Bataille, through to his staging of an extraordinary encounter between Stephane Mallarmé and Plato, through to his readings of Nietzsche, feminism and political philosophy. In each instance, I will be seeking to draw out a rather different understanding of deconstruction from the one we are used to, a Derrida who has much to tell us about life, embodiment, desire and sexuality. To re-deploy a phrase of Herman Rapaport (Rapaport 2002), we might say that Derrida is 'an existentialist of a different feather'.

Re-reading Derrida

It is clear from even Derrida's earliest texts on phenomenology that the intellectual influences on his work differ from what one might have expected. James Joyce, for example, appears rather unpredictably in Derrida's *Introduction à l'Origine de la Géométrie par Edmund Husserl* [hereafter *Introduction to Husserl's Origin of Geometry*],[2] published in 1962 (Derrida 1962/1989), but even in 1959 in his first published essay 'Genèse et Structure et la Phénoménologie' [hereafter 'Genesis and Structure and Phenomenology'] (Derrida 1967g/1978e), the introduction of the concepts of 'non-meaning' and 'death' strike a rather discordant note, and suggest a rather idiosyncratic framework. By 1963 and the publication of 'Force et Signification' [hereafter 'Force and Signification'] (Derrida 1967d/1978b), this subtext is becoming more explicit. Derrida's topic is 'literature', most especially interpretations of Stéphane Mallarmé's poetry (Mallarmé 2008), but he is now already invoking Maurice Blanchot (Blanchot 1997).

Throughout the next ten to fifteen years, Derrida will write a large proportion of his work around *avant-garde* themes or figures. Two essays on Artaud (Derrida 1967h/1967j), one on Bataille (Derrida 1967k), two essays on Jabès (Derrida 1967e/1967m), an essay on Leiris (Derrida 1972c), on Sollers (Derrida 1972l), on Mallarmé (Derrida 1972k) again, an essay on Valéry (Derrida 1972g), a book on Ponge (Derrida 1988), another massive text shared between Hegel and Genet, entitled *Gla*s (Derrida 1974a), perhaps one of his most interesting texts of the

---

also, by implication, indicating a clear *avant-garde* dimension to Derrida's own writing. This helps us to better understand the specificity of his work, most particularly his writing 'style'. Rather than see such a 'style' as ancillary, the *avant-garde* connection enables us to see Derrida's writing method as integral to his meaning. It also exemplifies a 'subversive' dimension to Derrida's work which is often lost in commentaries which portray the style as merely a superficial adjunct.

2   In the case of each of Derrida's texts, I refer in the first instance to the French title and thereafter to the translated title. In general, when quoting from Derrida, although I quote from the English versions, I give page references to both the French and English editions and I also quote the French if this is especially revealing. In some cases, the works have only appeared in English (e.g. Derrida 1986c) or only in French (e.g. Derrida 2002). There are, additionally, bilingual editions of some Derrida texts (e.g. Derrida 1979). I also note issues of problematic translation, where pertinent, and I draw attention to modified translations in a minority of instances.

period, and considerable late 1970s into the 1980s work on Blanchot (Derrida 1986a). In the 1980s, Derrida also turns to the work of Baudelaire in the book *Donner le Temps* or *Given Time* (Derrida 1991a/1992d).

Perhaps even more significantly however, throughout Derrida's work on more mainstream philosophical authors such as Plato, Hegel and Kant, one notices insistent and important referencing of these former *avant-garde* writers and texts. Thus, in two of the most important essays of Derrida's work, 'La Différance' [hereafter 'Différance] (Derrida 1972d/1982c) and 'Les Fins de l'Homme' [hereafter 'The Ends of Man'] (Derrida 1972e/1982d), the work of Georges Bataille (Bataille 2001) is invoked at crucial junctures of the argument, and affirmed as against the more dialectical philosophical approach which Derrida is critiquing. In the early 1980s, in an interview with Richard Kearney (Derrida 1986c), Derrida goes as far as to suggest that what distinguishes his work in the final analysis from Heidegger's can most clearly be seen in the specifics of the authors Derrida foregrounds as opposed to those whom Heidegger foregrounds. That is, 'Bataille, Ponge and Blanchot as against Rilke, Hölderlin and Trakl' (Derrida 1986c: 110).

One of the most important sub-themes of this book will be Derrida's consistent engagement with *avant-garde* authors and how this work significantly affects the themes of his own work. In his important foreword to Gilles Deleuze and Felix Guattari's *Anti-Oedipus* (Deleuze and Guattari 2004), Michel Foucault (Foucault 2004) contextualises a specific explosion of French thinking, within which (alongside Deleuze and Guattari) we can also include Derrida's work of this period. Foucault observes, 'during the years 1945–1965 (I am referring to Europe), there was a certain way of thinking correctly, a certain style of political discourse, a certain ethics of the intellectual. One had to be on familiar terms with Marx, not let one's dreams stray too far from Freud' (Foucault 2004: xl). But then the revolution happened: 'then came the five brief, impassioned, jubilant, enigmatic years' (Foucault 2004: xl). On Foucault's terms then, we are speaking of 1965–1970. Certainly, in looking at Derrida's work, it is clear that these years are key. Much of the second part of *L'Écriture et la Différence* [hereafter *Writing and Difference*] (Derrida 1967c/1978a) *De la Grammatologie* [hereafter *Of Grammatology*] (Derrida 1967a/1974b), *La Voix et le Phénomène* [hereafter *Speech and Phenomena*] (Derrida 1967b/1973), and the early drafts of the texts in *Marges De La Philosophie* [hereafter *Margins of Philosophy*] (Derrida 1972b/1982a), *La Dissémination* [hereafter *Dissemination*] (Derrida 1972h/1981a) and *Positions* [in English also *Positions*] (Derrida 1972a/1981f) all date from this period. These 'impassioned, jubilant, enigmatic years' will be my main focus in this book with regard to Derrida's work, although I will also seek to contextualise their import for Derrida's work more generally. What Foucault has to say about the significant influences of these years also has relevance for my thematic in Derrida's work. Foucault traces the paradigmatic period of original influence here as that of the time 'between the First World War and fascism' (Foucault 2004: xll): 'the dream that cast its spell between the First World War and fascism, over the dreamiest parts of Europe – the Germany of Wilhelm Reich, and the France of the

Surrealists – had returned and set fire to reality itself: Marx and Freud in the same incandescent light' (Foucault 2004: xll). On my terms, we can see here the crucial positioning of 'dissident surrealist' figures such as Bataille and Artaud (Artaud 1968a), whom Foucault refers to in terms of the 'utopian project of the thirties' which has now been 'resumed on the scale of historical practice' (Foucault 2004: xll). For Foucault, *Anti-Oedipus* (Deleuze and Guattari 2004) can thus be pictured as 'an erotic art, a theoretical art, a political art' (Foucault 2004: xll). If Deleuze's project can be described in these terms, I want to claim in this book that so too can Derrida's, even if the detail of their respective approaches to philosophical problems is distinct and often conflictual (Derrida 2000).

Indeed, my major theme of a Derridean 'writing of the body' ('l'écriture du corps', Derrida 1967h: 287) derives precisely from Derrida's intense reading of the work of Antonin Artaud over two separate essays in *Writing and Difference* (Derrida 1967h/1967j). The reason I foreground Artaud is that his position in the reading of *Writing and Difference* is unique. He is one of only two thinkers (the other is Edmond Jabès) to have two essays devoted to his work in a collection of eleven essays. This is no doubt significant in itself. But, more importantly perhaps, Derrida's essays on Artaud are placed strategically in the middle of the volume and also within the second half of the book (essays 6 and 8 respectively). This is also not without significance. There has been a good deal of speculation as to the precise ordering of the *Writing and Difference* (1967c) collection, as well as its place within Derrida's work as a whole.

In his 'Translator's Introduction' to *Writing and Difference* (Bass 1978), Alan Bass refers to a discussion in Derrida's text *Positions* (Derrida 1972a) relating to this very question. There, Derrida had put forward several hypotheses regarding the chronology of his early work, and claimed that one reading would suggest that the last five essays of *Writing and Difference* practice what Derrida calls a 'grammatological opening' (quoted Bass 1978: x). This can be defined as 'the deconstruction of philosophy by examining the structured genealogy of all philosophy's concepts; and to do so in order to determine what issues the history of philosophy has repressed' (quoted Bass 1978: x). According to this interpretation, *Of Grammatology* (Derrida 1967a) would be best placed in the middle of *Writing and Difference* in terms of a reading interpretation, as setting the scene and the conditions for the 'grammatological opening' to follow. Within the structure of *Writing and Difference* itself this would also set up a bi-partition, between the first half and second half of the book. As Derrida notes, 'between the sixth and seventh essays, a theoretical matrix was elaborated whose principles are to some extent derived from the first six essays and are more systematically put to work in the last five' (quoted Bass 1978: xi).[3] Alan Bass also nuances this reading in a

---

3 The inter-relation between Derrida's early texts is a matter for significant conjecture. Derrida himself provides several (sometimes contradictory) readings, especially of the relation between *Writing and Difference* and *Of Grammatology*. Competing interpretations tend to view one or the other text as the key text for reading Derrida's subsequent evolution.

way which I would like to follow in this book. As Bass observes, 'I would like to propose another division of the book; a division between the fifth and sixth essay' (Bass 1978: xii) thus making 'La Parole Soufflée' (Derrida 1967h) the first of the new application of deconstruction, signalling Artaud's distinctive importance for the 'grammatological opening'. It should also be noted that it is Mallarmé who provides the epigraph to the volume, 'the whole without novelty except a spacing of reading' (Derrida 1967c), exemplifying how the *avant-garde* more generally plays such a powerful role in the development of Derrida's thinking from the mid-1960s onwards. As we will see, this is a significance and influence which remains insistent in Derrida's writings, right up until and including the final works. Thus, we can say that *Writing and Difference* (Derrida 1967c) remains a crucial but under-analysed aspect of his *oeuvre*. Its primary focus on figures of the French *avant-garde*, such as Antonin Artaud (Artaud 1968a) and Georges Bataille (Bataille 2001) is pivotal to an understanding of the relation between deconstruction and a 'writing of the body'.

It is not immediately clear how one is to understand the relationship between Derrida's deconstructive approach to philosophy and the other respective philosophical movements which both pre-date and serve as contemporaneous to Derrida's work. If one looks firstly at those earlier philosophical approaches, one sees in each case both affinities and disaffinities. Though Derrida shares in the critique of positivism which is undertaken by phenomenology, existentialism and structuralism, his work also offers significant criticism of each of these interpretive perspectives (Kearney 1986: 1ff.). For example, he makes his break with structuralism very clearly in the essay 'La Structure, le Signe et le Jeu dans le Discours des Sciences Humaines' [hereafter 'Structure, Sign and Play in the Discourse of the Human Sciences'] (Derrida 1967l). He is positively scathing concerning what he claims is Sartre's fundamental misinterpretation of Heidegger in 'The Ends of Man' (Derrida 1972e). The relationship between deconstruction and phenomenology is undoubtedly more complicated (and more positive) but, again, there is both a clear critique of phenomenology put forward in his early (1960s) texts on Husserl (e.g. Derrida 1962) and a move away from substantive discussion of Husserl from the early 1970s onwards. Nonetheless, as we shall see, Derrida's relationship to phenomenology remains especially important for what builds up to a specific paradigm-shift in Derrida's work, his invocation of the French *avant-garde* as a key philosophical resource from the late 1960s onwards. Tracing influences on Derrida's work is not without its problems, as indeed is the very attempt to present deconstruction as a unified philosophical system. As Derrida often reminds his readers, deconstruction is not a unified method of philosophy (Derrida 1986c).

For the most part, the emphasis has been on the latter text, *Of Grammatology*. In this book, I will focus on the former text, *Writing and Difference*, as setting much of the agenda for Derrida's work to follow.

In his dialogue with Richard Kearney, Derrida outlines how he has been seeking to develop a 'non-philosophical site' (Derrida 1986c: 108–9) from which to question philosophy. Is it this quest which has led Derrida to emphasise 'particularly the literary texts of Jabès, Bataille, Blanchot, Artaud and Mallarmé', asks Kearney? Derrida's answer is affirmative but also seeks to complicate the sense that there would be a strict literary identity of these texts, as distinct and separate from the philosophical canon:

> Certainly, but one must remember that even though these sites are non-philosophical they still belong to our Western culture and so are never totally free from the marks of philosophical language. In literature, for example, philosophical language is still present in some sense, but it produces and presents itself as alienated from itself, at a remove, at a distance; this distance provides the necessary free space from which to interrogate philosophy anew (Derrida 1986c: 108).

Crucially, Derrida goes on to say that it was his preoccupation with literary texts which enabled him to discern the 'problematic of writing' as one of the key factors in the deconstruction of metaphysics (Derrida 1986c: 108). This also leads Derrida to eschew the very categorisation or disciplinary identity of philosophy: 'I'm not happy with the term philosopher…I have attempted more and more systematically to find a non-site, or a non-philosophical site, from which to question philosophy' (Derrida 1986c: 108) Why did Derrida feel the necessity for such an approach? Although Derrida notes the formative importance of Husserl and Heidegger in his work, nonetheless he also makes clear his distance: 'but I never shared Husserl's pathos for and commitment to a phenomenology of presence' (Derrida 1986c: 109). Here, he also makes explicit mention of the more positive influence of Nietzsche's work: 'my discovery of the genealogical and genetic critique of Nietzsche and Freud also allowed me to take the step beyond phenomenology towards a more radical, non-philosophical questioning, while never renouncing the discipline and rigour of phenomenology' (Derrida 1986c: 109). This is a key sense of the paradigmatic change which takes place in Derrida's work in the mid to late 1960s.

Methodology

Peggy Kamuf, in her preface to *A Derrida Reader* (Kamuf 1991: xi) has foregrounded the importance of 'cutting' and 'grafting' in Derrida's work. She clarifies that she has 'employed no single principle but [has] grouped the sets of selections according each time to a loosely defined criterion' (Kamuf 1991: x). This discussion of criteria for the specific Derrida anthology has a wider significance for Derrida scholarship insofar as Kamuf tries to justify this approach in terms of Derrida's own 'repeated insistence on the partialness of any text':

a partialness that is not recuperable in some eventual whole or totality; moreover, the notions of cutting, grafting, piecing together – extracting – are everywhere in evidence in Derrida's texts, both as themes and as practices, until they are virtually co-extensive with the text he is always interrogating and performing (Kamuf 1991: xi).

Kamuf justifiably foregrounds Derrida's text *Glas* (Derrida 1974a) as significant here: '*Glas* may be read as a long reflection on cutting, which is always culpable, put into practice...ultimately, there is no final justification for his cutting or splicing' (Kamuf 1991: xi). Nonetheless, although there is no ahistorical final justification, the selection criteria are hardly arbitrary. Kamuf herself refers to the need to respect the evolution of Derrida's text from one period to the next: his work, she says, is 'always moving beyond itself and yet never leaving anything behind...the work advances by bringing its past along, it is necessary up to a point to respect its chronology' (Kamuf 1991: x). Another more recent interpretative text on Derrida, Herman Rapaport's *Later Derrida* (Rapaport 2002), while concentrating on a specific period, nonetheless disavows any attempt to be a definitive analysis of even that period of Derrida's work. 'In terms of discussion the so-called later Derrida, I make no attempt to be all-encompassing or definitive...because the fact is that Derrida has been working simultaneously on a large number of multiple fronts that are not only complex but in a state of strategic incompletion or suspension. He has published well over twenty books since 1990...' (Rapaport 2002: vii). So, this is certainly, on one level, a question of the sheer quantity of Derrida's texts. But it is also, more fundamentally, an issue in principle.

Like Kamuf and Rapaport, I will in this book respect the chronological development of Derrida's work. My focus will be most especially on Derrida's texts from 1965 onwards, or from essay five in *Writing and Difference* (Derrida 1967c) onwards. From here, I will focus on an extraordinarily productive period of Derrida's work, from 1965 to 1979 (but also the extension of this thematic into his 1980s, 1990s and last texts), where his emphasis on the *avant-garde* is very significant and telling. But as with Rapaport and Kamuf, my intention is not to reduce Derrida's work to *avant-gardism*, or to see such influence as definitive. Rather, like Kamuf, and indeed like Derrida himself, my analysis is unashamedly partial. Nonetheless, there are several good reasons for so focusing on the *avant-garde* relation to Derrida. In the first case, despite the extraordinary proliferation of texts on Derrida's work, there has been a relative neglect of his relation to *avant-garde* thinkers such as Artaud, Bataille and Mallarmé. Much of the recent secondary work seems to split into three main interpretive camps, two of which are positive and one negative. In the first case, there is the (positive) focus on Derrida's ethics and religious significance (Caputo 1997b). In the second case, there is the (positive) emphasis on Derrida's relation to phenomenology and Husserl (Lawlor 2002). Finally, there is the (negative) critique of Derrida as a rhetorician (as in Habermas 1990). Ironically, it is only in Habermas' text that any sustained analysis is given of the *avant-garde* (but only specifically in terms of

Bataille; there is no mention of Artaud, Mallarmé, Blanchot, etc.). Additionally, the reference to Bataille is almost exclusively negative.

It is in this context that an analysis of Derrida's relation to the *avant-garde* in positive terms, and which concentrates on the philosophical (as well as literary) implications of such a relation, can be said to offer a significantly original perspective on the relation between deconstruction and both those philosophies which pre-dated it and those which were contemporaneous with it. With regard to those philosophies which pre-date deconstruction, most significantly existentialism, we can say that the relationship with the *avant-garde* was always problematic. One paradigmatic example of this is the relation between Bataille and Sartre, which we will explore in Chapter 2. With regard to those philosophies which are contemporary with deconstruction, the matter is even more clearcut. Deleuze (Deleuze and Guattari 2004), Foucault (Foucault 2004) and Lyotard (Lyotard 2004) all cite the key influence of the *avant-garde*, as do specific feminist thinkers such as Kristeva (Kristeva 1984), and it can also be argued that the specific theme of a 'writing of the body' is especially important across these relationships, that it is constitutive for these thought-systems.

Development

In this book, I will thus foreground a dimension of Derrida's work which has been relatively neglected: the *avant-garde* emphasis in his early work which, I will argue, represents a kind of paradigm-shift away from phenomenology. Moreover, I will also make the case that although this is not a definitive statement about Derrida's work, that it does help us to understand certain emphases which become prominent in Derrida's work in the late 1960s and 1970s. I will use the conception of a 'writing of the body' ('l'écriture du corps', Derrida 1967h: 287) as an exploratory theme for looking at deconstruction.

The book will trace a complex movement from Derrida's early texts in *Writing and Difference* (Derrida 1967c) which focused on *avant-garde* figures (and thus moved away from the more traditional concerns of Derrida's very early texts on phenomenology). It will also look at how one might, following certain clues which are given by Derrida himself, piece together how the various early texts might be grouped together. Thus following the aforementioned hypothesis that *Writing and Difference* can be divided in two with *Of Grammatology* in between (Derrida 1972a, Bass 1978), one can see how the last five essays of *Writing and Difference* practice what Derrida has called a 'grammatological opening', beginning with an essay on Artaud. I will argue that the focus on *avant-garde* figures in these transitional texts of Derrida's is not coincidental. Thus, Chapter 1 ('Derrida, Artaud's *Theatre of Cruelty* and a 'Writing of the Body') will look at how Derrida's reading of Artaud's *Theatre of Cruelty* can already allow us to foreground a thematic of embodiment (the 'proper body') which was central to surrealism and which Artaud takes up in his own idiosyncratic way (as a 'dissident surrealist'). In Chapter 2 ('"Except for a Certain Laughter": Derrida, Bataille and the Transgression of Dialectic'), I look at how this *avant-garde* relation is developed in another of the essays practicing the 'grammatological opening' in *Writing and Difference*, Derrida's essay on Bataille, 'De L'Économie Restreinte à L'Économie Générale: Un Hegelianisme Sans Réserve' [hereafter 'From Restricted to General Economy: A Hegelianism Without Reserve'] (Derrida 1967k/1978i). This essay is especially significant insofar as, here, Derrida foregrounds the relation between Bataille (Bataille 2001) and Hegelianism. This relationship to Hegel is not the aspect of Bataille's work one might foreground most readily. Nonetheless, Derrida shows Bataille to be a careful and skilled reader of Hegel (Hegel 1979). Again we are faced with a dialectic of embodiment, in the initial case, the dialectic of desire in Hegel. But this is a desire which is consummated and fulfilled in an overarching synthesis. In contrast to this, and against Alexandre Kojève's (Kojève 1980) reading of Hegel (although nonetheless influenced by it), Bataille takes up a position which posits an 'accursed share' in desire, an inability for desire to reach fulfilment (Bataille 2001). Both Bataille and Artaud can be seen as crucial in influencing Derrida to develop a notion of *différance* (Derrida 1972d) which emphasises deferral and delay and refuses the Hegelian synthesis. This is truly a deconstruction of the body and desire – a 'l'écriture du corps' (Derrida 1967h: 287).

In the next two chapters, I look at the way this problematic develops in Derrida's work after *Writing and Difference* (Derrida 1967c), concentrating especially on that book which is a not a book, *Dissemination* (Derrida 1972h). There, I look firstly at Derrida's essay on Platonism, 'La Pharmacie de Platon' [hereafter 'Plato's Pharmacy'] (Derrida 1972j/1981c), at how Derrida complicates the traditional position of Platonism *vis-à-vis* the Sophistic movement. In a provocative essay, Derrida gives the lie to those who would present him as simply offering a critique of speech-centred, 'phonocentrism' in the name of some writing-centred, 'graphocentric' philosophy. Rather, Derrida shows how Plato's text deconstructs itself. Similarly, in my analysis of 'La Double Séance' [hereafter 'the Double Session'] (Derrida 1972k/1981d) in Chapter 4, I explore how Derrida reintroduces the problematic of the *avant-garde* through the complex figure of Mallarmé (Mallarmé 2008) and how Derrida shows the Plato and Mallarmé relation to be one of co-dependency rather than mutual opposition. Central to his discussion is Derrida's reading of 'mimesis' and the 'double' (Derrida 1972k).

In the next chapter, I foreground Derrida's reading of Nietzsche and the 'question of woman' in his text *Éperons: Les Styles de Nietzsche* [hereafter *Spurs: Nietzsche's Styles*] (Derrida 1979). Surprisingly, the Nietzschean element of Derrida's work has been underplayed in favour, for example, of an emphasis on Emmanuel Levinas (Critchley 1999). In this chapter, I argue that this doesn't do justice to a strong Nietzschean influence which permeates all of Derrida's work. In *Spurs: Nietzsche's Styles* (Derrida 1979), the Nietzschean influence becomes most pronounced and I look at this text in Chapter 5, with especial emphasis on the Heideggerian reading (Heidegger 1991) of Nietzsche (which Derrida resists here) and on the relation between Nietzsche and feminism. I also look at Nietzsche's own understanding of the relation between 'truth and appearance', as he develops it in his Notebooks or *Nachlass* (Nietzsche 1990a).

It is the latter topic which brings me into the next chapter which explicitly addresses the question of feminism and Derrida. There has been considerable feminist response to *Spurs: Nietzsche's Styles*, some of it positive, some of it negative. In Chapter 6, I look at two seminal anthologies of feminist essays on Derrida's work (Holland 1997, Feder et al. 1997) which focus on *Spurs: Nietzsche's Styles* most especially but which also take account of Derrida's later work in relation to feminist thinking, for example in 'Choréographies' [hereafter 'Choreographies'] (Derrida 1992b/1982g) and 'Geschlecht: Différence Sexuelle, Différence Ontologique' [hereafter 'Geschlecht: Sexual Difference, Ontological Difference'] (Derrida 1997d/1991). It is these latter two Derridean texts which I look at in conclusion to this chapter, demonstrating how Derrida has shifted his emphasis away from a critique of Heidegger to a sense that Heidegger's philosophy provides a springboard to a critique not of sexual difference but of sexual duality or opposition, thus opening the way for a new kind of (Derridean) sexual difference. I also explore how we can make sense of this affirmative reading of sexual difference with regard to key female and feminist thinkers who are contemporaneous with Derrida, such as Julia Kristeva (Kristeva 1984), Luce Irigaray (Irigaray 1985) and especially Hélène Cixous (Cixous 1994).

In the final chapter, Chapter 7, I look at how Derrida's work has become increasingly political. Here, there is a sense that while the early texts are all implicitly political, nonetheless it seems that Derrida's encounter with feminism (post-*Spurs*) radicalised his political thinking. Another influence here was the strong political agenda of many of the *avant-garde* figures who influenced Derrida. I begin the chapter with an analysis of the politicisation of the *avant-garde*, for example in Artaud (Artaud 1968a), Bataille (Bataille 2001) and Blanchot (Blanchot 2004). Thus, we can see in Derrida's later work the addressing of political issues in two texts which I focus on as exemplary, *Cosmopolites de tous les pays, encore une effort!* [hereafter 'On Cosmopolitanism'] (Derrida 1997a/2001c) and 'On Forgiveness' (Derrida 2001d). I conclude the chapter by trying to contextualise how Derrida's political thinking relates to the current milieu of political philosophy, most especially with regard to his dialogue with Habermas (Habermas 1990) and Charles Taylor (Taylor 2007), amongst others.

In the Conclusion to the book, I reiterate the main themes of my analysis and critically assess the evolution of Derrida's work in terms of a close analysis of one of Derrida's later and more developed texts, *Le Toucher – Jean-Luc Nancy* [hereafter *On Touching – Jean-Luc Nancy*] (Derrida 2000/2005). Originally published in French in 2000, this text provocatively engages with the very conceptions of embodiment, 'flesh' and desire which I have sought to foreground throughout my own analysis. It is tempting to see this book as a kind of 'settling of account' with many of Derrida's forerunners and contemporaries, most notably with Maurice Merleau-Ponty (Merleau-Ponty 2002) and Gilles Deleuze (Deleuze and Guattari 2004). While critical of specific points in many other philosophers' work, the tone of

On Touching – Jean-Luc Nancy (Derrida 2005) is also extraordinarily affirmative, and one can say, somewhat transgressive. It reminds one of the explosive and recalcitrant dimension of deconstruction which is too often lost in attempts to subsume Derrida's thought under, for example, attempts to 'return' to more or less orthodox versions of ethics or religion. As with Deleuze and Guattari's *Anti-Oedipus* (Deleuze and Guattari 2004), as Foucault (Foucault 2004) notes, Derrida's texts are also always directed against a certain kind of 'fascism'; 'the fascism in us all, in ours heads and in our everyday behaviour...the tracking down of all variations of fascism, from the enormous ones that surround us and crush us to the petty ones that constitute the tyrannical bitterness of our everyday lives' (Foucault 2004: xiv). Derrida's 'l'écriture du corps', I will argue, is an extraordinary attempt to redirect the human being away from this *ressentiment* (Nietzsche 1967) which Nietzsche so well described.

Chapter 1

Derrida, Artaud's *Theatre of Cruelty* and the 'Writing of the Body'

Introduction

This chapter will argue against the oft-quoted accusation that the 'formal' aspects of Derrida's work mean that deconstruction has more affinity with discourse (understood exclusively as 'theory') than with the non-discursive, visual, spatial or performative dimensions of embodiment and sexuality. Rather, the opposite interpretation of deconstruction is the one I will take up here. That deconstruction, in specific instances, constitutes exactly a performative attack on discourse in the name of the non-verbal, the embodied, the spatial, the visual. This aspect of deconstruction can be linked to Derrida's reading of the concept of non-sense in *Speech and Phenomena* (Derrida 1967b/1973) and to the elliptical typography and content of a work such as *Glas* (Derrida 1974a/1986a), but here my primary focus will be on Derrida's readings of Artaud in seminal essays in *Writing and Difference* (Derrida 1967c, 1978a). Derrida's interest in Artaud extends across the chronological breadth of his work and, to conclude this chapter, I will look at Derrida's return to Artaud and specific questions of *avant-garde* poetics in his later writing (Derrida 1998a/2002a).

Artaud's *Theatre of Cruelty* called for a re-inspiration of 'breath' – 'the question of breathing is of prime importance' (Artaud 1970: 89) – against the degenerative affects of classical metaphysics and its lingering influence on modern philosophy and art. The dualisms between body and mind, text and performance, instituted a breathless death of what Artaud affirmed as the 'life-force' or 'existence'. Derrida's early essays on Artaud (Derrida 1967h/j, Derrida 1978f/h) initially portray his work as instigating an original and powerful critique of philosophy. Derrida credits Artaud both with overcoming a certain 'naïve' metaphysics and with being irreducible to the 'essentialist' interpretations of *avant-garde* readers such as Maurice Blanchot. Derrida's own work here seems to take its cue from Artaud's radicality, as if deconstruction was carrying on the work of the *Theatre of Cruelty*. Derrida comes close in these early essays to saying that deconstruction is also a kind of theatre, a performance of philosophy which takes us beyond philosophy to the very 'breath' and 'life-force', the very 'existence' which constitutes philosophy itself. Characteristically, however, Derrida's deconstructive reading also presents some of Artaud's key concepts (such as 'breath') as falling victim to the very metaphysical system which *The Theatre of Cruelty* is meant to overcome. That is, Derrida posits a certain revenge of philosophy against Artaud's 'breath' of existence.[1] This chapter will reinterrogate the boundaries of this encounter.

Derrida's philosophy has always paid due respect to the originality and radicality of Artaud's theatre, from early essays in the 1960s right up the work before Derrida's death, such as *Artaud le Mômo* (Derrida 2002). Here, I will be concerned primarily with the essay 'La Parole Soufflée' (Derrida 1967h/1978f, originally published in *Tel Quel* in 1965) or 'The Breathed Speech' (or 'The Stolen Speech'), where Derrida brilliantly aligns deconstruction with Artaud's reinvocation of 'breath' while also cautioning about the complicity between Artaud's theatre and the very metaphysics which he seeks to transgress.[2]

Artaud, Breath and Writing the Body

Writing and Difference (Derrida 1967c, 1978a), published in 1967 in France alongside *Speech and Phenomena* (Derrida 1967b, 1973), represents a rupture in Derrida's phenomenological methodology in the measure to which much of the analysis no longer stems from an intra-phenomenological critique, as with *Introduction to the Origin of Geometry* (Derrida 1962/1989) or *Speech and Phenomena*. Two key essays in the collection do engage with phenomenology, the early essay on 'Genesis and Structure in Husserl' (Derrida 1967g) and the infamous critique of Levinas's phenomenology, 'Violence et Métaphysique: Essai Sur La Pensée D'Emmanuel Levinas' [hereafter 'Violence and Metaphysics'] (Derrida 1967f/1978d). But the overarching significance of *Writing and Difference* is its shift from a focus on phenomenology to a focus on the *avant-garde*: 'Force and Signification' (Derrida 1967d/1978b) engages a reading of Mallarmé, 'Structure, Sign and Play' (Derrida 1967l/1978j) engages Nietzsche, 'A Hegelianism Without Reserve: From a Restricted to a General Economy' (Derrida (1967k/1978i) engages Bataille and two essays in the collection offer readings of Antonin Artaud's *Theatre of Cruelty* (Derrida 1967h/j, 1978f/h). This is nothing less than a paradigm-shift in Derrida's work, which sets the framework for Derrida's work in the 1970s and beyond, in *Margins of Philosophy* (Derrida 1972b, 1982a), *Spurs: Nietzsche's Styles* (Derrida 1979), *Glas* (Derrida 1974a, 1986a), etc.

---

1   Although I wish to claim a close connection between Derrida and the *avant-gardists*, I do not wish to make them synonymous. There are very clear differences between Derrida and Artaud, both in terms of the form *and* content of their respective work. Despite these rather obvious differences, it is extraordinary how close Derrida brings his own thought to that of Artaud in the relevant essays. It is also arguable that the more performative dimension of Derrida's style in these very essays, from *Writing and Difference* and his later work such as 'Tympan' and *Glas*, exemplifies a specific *avant-garde* inheritance.

2   This is primarily a question of what Derrida refers to as 'force' and 'form'. As Derrida puts it in 'To Unsense the Subjectile', it is a question of 'force before form' (Derrida 1998a: 76). We will return to this issue below.

A Non-Hegelian Difference

The conception of 'écriture' (or writing) is paradigmatic in this context, giving the title to the very collection of essays. One can also see how this conception underwrites the invocation of a non-Hegelian difference in the essay on Bataille:

> a difference which would no longer be the one which Hegel conceived more profoundly than anyone else: the difference in the service of presence, at work for (the) history (of meaning). The difference between Hegel and Bataille is the difference between these two differences (Derrida 1978i: 263).

Derrida thus looks not to phenomenology but to the French *avant-garde* for a basis for his conception of 'différance', which would be Bataille's difference rather than Hegel's. Artaud too, Derrida tells us, understood this:

> Artaud knew this well: 'a certain dialectics...'. For if one appropriately conceives the horizon of dialectics – outside a conventional Hegelianism – one understands, perhaps, that dialectics is the indefinite movement of finitude, of the unity of life and death, of difference, of original repetition, that is, of the origin of tragedy as the absence of a simple origin (Derrida 1978h: 248).

Différance would from the beginning then be *avant-garde*; surrealist rather than phenomenological, Artaudian rather than Levinasian.

Here, I will focus specifically on the longer of the two texts which Derrida devotes to Artaud in the *Writing and Difference* collection, 'La Parole Soufflée' (Derrida 1967h, 1978f), this title capturing the ambiguity of either a 'stolen speech' or 'inspired speech', or both: 'soufflée: entendons dénobée par un commentateur possible...entendons du même coup inspirée depuis une autre voix' (Derrida 1967h: 261–2). The authentic self has been displaced, according to Artaud, by the machinations of Western metaphysics and its infiltrating influence on all art and social forms. Our breathing has been suffocated by over-conceptualisation and over-textualisation. But here, Artaud also holds out for a different reality, a breathing (inspiration) which can be said to exist, or which at least re-exist, if his own project of a *Theatre of Cruelty* can be brought to fruition. What Artaud calls 'cruelty' signifies a new rigor and consciousness of the tragic theft of our very breath and 'life-force', by metaphysics. It also seeks to reinstantiate what Artaud calls the 'body without organs', a pure body ('un corps sans souillure', 1967h: 271) in effect the authentic self who breathes for him/herself, and who can inspire cultural and social revolution.

Artaud applies this understanding to the history of theology: 'do you know anything more outrageously fecal/than the history of God' (quoted Derrida 1978f: 121). After Nietzsche, but in a slightly different key, Artaud seeks to drive the death of God to its most radical conclusion. God is the apex of the metaphysical mindset and has reduced the life-force of the divine to a pathetic anthropomorphism ('et qu'as-tu fait de mon corps, Dieu?' (quoted Derrida 1967h: 269). Far from constituting idealism or utopianism, modern religion is nothing but human excrement, a fecal excess. The divine must be restored through the de-excrementalisation of human culture and society.

A Writing Against Writing

The status of 'writing' within Artaud's project is problematic: *writing is all trash.*[3] Artaud is a writer who, on one level, disavows writing *de jure*. Instead of words, Artaud calls for a physical theatre and a physical language, of shouts, gestures, expressions; 'we could listen more closely to life' ('nous pourrions mieux écouter la vie', Derrida 1967h: 282) and return to sonority, intonation, intensity. Derrida commends Artaud's work for overcoming the 'naïvete' of traditional metaphysics but also that of contemporary 'critical and clinical discourse', where Derrida is referring to psychoanalysis and the work of philosophers such as Foucault and Blanchot. Despite the subtlety of the latter theorists, in effect they get Artaud wrong. Artaud's work presents more of a challenge to critical and philosophical discourse, and its conceptualisations, than has previously been allowed. Here, Artaud's central notion of 'breath' (le souffle) is crucial for Derrida. Paradoxically, this must be reinforced by writing itself, but a nonphonetic, 'hieroglyphic' *writing of the body* ('l'écriture du corps', 1967h: 287), to bring about *'the alienation of alienation'* (Derrida 1978f: 230). 'C'est de créer une maîtrise absolue du souffle dans un système d'écriture non phonétique' (Derrida 1967h: 287).

Susan Sontag's defence of a more revolutionary conception of theatre (Sontag 1994) throws into relief some of the key innovations which Artaud's discourse on theatre made *vis-à-vis* previous art and theatre criticism, and also its implications for our thematic of embodiment, a writing of the body. Sontag seeks to defend Artaud against the presumption of what might be termed a 'psychological theatre' or a 'theatre of character', which stress the verbalisation of emotion through text-based drama and then development of character through dialogue.

Such theatre sees the stage itself as merely a means to an end, the performance of the theatrical event itself reduced to a means to the semantic transmission of authorial meaning. For Artaud, it is the hegemony of such theatre which constitutes the crisis of contemporary theatre, which is also to be identified with a very crisis in existence or life itself. 'This obstinacy in making characters talk about feelings, passions, desires, and impulses of a strictly psychological order, in which a single word is to compensate for innumerable gestures, is the reason...the theatre has lost its true *raison d'être*' (Sontag 1994: 100). This psychological theatre must be replaced by a 'theatre of the senses' or a 'pure theatre language' ('ce langage théâtral pur', Derrida 1967h: 287) which ironically, as Sontag observes, constitutes a move from psychological theatre to a theatre which

---

3   The situation here bears similarity to that of Plato, whose conception of 'writing' we will address in Chapters 3 and 4. Both Artaud and Plato simultaneously castigate *and* affirm writing.

is more heroic (and also more philosophical). This de-psychologisation of the theatre and its re-philosophisation is no doubt one of the attractions of Artaud's work for Derrida. It involves a move from a Brechtian paradigm to a paradigm which bears closer resemblance to other art forms, most notably the Happenings of performance art or the cinema of Antonioni and Godard, where we move beyond the binary 'positives and negatives' of psychology.

This moves us also away from the paradigm of humanism (again, a link to Derrida), and away from not simply the moral dimension but even the replacement of morals by aesthetics (à la Nietzsche), towards what Sontag describes as the 'ontological' plane (Sontag 1994: 101). In contrast, the Artaudian theatre, what Sontag refers to as a 'theatre of the senses', disavows the textual author, privileging instead the 'person who controls the direct handling of the stage'. If we can say that Sontag's work on Artaud (and the development of his thinking in works by Peter Brook and Peter Weiss) borders on the eulogistic in its conception of Artaud's revolutionary break, one can say that Derrida's essays on Artaud constitute a more problematical inheritance.[4]

A Radicalisation of Style

Derrida's early essays on Artaud initially portray his work as instigating an original and powerful critique of philosophy. Derrida credits Artaud with overcoming a certain 'naïve' metaphysics and with launching us into a space which seems genuinely transgressive and creative. Certainly, there is a clear sense that Derrida is uneasy with the status of traditional philosophical discourse and his own encounter with Artaud allows him to develop a different kind of (nonphilosophical) textual practice or performance. As Derrida observes, for example, in his dialogue with Richard Kearney:

> I have attempted more and more systematically to find a non-site, or a non-philosophical site, from which to question philosophy…I try to compose a writing which would traverse, as rigorously as possible, both the philosophical and literary elements without being definable as either (Derrida 1986c: 106).

Of course, we must also bear in mind that there is a simultaneous debt to and borrowing from the very philosophical tradition which is being subverted or

---

4   Derrida points out Artaud's romanticism concerning a 'pure body', while affirming the evolution of Artaud's thinking from such a physical purism to a more nuanced understanding of the complicity of the body with metaphysics. This latter would be Artaud's '*writing*' of the body'. The written element of embodiment signifies the impossibility of pure physical or conceptual immediacy. In theatre terms, it demonstrates the necessity of a certain 'text' and the impossibility of a pure spontaneous, 'physical' theatre. This Artaud is already practicing a certain deconstruction of the body and of theatre.

questioned: 'my philosophical formation owes much to the thought of Hegel, Husserl and Heidegger' (Derrida 1986c: 110).

Tracing the genealogy of Derrida's early work, one can see a gradual radicalisation of style, which can be linked to his attempt to create this 'nonphilosophical site' from which to question philosophy. This is methodologically no doubt what interests him in a thinker like Artaud, and indeed in *avant-garde poetics* more generally. Artaud's 'theatre' inscribes philosophy in a space in which it can be contested. Undoubtedly, both thinkers owe a significant debt to Nietzsche here, that the Nietzschean call to instigate a critique of all values (or a 'transvaluation of values') would also apply to the value of philosophy itself. All the internalist critiques of philosophy would have come to nought insofar as they assumed the worth of philosophy as an arbiter of philosophical value.

But instead of asking whether it should be this philosophy or that which wins out, Artaud and Derrida, as with Nietzsche, are asking: whether philosophy at all? *What is the value of philosophy*? This is a question which philosophy itself cannot ask of itself without the answer already being in the question. And this is, for Derrida, as for Artaud, a question of desire, of erotics: the desire to have or not to have philosophy, but also a question of meaning. Here, we see the connection back to Derrida's earlier readings of Husserl. Is Artaud's *Theatre of Cruelty* an attempt to stand outside the need for philosophical meaning, to assert a (physical) independence of meaning? For Derrida, such a pure outside of philosophy is impossible. By the same token, however, Husserl's project fails because it tries to make too inflexible a distinction between meaning and nonmeaning (Derrida 1962, 1967b). At its best, Artaud's *Theatre of Cruelty* overcomes its tendency to physical purism and affirms the 'difference, of original repetition, that is, of the origin of tragedy as the absence of a simple origin' (Derrida 1978f). It is in this way that one can overcome metaphysical but also anti-metaphysical naïveté.

This then will also be a question of style, of a 'writing of the body' ('l'écriture du corps'). While Derrida's first works, from a content perspective, radicalise phenomenology, in form they remain internalist phenomenological critiques (Derrida 1967e, 1967g, 1962). But this starts to change with the essays developed in the *Writing and Difference* collection. Now, something else is happening, and often it is noticeable in the prefaces. Derrida writes contorted prefaces, they are obscurantist. They distract and accumulate confusion and one feels, as a reader, that one is not being guided into something but being thrown deliberately into a space which has no real orientation. Derrida's prefaces inscribe us within a labyrinth, we feel paralysed and lost. To quote a later Derridean text, discussed below, these texts act as 'subjectiles' (Derrida 1998b), taking the reader to a place 'outside-sense'.

This, we might argue, is Derridean theatre, Derrida's performance art. What must be overcome is what Derrida refers to in 'La parole soufflée' as 'the naivete of the discourse' (Derrida 1978f: 169); 'naiveté du discours' (Derrida 1967h: 253). According to Derrida, Artaud's designation of the theatre of cruelty as 'life' or 'breath', for all its apparent utopianism, 'absolutely resists [résiste absolument] –

as was never done before – clinical or critical exegeses; he does so by virtue of his adventure [son aventure]; attempting to destroy the history of dualist metaphysics' (Derrida 1978f: 174, 1967h: 261). Artaud's resistance to 'clinical' exegeses is, of course, more than simply an academic or even aesthetic issue.

As is well known, Artaud was institutionalised for a long period of his life and received severe electro-shock therapy in large quantities, which had a dreadful affect on his mind and body. His hair and teeth fell out and the cancer which killed him was a direct result of an infection which had been caused by the electro-shocks.[5] According to Derrida, Artaud 'exhumes' the 'ground of the clinic': 'what his howls [ses hurlements] promise us, articulating themselves under the headings of existence, flesh [de chair], life, theatre, cruelty, is the meaning of an art prior to madness and the work; an artist's existence [l'existence d'un artiste]' (Derrida 1978f: 174, 1967h: 260). Artaud (and Derrida's) emphasis on existence here demonstrates a key (but underestimated) connection between deconstruction and existentialism. As Herman Rapaport has noted, Artaud (and Bataille) can be seen as 'existentialists of a different feather' (Rapaport 2002: 138). As Bruce Baugh has observed, 'Derrida is more existentialist than existentalism' (Baugh 2005).

A Question In Which We Are Posed

The very title of Derrida's essay captures the pivotal and indispensable tension at the heart of Artaud's project; 'spirited [*soufflée*] let us understand stolen by a possible commentator…at the same time let us understand inspired [inspirée] by an other voice'(Derrida 1978f: 174, 1967h: 262). Our bodies, and our very breath, our very sources of 'life-force' are both poison and cure. Poison in the sense that they allow our identities to be lost, or 'spirited away' in the alienation of everyday existence. Nonetheless, these bodies can also be 'inspired' or 'spiritualised'. For Derrida, when Artaud refers to 'my Body, my Life', these expressions must be understood 'beyond any metaphysical determinations and beyond the limitations of being' (Derrida 1978f: 176) ['au-delà des déterminations métaphysiques et des limitations de l'être'] (Derrida 1967h: 263).

This would be a body which would overcome alienation through taking possession of itself in 'a place where property would not yet be theft' (Derrida 1978d: 178). But this vocation to propriety, to re-establish a proper body and life-existence, is constantly deferred in the quest for and consolidation of form. This, for Artaud, is the great tragedy of contemporary existence and constitutes a crisis in society, a truly political crisis: 'if there is still one hellish, truly accursed thing in our time, it is our artistic dallying with forms, instead of being like victims burnt at the stake, signalling through the flames' (quoted Derrida 1978f: 178). For Derrida, the *Theatre of Cruelty* text can be read as 'a political manifesto' (Derrida 1978f: 328), making connections between Artaud and the young Marx.

---

5   See C. Eshleman 'Introduction' in Eshleman, C. et al. (eds) (1995) *Antonin Artaud – Watchfiends and Rack Screams: Works From The Final Period* (Boston, Exact Change).

Derrida also delineates affinities between Artaud and Jacques Lacan in this context and between Artaud and Nietzsche. In the case of Lacan, Derrida speaks of 'the necessity of unconscious formations; he [Artaud] traces the form of theatrical writing from the model of unconscious writing' (Derrida 1978f: 192). Artaud also refers to psychoanalysis positively as 'giving words the importance they have in dreams' (quoted Derrida 1978f: 328). Of course, in relation to psychoanalysis, one can also cite Artaud's more specific dislike of Lacan because of the latter's institutional authority over his condition. As Artaud unequivocally comments, Lacan is a 'filthy, vile bastard' (quoted Eshleman 1995: 19). Lacan had been chief psychiatrist at one of the clinics where Artaud had been interred and had in fact delivered a diagnosis of 'fixed' with regard to the possibilities of Artaud overcoming his psychological predicament (Eshleman 1995: 19).

With regard to Nietzsche, the affinity is less problematical. As Nietzsche observes, 'I love only what a person has written with his blood...I hate the reading idlers...another century of readers and spirit itself will stink' (quoted in Derrida 1978f: 328). Artaud, following Nietzsche, certainly also wrote 'in blood'. As he says of his own thought, and as a paradigm for all true thinking and art, 'no one has ever written, painted, sculpted, modelled, built, or invented except literally to get out of hell' (quoted Eshleman 1995: 34). Or in his early text, 'Umbilical Limbo', 'I do not consider any work apart from life...life consists of burning up questions' (Artaud 1968b: 49). It is this radicality[6] of Artaud's project which Derrida considers so important, and also so uniquely effective in attempting to transgress the limits of Western philosophical thinking about life. 'Artaud keeps himself at the limit, and we have attempted to read him at the limit. Artaud fulfils the most profound ambition of western metaphysics; but also affirms the law of difference; no longer experienced within metaphysical naïvete but within consciousness' (Derrida 1978f: 194).

Artaud thus achieves a 'consciousness' which goes beyond traditional philosophical understanding while also remaining enigmatically dependent upon philosophy. As Derrida observes in conclusion: 'the transgression of metaphysics always risks returning to metaphysics; such is the question in which we are posed' (Derrida 1978f: 194) ['telle est la question que nous avons voulu poser'] (Derrida 1967h: 292). There is thus no final answer for Derrida here, but 'a question in which we are posed'.[7] Artaud remains an 'enigma of flesh' ['l'énigme de chair'] (Derrida

---

6 But this Artaudian radicality is significant for Derrida precisely insofar as it maintains a tension or ambiguity within itself, which remains irresolvable. '*Writing*' in blood involves an ambiguation of a more straightforward blood or body purism.

7 This seems the most appropriate way to read Derrida's encounter with Artaud and indeed with the *avant-garde* more generally. That is, this encounter opens up questions 'in which we are posed'. What Derrida suggests here is that this questioning constitutes a *radicalisation* of the questioning which was opened up in the earlier encounter with phenomenology. This would then be the 'grammatological opening'.

1978f: 194, Derrida 1967h: 292). As Artaud observes searingly in another early text, 'Nerve Scales', 'nothing, except fine Nerve Scales. A sort of impenetrable stop in the midst of everything in our minds' (Artaud 1968c: 75).

This is a significant phrase, 'impenetrable stop'. Artaud's work would remain irreducible to a straightforward reading; it would continue to be 'impenetrable' and 'enigmatic'. This would symbolise the self-deconstruction at work in Artaud's thinking and writing. In the next section, I will look at how this extraordinary Derrida/Artaud encounter develops through Derrida's later work and especially his text 'To UnSense the Subjectile' (Derrida 1998b), and how we might make sense of this encounter in terms of Derrida's wider relation to the *avant-garde*.

On *Différance* and the Subjectile: The Wider Implications of Derrida's Relation to the *Avant-Garde*

Jacques Derrida's insistent motif of 'différance' is arguably the most important 'concept' (or 'non-concept') developed in Continental philosophy in the twentieth century. Originally suggested as far back as 1959 in an essay on Edmund Husserl ('Genesis and Structure', Derrida 1967g), the concept also appears in 1962 in Derrida's *Introduction to Husserl's Origin of Geometry* (Derrida 1962/1989) and is developed throughout the essays collected in *Writing and Difference* (Derrida 1967c/1978a). The concept is finally systematically foregrounded in Derrida's essay 'Différance' (Derrida 1972d, 1982c), included in *Margins of Philosophy* (Derrida 1982a). Although often misunderstood as emphasising difference *per se*, the notion is rather introduced by Derrida originally to complicate the binary opposition between difference and identity, critiquing simultaneously the unitary identitarianism of Husserl but also (and this is often underplayed) the naive emphasis on difference (or 'otherness') in thinkers such as Levinas. This latter is especially made clear in essays from *Writing and Difference*, such as the seminal 'Violence and Metaphysics' (Derrida 1967/1978d) on Levinas.

A Différance Under Erasure

The notion of différance is (in)famously slippery. Indeed, I can barely write this word on my computer, it keeps getting erased and rewritten as the word 'difference'. This, in a sense, encapsulates what Derrida means to indicate by the notion. We have come to designate something tried and tested by the notion of 'difference' in our language. We think we know what it signifies; its semantics are fixed. What Derrida is suggesting is that this notion we have doesn't do justice to the real thrust, the real complexity and radicality of what difference involves; we have domesticated such difference. For example, the French verb for difference, 'différer', Derrida tells us (Derrida 1982c: 7), already focuses on the meaning of difference as to differ from a spatial point of view; for a thing to differ from itself in space, to differ with itself as a thing, or to differ with other things in space. This neglects an earlier notion of difference encapsulated in the Latin conception of difference (*differre*) which also involved temporal deferral or delay; differing in relation to taking a different route or a detour, a delay, a deferral. Moreover, a third notion of difference in French which is captured by a word such as *le différend*, measures the difference of polemic (Derrida 1982c: 8). Creating differences or disagreement in debate with another, which derives in spirit from the Greek term 'polemos'.

Part of Derrida's motivation then in creating this new word, this non-word, difference spelt with an 'a', is to show the difference between traditional difference and difference as such (if one can say such a thing). Because, of course, one can't say such a thing – there would be no difference *as such*, because once we try to define it, it loses its differential quality. That is why we shouldn't get too hung up on 'différance', Derrida tells us. It is an approximation, a nonconcept, it should not be treated as a transcendental (Derrida 1982c: 7ff.). In Husserlian terms, it does not express the essence or intuition of difference but rather only serves as an 'indication' of difference (Derrida 1962/1989). Derrida here is seeking to use the subordinate notion of phenomenological indication to undermine the privileging of phenomenological expression. He also claims that *différance* tells us something about our era today; there is something contemporary about *différance*, something then also contemporary about deconstruction. But it is, he says, a notion which we must also be prepared to give up, to move on from (when the time comes). As he observes:

> there is nowhere to begin to trace the sheaf or the graphics of *différance*. For what is put into question is precisely the quest for a rightful beginning, an absolute point of departure, a principal responsibility. The problematic of writing is opened by putting into question the value *arkhē* (Derrida 1982c: 7).

Derrida and Surrealism

But if one is to reinterpret or reposition the concept of *différance*, what are the implications, not only for an understanding of Derrida's work, but also for an understanding of his relationship to extra-philosophical discourses? As John Brannigan has noted in an important essay on Derrida and surrealism (Brannigan 1999b), the importance of surrealism for Derrida is its obsession with the production of language that operates at a remove from being. This is why it is particularly significant that Derrida's tracing of the word *différance* articulates both a spatial differing and a temporal deferring. In both cases, there is a close affinity between surrealist writing and Derrida's writing in the temporal and spatial distance of being removed or at a distance from self. That is, difference as a temporal deconstruction of self but also as a spatial deconstruction of self.

It is clear that Derrida's invocation of this notion owes a considerable debt to the work of the French *avant-garde* in the 1930s and 1940s, especially the work of Georges Bataille and Antonin Artaud, both surrealists of a sort; we might call them *dissident surrealists*. Such a thematic helps us to throw light on what has been termed Derrida's 'intertexts' (Brannigan 1999a: ix). This is a highly complex thematic, with numerous (disseminated) authors and texts involved or embroiled from Alfred Jarry's 'oulipian grammatology' (Tufail 1999: 122ff.) to Mallarmé (Temple 1999) to Baudelaire and Valéry (Robbins and Wolfreys 1999), and beyond. Again here, however, my focus will be specifically on Artaud.

As Brannigan argues persuasively (Brannigan 1999b: 55), there is a powerful series of intellectual and theoretical resonances between Derrida and surrealism (here Artaud being seen as a 'dissident' surrealist). Both thinkers, Derrida and Artaud, can be seen to 'transform the relationship between art and the body' (Brannigan 1999b: 56). Rather than being a localised or internalist aesthetic critique, Artaud's *Theatre of Cruelty* is rather profoundly political, 'cruelty' being another name for life or desire, 'the theatre of cruelty is life itself; the space it inhabits is that of original representation, the *archi*-manifestation of force or of life' (Brannigan 1999b: 59). If surrealism is a 'brilliant obsession' (as Blanchot evocatively comments), then 'no one bears this ghost, this brilliant obsession, after surrealism to quite the same extent as Jacques Derrida' (Brannigan 1999b: 62).

Of course, there is also a strong existentialist element to Derrida's thinking, in this context (and as we noted earlier through Rapaport, Artaud would also be an 'existentialist of a different feather'). Much has been made of Derrida's disavowals of Sartre and of a certain 'existentialist humanism (after the War)' (in, for example, the essay 'Ends of Man', Derrida 1982d) but it is clear that, even in his radical critique of *Existentialism and Humanism* (Sartre 1980), Derrida still cites Sartre's *Nausea* as a key anti-humanist text. As he states in his later text, *A Taste for the Secret* (Derrida 2001):

> my intention was certainly not to draw away from the concern for existence itself, for concrete personal commitment, or for the existential pathos that, in a sense, I have never lost. Rather, what I did stemmed from my critical reflections on the reading of Husserl and Heidegger advanced by certain French existentialists such as Sartre and Marcel; and my dissent did not mean of course that I turned my back on existential questions. In some way, a philosopher without this ethico-existential pathos does not interest me very much (Derrida 2001a: 60).

I think that it is within the context of this 'ethico-existential pathos' that we can best understand Derrida's recourse to the radical *avant-garde* and their more singular thematics, which he argues consistently, have been excluded and marginalised by the more mainstream philosophical and phenomenological traditions.

What is perhaps most striking for our purposes is that Derrida returns most explicitly to the theme of Artaud's thought in his later work. Having devoted two texts to Artaud in *Writing and Difference* (Derrida 1967c/1978a), this is again symptomatic of Artaud's importance for the project of deconstruction, taken from early to late. Derrida focuses on Artaud in two key later texts, 'To Unsense the

Subjectile' (Derrida 1998a) and *Artaud le Mômo* (Derrida 2002). It is the former text which I will concentrate on here.

Conclusion: The Dramaturgy of the Subjectile

In 'To Unsense the Subjectile' (Derrida 1998a), Derrida takes up the theme of an obscure, improper or nongrammatical word ('subjectile') which Artaud uses three times in his texts (at Derrida's counting). A little like the Derridean notion of *différance*, the concept of the 'subjectile' comes to take on a generalised significance for Derrida's reading, both with regard to Artaud's thought but also to the more overall relationship of philosophy to embodiment.

The scene of the 'subjectile' in Artaud constitutes a 'dramaturgy', according to Derrida (Derrida 1998a: 62). Even the word itself, which can be said to have no definitive meaning, designates a mini-drama: 'between the beginning and the end of the word (sub/tile); the subjective and the projectile' (Derrida 1998a: 62). The term 'subjectile' would mean *neither/nor* the subjective or the projectile, but it would carry resonances of both. With regard to the traditional notion of the subjective, Artaud would be declaring that 'the body must be reborn' (Derrida, 1998a: 99), and calling for a new 'bodily writing' (Derrida 1998a: 85). This would also relate to the question of 'beingness': as Derrida notes, 'the way Artaud treats the question of beingness; being starts with movement and not the inverse' (Derrida 1998a: 75).

This would be a new philosophy of *becoming*, again showing the connections between Artaud and Nietzsche (as well as with Derrida). It would also constitute a liberation, a 'delivery from a domination' (Derrida 1998a: 69). This would be the 'projectile' aspect of the subjectile, a 'force before form' (Derrida 1998a: 76) and an emphasis on radical *expression* (Derrida 1998a: 102/3).[8] And there would also be, Derrida tells us, a great consistency here in Artaud's work: 'the machinery of the breath has always been at work' (Derrida 1998a: 120). From *The Theatre and its Double* right up until Artaud's last work, there would be an emphasis on breathing, on the sustaining expression of *breath*:

> Ten years ago language left,
> and in its place there came
> this atmospheric thunder,
>   this lightning
>
> ....

---

8 'Force before form', as a principle, would be an *aspect* of Artaud and Derrida's thinking. That is, we shouldn't interpret this as a privileging of force over form, *as such*. Much as Derrida will talk of the 'between' ('l'entre') in *Dissemination* and '*l'entre*lacement' in *On Touching*, we can see the relation between force and form in Derrida as an 'inter-lacing', a mutual complication. I will return to this problem of the 'l'entre' in Chapters 3 and 4.

> I say then that language distanced is a lightning that I brought on now in
> the human fact of breathing, sanctioned by my pencil strokes upon
> the paper

(quoted Derrida 1998a: 113).

Of course, this is no neutral reading by Derrida. As the enigmatic title suggests, the 'subjectile' is being 'unsensed'. Mary-Ann Caws seeks to explicate the term as follows: 'forcené/for-sené – unsensed by genius but not senseless; for unsense has in it the peculiar echo of an incense…something is consecrated here…sense is not simply lost…it is gravely undone…there is a serious difference' (Caws 1998: xiii). Derrida looks to Heidegger on Georg Trakl for some help: 'the demented person dreams and he dreams as no one else could…he is gifted with another sense…' (quoted Derrida 1998a: 69/70).

Ultimately, however, Derrida would not simply be talking of or on Artaud as intellectual object. He would also be speaking, in relation to the 'unsense' and to the 'subjectile', of deconstruction, and indeed of desire, more generally. Here, in 'To Unsense the Subjectile', we would have significant evidence of Artaud's influence on the very 'trajectory' of Derrida's work as a whole: 'the *trajectory* (as well as the spurt or the -ject of a projectile) in other words, the path (*sent, set*) of the *forcènement*' (Derrida 1998a: 150). It would be a matter, once more, of 'force before form': 'Will I have been forcing things?…But first of all no reading, no interpretation could ever prove its efficacy and its necessity without a certain forcing. *You have to force things*' (Derrida 1998a: 156) [Derrida's emphasis].

This would then be precisely the performative dimension of Derrida's work, which would be more than merely a strategic adjunct. In *performing* philosophy in this way, Derrida would put the whole identity and self-understanding of the discipline into question, each time he undertakes a deconstructive reading. And in this radicality and iconoclasm, this 'force before form',[9] Derrida would be precisely following (with significant digression and drift, by definition) an Artaudian trajectory.

---

9 For Derrida, 'form' can also be a force, and 'force' a form. Derrida replaces the binary opposition between these two terms with a conception of 'inter-lacing' ('*l'entre*lacement'), which he develops, for example, in *On Touching* (Derrida 2005). I return to this problem in the Conclusion. See also Derrida 1967d, 'Force et Signification'.

Chapter 2

'Except for a Certain Laughter': Derrida, Bataille and the Transgression of Dialectic

Introduction

In the last chapter, we saw how Derrida's *Writing and Difference* (Derrida 1967c) constitutes a paradigm-shift in Derrida's work, away from the phenomenological emphasis of his early work (however radical) towards precisely a new *avant-garde* thematic. There, we looked specifically at Derrida's relation to Antonin Artaud. Here, in Chapter 2, I will explore how Derrida also develops a complex and important relationship to Georges Bataille in *Writing and Difference* and how this relation will remain important for deconstruction right through to Derrida's last texts in the late 1990s and early twenty-first century (Derrida 2000/2005). Georges Bataille stands as perhaps the most idiosyncratic but also prolific of the early twentieth century *avant-garde* intellectuals who were to have such an immense effect on the thought of Derrida and later French philosophy.

Born in 1897, Bataille's early writings stem from the late 1920s, with his infamous pornographic novel *The Story of the Eye* (Bataille 2001b). Simultaneously influenced by Hegel, Marx and Sade, Bataille's work in the 1930s developed a more explicitly political agenda as a counter to the increasing threat of Fascist politics. Essays such as the 'Psychological Structure of Fascism' (Bataille 1985c), 'The "Old Mole" and the Prefix *Sur* in the Words *Surhomme* [Superman] and Surrealist' (Bataille 1985b) and the novel *Blue of Noon* (Bataille 1986b), each evolve a complex and ambiguous politics, attempting to counter Fascism but also aware of the erotic lure of the latter ideology. Bataille's own focus on eroticism, developed most systematically in his seminal *Eroticism* (Bataille 2001a), is already implicit in these earlier texts and is also developed in his controversial literary work, such as *Madame Edwarda* and *Ma Mère* (Bataille 1986a). Bataille's later work also develops an interest in the relationship between the erotic and the sacred, most notably in his trilogy *La Somme Athéologique*, comprising *Inner Experience*, *On Nietzsche* and *Guilty* (Bataille 1988b).

Since the 1970s, Bataille's work has increasingly come to be seen as an important precursor to the development of postmodernist thinking. This chapter will focus on the complexity of Derrida's relation to Bataille's work. I will begin by analysing the detail of Derrida's most sustained treatment of Bataille's work, in the essay 'From Restricted to General Economy' (Derrida 1967k/1978i), from *Writing and Difference* (Derrida 1967c/1978a). I will foreground here Derrida's focus on the Bataille-Hegel relation. In the following section, I will look at how we might best understand the mediation of Hegel by Bataille and its influence on Derrida's work, by looking at Bruce Baugh's seminal interpretation of the 'French Hegel' (Baugh 2005). However, in many respects, Derrida's focus on Hegel serves to occlude other influences from Bataille's work, such as his conception of embodiment and desire, and especially his conception of the relationship between prohibition and transgression. I will argue that these aspects of Bataille's work have been a pivotal resource for Derrida's own thinking of the relation between philosophy and what he calls 'nonphilosophy'.

A Genealogy of Dissidence

As with Artaud, it can be difficult to categorise Bataille in relation to philosophical or cultural movements. One strand of thinking which they share relates to the surrealist movement. Artaud, for example, for a time was a key figure within surrealism and celebrated by Breton (although he moved away from the movement soon after). Bataille's relation to Breton was always more conflictual, with Bataille consistently criticising Breton and the wider surrealist movement for its 'idealism' in relation to the interpretation of eros (Mundy 2006). Both may most cogently, with regard to surrealism, be seen as 'dissident' thinkers (Ades and Bradley 2006: 11) Charles Taylor, in his recent text *A Secular Age* (Taylor 2007) has foregrounded another possible way of interpreting Bataille's line of development. Here, Bataille can be seen to have inherited the spirit of what Taylor refers to as the 'immanent Counter-Enlightenment' in French literature, the poet *maudits* or damned poets, such as Rimbaud, Baudelaire, Lautréamont and Mallarmé, espousing an 'immanent transcendence' (Taylor 2007). These poets vehemently reject the rationalism of the Enlightenment and instead revive a mystical tradition (at least in aesthetics) with a focus on the irrational, sin and thanatology. This view also ties in with the portrayal of Bataille's significance which comes through the work of Susan Sontag. Sontag in her essay 'The Pornographic Imagination' (Sontag 2001) focuses on Bataille as a reader of the Marquis De Sade. Here, she cites (Sontag 2001: 96) the crucial 'importance of the reinterpretation of Sade after World War II by French intellectuals…a crucial point of departure for radical thinking about the human condition' (Sontag 2001: 102). She notes what she terms 'the prevailing view of sexuality as a perfectly intelligible source of emotional and physical pleasure' (Sontag 2001: 102). It is 'these assumptions [which] are challenged in the French Sadean tradition' (Sontag 2001: 102). In this alternative tradition, the obscene is a primary notion of human consciousness, human sexuality is a highly questionable and contested phenomenon and there are extreme and demonic forces in consciousness which are linked to the desire for death. Bataille is, for Sontag (as indeed for Jane Gallop in her text *Intersections*, Gallop 1981), the key figure in this paradigmatic re-reading of Sade.

Finally, we can refer to Michel Foucault as a reader of Bataille (we will return to Foucault *vis-à-vis* Derrida's reading below). In his seminal text 'A Preface to

Transgression' (Foucault 1998), Foucault champions Bataille's development of the Nietzschean legacy. Here, Foucault makes an intrinsic connection between the new thinking of 'sexuality' and the crisis engendered by the 'death of God'. For Foucault, this is a legacy which is inherited not only from Nietzsche but earlier from Sade, but it is Bataille in the twentieth century who has radicalised this inheritance most forcefully (and here Foucault is also acknowledging the influence of Bataille on his own work): 'And from this perspective, the thought that relates to God and the thought that relates to sexuality are linked in a common form, since Sade to be sure, but never in our day with as much insistence and difficulty as in Bataille' (Foucault 1998: 72). As we shall see below, these extraordinarily affirmative readings of Bataille by Sontag, Gallop and Foucault are not shared by all commentators. Indeed, most especially Jean-Paul Sartre's almost wholly negative and reductionistic reading of Bataille has become infamous (Sartre 1947). It is precisely into such a contested space of interpretation that Derrida's reading of Bataille arrives in 1967.

'From Restricted to General Economy: A Hegelianism Without Reserve': A Very Derridean Bataille

Derrida's philosophical encounter with Bataille extends from the ninth essay of *Writing and Difference*, 'From Restricted to General Economy: A Hegelianism Without Reserve' (Derrida 1967k/1978i), which had been originally published in *L'arc* in May 1967, right through to Derrida's texts in the early 1970s, and up until some of his very last texts, such as *Le Toucher – Jean-Luc Nancy* (Derrida 2000).[1] In the 1970s, Derrida employs Bataille to play a significant role in essays such as 'Tympan' (Derrida 1982b), 'Différance' (Derrida 1982c) and 'The Ends of Man' (Derrida 1982d) and perhaps, most notably, Bataille is introduced in *Glas* (Derrida 1974a) to explore a complex reading of Jean Genet's work *vis-à-vis* Hegel. Bataille, for Derrida, is perhaps the most accurate and radical of Hegel's commentators in the 1930s and beyond, and Bataille's own *avant-garde* status also makes him a paradigmatic interlocutor of Genet (Derrida 1974a). In the 1980s, Bataille's thinking is introduced in a very important reading of Levinas (Derrida 1997c/1994) and he is also referred to in numerous interviews by Derrida (for example, Derrida 1986c). I will return to these many references below. To begin, however, I will focus on Derrida's earliest and most extended treatment of Bataille's work, in the essay 'From Restricted to General Economy: A Hegelianism without Reserve' (Derrida 1967k/1978i).

We have already spoken in the last chapter about the paradigm-shift in Derrida's work from phenomenology to the *avant-garde*, which we are locating specifically in *Writing and Difference* (Derrida 1967c/1978a) and most especially in the last six essays which offer what Derrida has called a 'grammatological opening'. As we

---

1   Bataille is also an acknowledged influence on Nancy.

saw in the case of the reading of Artaud, the work of the *avant-garde* constitutes what could be referred to as 'a nonphilosophical' (Derrida 1986c: 6) practice which can be seen to influence the very obvious radicalisation of style in Derrida's work from this moment onwards. Again, as with Artaud, in the case of Bataille, we once more see Derrida's complex relation to surrealism being foregrounded, what Brannigan has referred to as Derrida's 'inter-texts' (Brannigan 1999a: ix). It is once more a question of the relation between the body and philosophy, or the question of the relation to the 'other' of philosophy. 'Force before form' as Artaud said of André Masson's surrealist drawings and paintings, and Bataille too can be seen in this light.[2] As always with Bataille, many issues finds themselves interconnected here. Formalism is constantly seeking to keep 'force' in check, to repress it or to sublimate it. One paradigmatic example which Bataille gives in his text *Theory of Religion* (Bataille 1990) relates to the notion of God or a Supreme Being, which he interprets as an 'impoverishment'.

In his analysis of this phenomenon, Bataille would appear to be also implicitly critiquing pre-Christian concepts of the Supreme Being, whether of the Neo-Platonists or the Judaic tradition. 'There is doubtless, in the positing of a supreme being, a determination to define a value that is greater than any other. But this desire to increase results in a diminution' (Bataille 1990: 34). Bataille regards such monotheism as a diminution of the force of the sacred:

> The sacred is that prodigious effervescence of life that, for the sake of duration, the order of things holds in check…The sacred is exactly comparable to the flame that destroys the wood by consuming it. It is that opposite of a thing which an unlimited fire is; it spreads, it radiates heat and light, it suddenly inflames and blinds in turn (Bataille 1990: 53).

This anarchic religious or sacred force is reduced, through more conventional religious orthodoxy, to the orderly point of a Supreme Being. This, for Bataille, is not exclusively a theological issue but also relates to the whole socio-political and moral infrastructure which is attendant on monotheism. The sacred is translated into a moral and political set of commandments. In surrealism, by contrast, Bataille finds an approach to life which embodies an 'elementary state of revolt' to this state of affairs: 'it is genuinely virile opposition – nothing conciliatory, nothing divine – to all accepted limits, a rigorous will to insubordination' (quoted Richardson 2006: 24).

On first inspection, this more prominent (and insurrectionary) dimension of Bataille's work remains underplayed by Derrida in 'From Restricted to General Economy' (Derrida 1967k/1978i). What Derrida rather comments on first in this

---

2   As with Artaud, however, this principle of 'force before form' should not be taken as absolutist. In both Artaud and Bataille, it would be subjected to a process of ambiguation, primarily through the activity of 'writing' ('l'écriture'). As we will see below, in Bataille, writing subjects everything to a process of 'glissement' or 'sliding'.

essay (and develops throughout as his theme), is precisely Bataille's relation to Hegel. This is not the most obvious route into Bataille's work but it is the one which Derrida has chosen to emphasise; the title of the essay makes this clear; 'a Hegelianism without Reserve'. This, already we might say, is indicative of a certain *différance* being at work in Derrida's reading. The reader is not getting what they might expect, on at least two counts. In the first case, as a work of philosophy, it is strange to see an *avant-garde* figure like Bataille being introduced.

Second, when treating of an *avant-garde* figure like Bataille, so renowned for his radical work on eroticism, why the focus on Hegel and Bataille's relation to Hegelianism? Derrida is once more confounding expectations, and, as we discussed in the last chapter, this is part of the insistent strategy of deconstruction. Derrida proceeds to mention Bataille's discussion of Hegel and Kierkegaard, which is instructive. While one might expect that Bataille would favour the latter over the former, it is rather Hegel who Bataille admires; 'for two years he [Hegel] thought he would go mad...in a sense, Hegel's rapid phrase has a force ('une force')[3] that Kierkegaard's long cry does not have. It is not any less within existence – which trembles and exceeds – than this cry' (quoted Derrida 1967k: 372, 1978i: 334). This is unexpected; that Bataille would favour Hegel, the great philosopher of the Absolute, over Kierkegaard, the supposed philosopher of the fragment and the individual.

Exceeding the Dialectic

But, says Derrida, it shouldn't surprise us if we look more closely at Bataille's relation to Hegel and his constant (but almost always respectful) interrogation of the latter. Bataille takes Hegel and Hegelianism very seriously, he does not underestimate the significance of Hegel's analysis of dialectic. 'Souvent Hegel me semble l'évidence, mais l'évidence est loured à supporter' (quoted Derrida 1967k: 369). There would be no 'simplification', Derrida clarifies, in Bataille's reading of Hegel (Derrida 1978i: 251). According to Bataille, Hegel would almost have the last word on existence. The Hegelian system would be a 'philosophy completing itself...except for a certain laughter' ['hommis peut-être un certain rire'] (Derrida 1967k: 370, 1978i: 252). Thus, according to Bataille, Hegel's system would finally fail and falter in trying to complete the circle of existence, in trying to found an Absolute truth. There would always be something which would exceed this attempt at finalised philosophical mastery – whether it be laughter, tears, nonsense, death, or sex (Bataille employs a long list of 'exceeding' phenomena here). But Derrida also adds a crucial 'and yet' ('et encore') in this context (Derrida 1967k: 370, 1978i: 252). We shouldn't jump to any conclusions, just yet. This would be what Bataille claims for his own thinking, that after a long and intimate rapport with Hegel, it can finally exceed the dialectic. But 'and yet' signifies Derrida's own partial distancing

---

3   This reference to Hegel shows the complexity of the thematic of 'force' in Derrida. Here, Hegelianism is seen as on the side of force, and Kierkegaard as more formalistic.

from this assurance. Derrida's essay will take up this question ('the question in which we are posed'), and there can be no certain answers, as yet.

Still, Derrida makes clear that Bataille has come very close to this ultimate transgression of the Hegelian system, and thus, we might say, of philosophy itself. What is at stake here is the very 'nonphilosophical' site which Derrida has talked about as one of the guiding motivations of his work (Derrida 1986b). This demonstrates the importance of Bataille to Derrida's overall task of deconstruction. In the case of Bataille, Derrida argues that 'rarely has a relation to Hegel been so little definable; the extreme point of experience, laughter, ("un certain éclat de rire") destroys and exceeds the sense' (Derrida 1967: 253). What is generated is thus a 'new configuration' (Derrida 1978i: 253). He also goes on to signal the connection between this move away from Hegel and the 'genealogical and genetic critique of Nietzsche and Freud':

> my discovery of the genealogical and genetic critique of Nietzsche and Freud
> also allowed me to take the step beyond phenomenology towards a more radical,
> non-philosophical questioning; while never renouncing the discipline and rigour
> of phenomenology (Derrida 1986b: 105).

In 'From Restricted to General Economy' (Derrida 1967k), Derrida is seeking out this nonphilosophical site in the work of Bataille (who is, amongst other affiliations, a 'neo-Nietzschean').

We can also say that this Derridean reading of Bataille is a very public re-reading. Derrida is seeking to defend Bataille's system of 'general economy' against the various accusations which had been brought against it, most especially by Jean-Paul Sartre (Sartre 1947). Sartre had a very complex relation to Bataille. Bruce Baugh, for example, comments that Sartre's work is very close to Bataille's in spirit, even in letter (Baugh 2005). Perhaps it is precisely such proximity which leads to the vehemence of Sartre's dismissals of Bataille. In *Situations*, for example, Sartre accuses Bataille of being a 'new mystic' ['un nouveau mystique'] (quoted Derrida 1967k: 394). As Derrida observes (*contra*-Sartre), Bataille 'is above all not a new mystic' (Derrida 1967k: 394). Sartre also reads Bataille's conception of laughter as 'negative in a Hegelian sense' (Derrida 1978i: 256). That is, Sartre reads Bataille's attempt to exceed the Hegelian dialectic as a 'failure'; the dialectic can simply recuperate such laughter or whatever excess Bataille chooses for its meaningful march towards the truth. But, for Derrida, Bataille's laughter is in no way negative ('laughter is not negative', Derrida 1978i: 256). Rather, for Derrida, Bataille's laughter laughs at the philosophical system of Hegel: 'rit de l'Aufhebung' (Derrida 1967k: 377).

It is rather (and here he borrows from Michel Foucault's reading of Bataille in 'A Preface to Transgression) a 'nonpositive affirmation' (Foucault speaks of a 'nonpositive affirmation': Derrida 1978i: 335) ['d'une affirmation non positive', Derrida 1967k: 380]. Foucault's reading is important in its very distinction from Derrida's. Foucault's essay had been written on Bataille's death and thus 'A

Preface to Transgression' (Foucault 1998) is crucial for the reception of Bataille, but it differs from Derrida's interpretation considerably. Foucault traces a line from Emile Durkheim through Marcel Mauss and Roger Caillois to Bataille; a more anthropological or sociological analysis of his work which will later go on to influence Jean Baudrillard (Baudrillard 1994).

A Peculiar Negligence

Derrida stresses Hegel more substantially in his reading of Bataille. Bataille was a careful reader of Hegel under the influence of Alexandre Kojève (Kojève 1969) but what Derrida singles out is Bataille's avoidance of an overly anthropological approach to Hegel. Bataille takes the existential dimension of Kojève's reading of Hegel but loses the anthropologism (at least according to Derrida). For Bataille, Kojève is still too focused on a 'mastery' of the phenomena of life; he seems convinced of the 'totality' of human existence and of 'absolute knowledge'. As Kojève observes of Hegel: 'He therefore knows the totality of human existence, and consequently sees it as it is in reality or in truth (in der Tat). Thus possessing "absolute knowledge…"' (Kojève 1969: 261).

Bataille rather foregrounds the themes of prohibition and transgression, of the intrinsic relation between tradition and its other, and the deconstruction of the subject in *Inner Experience*, which owes a debt to Heidegger. As an affirmation, Bataille's excess cannot be so easily recuperated by Hegel's dialectic. Derrida seems to be telling us that this is an authentic excess and not still intra-Hegelian, as Kojève would have claimed. It is in returning to a disagreement with Sartre (in terms of their respective readings of Bataille) that one can see how Derrida might imagine Bataille to free his thought from a Hegelian grip.

The last word which Derrida has on the Sartre interpretation in this essay is in relation to the question of form and content, and Sartre would have remained intra-Hegelian, at least for Derrida. 'Sartre's study of Bataille joints its first and second parts with the hinges of this proposition; 'but form is not everything; let us look at the context' ['voyons le contenu'] (quoted Derrida 1967k: 393). Here Sartre is interested only in the 'matter' of Bataille's discourse; he sees the style of Bataille's discourse, his strange use of language, as irrelevant. On Derrida's terms, Sartre is abstracting from the problematic aspect of Bataille's language (and this abstraction would be Hegelian). Other commentators, more sensitive to the nuance of Bataille's writing style, have commented on the extraordinary specificity of Bataille's writing style as an 'event of twentieth century language', Denis Hollier for example (who edited Bataille's *Oeuvres Complètes*):

> Bataille, who always wrote a great deal, always manifested a peculiar negligence when it came to books; …yet the rigor of his often anxious, sometimes insolent indifference to literature positions his writings among the major events in twentieth-century language; a throttled, ragged voice, struggling in the labyrinth of language (Hollier 1997: 69).

Derrida also begs to differ with Sartre on the form/content distinction: 'Bataille's writing, in its major instance, does not tolerate ["ne tolère pas"] the distinction of form and content' ['la distinction de la forme et du contenu'] (Derrida 1967k: 393/1978i: 267). For Derrida, the relationship, in Bataille, between form and content is constitutive of the whole Bataillean discourse. It is what allows Bataille to exceed Hegelianism while nonetheless often appearing to be superceded by Hegel. This is where Sartre goes wrong. He interprets the detached content of Bataille's discourse, he fails to look at the context, at the relation between what Bataille is saying and the form in which he is saying it. Derrida also makes this point in relation to many of the concepts which Batailles uses – 'sovereignty', 'continuum', 'communication', 'instant'.

Taken literally as formless contents, these are Hegelian, Derrida says. But to properly read Bataille's text is to see how Bataille's formal discourse makes the normal meaning of these terms become excessive; 'le texte de Bataille est piége' ('Bataille's text is booby-trapped') (Derrida 1967k: 393). The methodological phrase Bataille uses (and Derrida follows him in this) is 'sliding' ('glissement' from 'glisser', Derrida 1967k: 386). 'Sliding' is an approximate translation here; it could also be translated as 'slipping, gliding, skating, whispering, creeping, grooving'. But we shouldn't lose sight of the irreducible precariousness: 'ce glissement est risqué' (Derrida 1967k: 386). This also relates to Bataille's insistent 'accent on simulacrum and subterfuge' (Derrida 1967: 258). This latter brings Bataille's thought close to that of Pierre Klossowski, whose essay on Bataille (precisely on the employment of the 'simulacrum') Derrida cites here. Additionally, Derrida mentions the Husserlian concept of 'indication' in this context. For Husserl, indication is always inferior to expression. But the terms which Bataille uses only 'indicate' their meaning; they should not be understood as expressive but as indicative terms, Derrida suggests. This introduces difference and otherness into the employment of philosophical language, what Derrida calls the 'the difference of sense; the unique interval which separates meaning from a certain nonmeaning; this dissymetry' (Derrida 1967: 259). A certain 'glissement' is irreducible.

It is this 'dissymetry' which Hegel 'misses'; 'poetry, laughter, ecstasy are nothing; Hegel knows no other aim than knowledge; his immense fatigue is linked to his horror of the blind spot' (Derrida 1978i: 256). Hegel cannot seem to philosophically register the absence of meaning or the dissymmetry of meaning. He tries to turn the blind spot into some kind of meaningful vision. This is nowhere more apparent than in his interpretation of the phenomenon of death, which Bataille treats as paradigmatic. In seeking to understand the full totality of existence, Hegel must also provide a philosophical understanding of death. For Hegel, although death represents a negativity, a negative moment in the dialectic, it is possible for this negativity to be turned into something positive, to be superceded and overcome into a meaningful totality. Hegel refuses to give into a scepticism here. As Kojève observes, 'man's transcendence with respect to his death "manifests" itself in yet another way than by the mistaken "subjective certainty" of an afterlife;

this transcendence also "appears" as a truth (*Wahrheit*), being the revelation of an "objective reality"' (*Wirklichkeit*) (Kojève 1980: 256).

But, for Bataille, this is a 'comedy':

> sacrifice and the absolute risk of death; the comedy of the *Aufhebung* to which Hegel is indifferent; thus is sketched a figure of experience irreducible to any phenomenology, which is displaced in phenomenology, sacrifice and the absolute risk of death; the impossibility of reading a sense or truth in death (Derrida 1978i: 257).

For Bataille, the supposed meaning which Hegel finds in death is a mere philosophical or metaphysical ruse: 'death, in truth, reveals nothing; the revelation never takes place' (Derrida 1978i: 257). While Bataille's own discourse has thus followed Hegel to this ultimate point, this is also where we see the very significant divergence and disagreement between Hegel and Bataille; 'the *Aufhebung* profits from everything and wastes nothing; Bataille is not a speculator because he is concerned precisely with what is left behind; with what cannot be profited from' (Derrida 1978i: 335). It is this 'left behind' which Derrida and deconstruction are also interested in; what Derrida refers to as *différance*. It is this difference which leads Derrida to take up and develop Bataille's distinction between a 'restricted' and a 'general' economy. Hegelianism, for all its concern for negativity, would be a restricted economy.

A general economy, in contrast, must take account of the 'other' of philosophy without seeking to simply subsume it, on philosophy's own terms. Sometimes, this will require an 'accent on simulacrum and subterfuge' (Derrida 1978i: 258). While we must take Hegel seriously, we mustn't take him too seriously. This excess of dialectic leads to what Bataille calls 'gay anguish; absolute rending...my joy finally tears me asunder' (Derrida 1978i: 259). This is what Derrida means by a 'Hegelianism without reserve', that is, a Hegelianism which cannot fall back upon a reserve. This is a Hegelianism which must face up to the irreducible elements of existence, that which remains resistant to any dialectical or philosophical understanding. Again, we can see how this concern in Derrida's work derives from his aforementioned focus on a nonphilosophical site from which to question philosophy. Hegelianism ultimately, for Derrida, remains too intra-philosophical, too closed to any questioning outside of its own terms. This is a place of questioning which Derrida refers to, in *Dissemination* (Derrida 1972h), as the 'hors livre' (the 'out of book').

Therefore, for Derrida, Bataille moves beyond the 'legacy of Hegel and Kant' (Derrida 1978i: 259). For Bataille, Hegel was wrong 'for (always) being right', for having (supposedly) triumphed over the negative. This was only an empty triumph, and Bataille thus 'uncovers the limit of discourse and the beyond of absolute knowledge' (Derrida 1978i: 261). Against Sartre, who read this Bataillean discourse as negative (and thus subsumed by the dialectic), Derrida follows Foucault: 'Foucault speaks of a "nonpositive affirmation", this is the experience of absolute difference which is non-Hegelian' (Derrida 1978i: 263). Here, Bataille introduces one of the paradigmatic terms ('sovereignty') which Derrida describes as linking form and content inextricably. Although we can read these terms literally (as Sartre does) as falling back into Hegelianism, Derrida says we should be attentive, as good readers, to their conceptual 'sliding' ('glissement'). This emphasis on the importance of style and context in reading philosophy is a recurring theme of Derrida's. We will return to it in Chapter 3 when we look at Barbara Johnson's attempts to understand Derrida's own writing strategems and ploys (Johnson 1981). It is also the overarching theme of Derrida's reading of Nietzsche in *Spurs: Nietzsche's Styles* (which we examine primarily in Chapter 5, but also in relation to feminist thought in Chapter 6).

Here, our concern is with Bataille's term or concept of 'sovereignty', which Derrida gives significant emphasis to in the reading. We are told that 'sovereignty is not self-consciousness; it is not phenomenological' (Derrida 1978i: 264). As with Nietzsche, it must 'practice forgetting; it must no longer seek to be recognised … sovereignty has only the kingdom of failure' (Derrida 1978i: 336). And again: 'sovereignty must not seek recognition, as does the master, for this inevitably leads to servility' (Derrida 1978i: 336). Another way of understanding this emphasis is, Derrida tells us, in relation to the 'simulacrum' (Derrida 1978i: 283). Derrida here cites Pierre Klossowski's essay on Bataille and the 'simulacrum' and Klossowski's own readings of 'simulacrum' are obviously implicit throughout this reading of Bataille (Klossowski 1991). What is significant for our purposes here is that a complex and subtle reading of Bataille is required here, according to Derrida. Again the key target is Sartre, who represents a constant enemy presence within the ranks of dissident surrealists, such as Klossowksi and Bataille. Sartre's aforementioned attempt to separate form and content in Bataille (Sartre 1947) is seen as paradigmatically mistaken and misleading (much as Sartre's later reading of Heidegger's concept of *Dasein* will similarly be seen, by Derrida, as having a catastrophic effect on the French reading of phenomenology).

Through Bataille's discourse, according to Derrida, one has a 'renunciation of recognition' (Derrida 1978i: 265). Against the attempts by the Hegelian dialectic to recuperate meaning and some overall project for mankind, Derrida cites Bataille's thought as authentically transgressive: 'man is irreducible to the project, nondiscursive existence, laughter, ecstasy…Hegel has suppressed chance and laughter' (Derrida 1978i: 335). This chance and laughter would now be exposed and developed by Bataille and also by deconstruction. But this 'sovereignty' would not be nihilistic: '[sovereignty] is not the loss of meaning but *the relation to this loss of meaning*; the effect of unknowledge' (Derrida 1978i: 270). Derrida cautions against seeing such a move as a new enlightenment or a new emancipation. And he credits Bataille with also seeing such limitations: 'this knowledge which might be called liberated, but which I prefer to call neutral' (Derrida 1978i: 270). One can argue that this represents a significant methodological influence on Derrida and that this reading of Bataille is paradigmatic insofar as it also seems to represent Derrida working out his own strategy of deconstruction.

At times, Derrida reading Bataille would seem to be, more or less, Derrida reading Derrida. Bataille's writing (and Derrida's) would thus constitute, on this interpretation, 'the simulation of meaning in play' (Derrida 1978i: 268). This writing would 'inscribe ruptures' and would involve the 'absolute excess of every episteme, of every knowledge' which only a 'doubling position' can account for (Derrida 1978i: 268). Only a 'double position' can account for this Bataillean discourse, 'which is neither scientism nor mysticism' (Derrida 1978i: 269). In line with further readings of Levinas in particular, Derrida cites the need to go beyond gratitude or respect ('sovereignty must be ungrateful', Derrida 1978i: 269). This might also be applied to his later and very controversial readings of Hans-Georg Gadamer (Michelfielder and Palmer 1989) where Derrida eschews a grateful or even gracious reading.

Indeed, in the later Levinas reading, 'En ce moment même dans cet ouvrage me voici' [hereafter 'At this moment in this work here I am'] (Derrida 1997c/1994a), Bataille is invoked at a key juncture. This very essay ('From Restricted to General Economy', Derrida 1967k) is cited. The conclusion of the Bataille essay is cited at a key moment of the Levinas essay. Derrida seems to affirm the conception of difference in Bataille which takes it beyond any Hegelian recuperation:

> a difference which would no longer be the one which Hegel conceived more profoundly than anyone else: the difference in the service of presence, at work for (the) history (of meaning). The difference between Hegel and Bataille is the difference between these two differences (Derrida 1978i: 263).

Here, Derrida is clearly privileging Bataille's conception of difference as not reducible to Hegelian difference despite the complexity of the latter. This conception of Bataille's difference, outlined in texts such as *The Accursed Share* (Bataille 1991), is, I would claim, an important precursor of Derrida's notion of *différance* and indeed Bataille appears as an ally in the crucial essay in *Margins of Philosophy*, 'Différance' (Derrida 1982c).

Derrida also makes several comments in passing and, sometimes in footnotes here, which are most instructive for his later work. Unsurprisingly, a lot of Derrida's most important work takes place in footnotes and endnotes, away from the 'centre of the text'. Indeed, in some essays, especially in *Margins of Philosophy* (Derrida 1982a), the footnotes become so significant as to marginalise the supposedly central text. This happens also most notably in *Glas* (Derrida 1986a), in *Circumfession* (Derrida 1999) and in 'Living On: Borderlines' (Derrida 1986a), the latter title capturing the very performative aspect of such complicating textual and (non) philosophical strategies. Here, in *Writing and Difference* (Derrida 1978a), where the form/content distinction is already problematised, but not so much the typographic integrity as yet, Derrida speaks of the important relation between 'Bataille and Marx' (Derrida 1978i: 337), which we will return to later in our discussion of some of Derrida's more explicitly political writings, in Chapter 7.

As we saw in Chapter 1, however, Derrida had also made similar, political remarks regarding Artaud's discourse. Thus, his emphasis on the *avant-garde* should not be seen as 'textualist' (as some critics would suggest): it is, at least on his own terms, radically political. The same can be said for his reading of Mallarmé. Mallarmé understood his own supposedly elitist work as radically democratic, in its transfiguration of everyday language, finding the extraordinary in the ordinary (McCombie 2008). A similarly 'literary' politics is also of course at work in the work of James Joyce, whom Derrida returns to at several junctures (e.g. Derrida 1962/1989). Derrida also makes important remarks here regarding the relation between Bataille and theology and, by implication, there are suggestive resonances for the relations between deconstruction and theology: 'god is also an effect of this nonknowledge' (Bataille quoted in Derrida 1978i: 337).

That is, for Bataille, 'god' would not be some ultimate ground, but rather an effect. God would be a literary or philosophical effect, although not just one effect amongst others. Derrida, following Bataille's own terminology, refers to this as an 'atheology'; 'Bataille's atheology is also an a-telelogy and an aneschatology' (Derrida 1978i: 331). This again is a reference in endnotes where it is accompanied by a citation of Bataille's *L'Expérience Intérieure* (Bataille 1988a) text, as part of 'a series to be called *La Somme Athéologique*' (Derrida 1978i: 331). Significantly, this is a term which Derrida will also use to describe the relationship of deconstruction to religion – as atheology (e.g. Derrida 1997f). Although Derrida does not cite them here, it is worth citing Bataille's own comments on religion (specifically in relation to Heidegger), as they are made in an essay on existentialism by Bataille which Derrida cites several times in other regards in this context. In the case of Heidegger, Bataille says:

> Heidegger requires admiration for the synthesis that he had successfully made of traditional religious experience and a philosophical school associated with atheism: his teachings proceed from the most sensible investigation that has been made of the profane and sacred spheres, of the discursive and the mythic, and of the prosaic and the poetic (quoted Rapaport 2002: 109).

This constitutes a complicity between Bataille and Heidegger often forgotten, but one would imagine not lost on Derrida, although he doesn't mention in it in this context. One can also see here an anticipation of Derrida's later engagement with negative theology.[4] Derrida, in fact, refers to Bataille's understanding of religion as close to, but also significantly distinct from, the specific predicative movements

---

4   The question of Derrida's relation to religion is not taken up directly in this book, although the implication of a more *avant-garde* and Nietzschean interpretation of Derrida which I develop would suggest a complicating of the rather simplistic readings of a Derridean 'religious turn'. However, atheology (for Bataille as for Derrida) is *not* atheism or, at least, not *simply* atheism. For a more explicit reading of this question with regard to a neo-Nietzschean tradition (Bataille, Klossowski, Foucault), see my forthcoming book, *Religion After Nietzsche: The Subversion of Atheism Following the Death of God* (Ashgate, Transcending Boundaries in Philosophy and Theology series).

of negative theology. Again, this important matter is take up in a footnote: 'negative theology as a phase of positive ontotheology...Meister Eckhart: this does not proceed along the lines of a negative theology' (Derrida 1978i: 337). Despite its claims, negative theology would only disavow god's essence so as to 'hyperessentialise' it in an ulterior move. This hyperessentialism (God as a hyper-essence beyond essence) would be very different in kind from a more radically deconstructive 'apophasis'. This anticipates many of Derrida's later texts (for example, Derrida 1997f). It also gives the lie to those who would want to posit a significant discontinuity in Derrida's work between an earlier (Nietzschean/*avant-gardist*) phase and a later (ethical/religious/Levinasian) moment. There is a clear (if nonetheless complicated and somewhat elliptical) continuity here between Derrida's early and later work.

There is also a reference back in this context to the earlier discussions of Husserl and his opposition between indication and expression, although the reference is implicit. Bataille's terms, in general (but here specifically in terms of his 'atheological' terms), 'indicate' rather than 'express' and so they do not achieve a full 'intuition of essence'. The danger for many interpreters of Bataille, Derrida warns, is that they take his indications for expressions: 'indication in Bataille; what indicates itself as mysticism...or as interior experience...[is] neither inner nor outer...above all is not a new mysticism' (Derrida 1978i: 273). Baugh makes a similar point in his *French Hegel* text when he argues that the 'atheist mystic' contemplates negativity but is never able to transpose it into being (Baugh 2005). This also shows that Bataille would have taken indication seriously, which might allow his general economy to do the work which was claimed for Husserl's understanding of signification. Certainly, Derrida's relation to Husserl is complex and one shouldn't underestimate the continuing influence of Husserl in the later work, for example his critique of Levinas is often Husserlian in some respects, even crucial respects. Even in recent texts such as *On Touching – Jean-Luc Nancy* (Derrida 2005), Derrida returns to a Husserlian critique, for example of Merleau-Ponty and indeed the whole 'French phenomenology of the flesh' (Derrida 2005). I think that this can also be said of his distance from the more mainstream phenomenology of religion, for example the work of Jean-Luc Marion. One might also argue that he often critiques Heidegger from a Husserlian perspective. Nonetheless, ultimately, Derrida moves away from Husserl. However, a good contemporary reading of this relationship in a positive light is that of Leonard Lawlor (Lawlor 2002).

Ellipsis, Adventure, Chance

To return to our discussion of Derrida's relation to Bataille in this essay, Derrida concludes in a tone which, for some, is perhaps surprisingly affirmative of Bataille. For Bataille, as with Derrida, 'writing is absolutely adventurous, is a chance and not a technique' (Derrida 1978i: 273). There is only the 'perhaps' of a transgression, but this 'perhaps' should not be seen as designating a failure on Bataille's part. Rather, transgression and taboo are always complicit. Transgression requires the limit to be reinforced for a transgression to be even possible, as a very condition of transgression. Bataille's writing thus cannot be ultimately categorised; 'neither this nor that'; and here he cites, in an important statement of intent, the affinities between Bataille and the work of Maurice Blanchot. Ultimately, Bataille rather than Hegel would seem to have the last word: 'Bataille is even less Hegelian than he thinks' (Derrida 1978i: 274). The essay ends enigmatically with an ellipsis (1978i: 276) marked in the text. There is a reference to 'vision' and 'illumination' and an affirmation of a 'sketch...of an opening'. This is no doubt the 'grammatological opening' which Derrida refers to elsewhere. This then can be seen as a crucial 'concluding' sentence and this is reinforced by Derrida returning to it in the Levinas essay (Derrida 1997c).

Another Existentialism

Bataille's reading of Levinas is also significant here. In a review of early existentialism which he published in *Critique* in 1947 (Bataille 1947), and which is insistently mentioned by Derrida in his essay on Bataille, Bataille speaks in response to an earlier article which had put his own work, alongside that of Blanchot and Klossowski, into the same grouping as existentialists such as Camus and Sartre. While Bataille doesn't reject this categorisation outright, his reading of the possibilities of existentialism takes it beyond how Sartre or Camus would have envisaged it. Existentialism has posed subjectivity in a way that its positioning implies 'the ruin of the subject' (quoted Rapaport 2002).

Although Derrida mentions this article in his essay, he interestingly doesn't take up two of its most interesting dimensions, its references to Heidegger and Levinas. We have already mentioned Bataille's reference to Heidegger on the subject of religion above. In the case of Levinas, Bataille says that Levinas' work on existence posits existence as nondialectical, as 'irremissible' (quoted Rapaport 2002). This, of course, is at odds with the reading of Derrida on Levinas in 'Violence and Metaphysics' (Derrida 1967f), but close to Derrida's later reading of Levinas in 'At this Moment' (1997c) where Bataille plays a crucial part in the interpretation.

But if Derrida is critical of Levinas (with Bataille), he nonetheless also sounds a word of warning in relation to the Bataillean discourse. As mentioned above, in concluding the essay on Bataille, Derrida refers to 'only the perhaps of a transgression' (Derrida 1978i: 273). Transgression is one of Bataille's most significant notions and it is instructive that Derrida does not speak about it until the very end of the essay. But one might assume that this is a potentially negative or critical reference of Derrida to Bataille: 'how can mediacy and immediacy be transgressed simultaneously? *Perhaps* through major writings. Only *perhaps*...' (Derrida 1978i: 273) [italicised twice by Derrida]. But this contingency of transgression is already recognised by Bataille in his own work. Indeed the dependency of transgression (its lack of self-sufficiency) brings us to Bataille's own discussion of transgression in his important text, *Eroticism* (Bataille 2001). This is a text little referred to by Derrida but more central to Foucault's reading of Bataille, and it most especially relates to the connection or dynamism between taboo and transgression. Bataille's discussion of the relation between taboo and transgression highlights the strong anthropological dimension of his work, and, in this case, his attempt to provide an anthropology of eroticism.

For Bataille, the genesis of taboo is tied to the very genesis of human society and community and this is particularly the case with the two most central human taboos, those concerning death and sexuality; 'thou shalt not kill' and 'thou shalt not perform the carnal act, except in wedlock' (Bataille 2001: 42). These prohibitions represent the most explicit face of a whole spectrum of taboos concerning death and sexuality, such as burial rites and disallowing any contact with corpses with regard to death and prohibitions of incest, bodily nudity and masturbation, with regard to sexuality (Bataille 2001: 55). Both sexuality and death require strict regulation because from the earliest civilisations they represent the introduction of what Bataille terms 'violence' into human culture, a violence which can never be eliminated but which must be kept under relative control if culture and society is not to unravel destructively. Here, Bataille is not arguing against taboo (Bataille 2001: 55). In foregrounding the intrinsic relation between human society and taboo, Bataille is precisely arguing against those modern liberals who would call for a complete liberalisation of mores, and specifically here, sexual mores. As Colin McCabe observes: 'For Bataille, the notion that sexual fulfilment resides in the abolition of taboos is a contradiction in terms. For the pleasures of eroticism are the pleasures of breaking a taboo which is, none the less, acknowledged as such. No taboo, no desire' (McCabe 2001: x). To allow eroticism to flourish in culture thus requires a necessary dimension of taboo.

Secondly, however, for Bataille we misunderstand taboo if we see it as only a prohibitionary force. Such an understanding is only possible if we interpret the phenomenon of taboo in complete isolation from its surrounding context:

> Taboos...are not only there to be obeyed. There is always another side to the matter. It is always a temptation to knock down a barrier; the forbidden action takes on a significance it lacks before fear widens the gap between us and it and invests it with an aura of excitement (Bataille 2001: 48).

The 'other side to the matter', as Bataille puts it, is thus the relation between the taboo and that which it apparently prohibits, the transgression of the taboo. Far from being mutually opposed, taboo and transgression for Bataille operate as 'complicit' functions: 'the taboo is there to be violated'. At the same time, however, if transgression does take place, it never overcomes the taboo but rather can only be a transgression if it recognises the limit set by the taboo. Taboo and transgression thus become inter-dependent.

For Bataille, such examples are nothing new. They are rather part of an age-old dynamic of duality within human culture and morality: 'When one considers the most striking manifestations of the principles enunciated, one cannot fail to observe mankind's double nature throughout its career' (Bataille 2001: 186). Eroticism is Bataille's general term for the phenomena which result from this duality, phenomena which distinguish us from the more cyclical aspect of animal life but which also point to a problematicity at the heart of human existence. Here, Bataille refers back to the teaching of the anthropologist Marcel Mauss and his pupil, Roger Caillois. Both read the duality between taboo and transgression as the very motor and structuring principle of the development of human society and culture:

> Man's time is divided into profane time and sacred time, profane time being ordinary time, the time of work and of respect for the taboos, and sacred time being that of celebrations, that is in essence the time of transgressing the taboos. As far as eroticism goes, celebrations are often a time of sexual licence (Bataille 2001: 257).

When Derrida thus tells us that Bataille's work only possibly or 'perhaps' transgresses the Hegelian dialectic, this is clearly in line with Bataille's own self-understanding. As Derrida goes on to observe (although it could be Bataille speaking):

> only perhaps, and this is 'after all superfluous' [a quotation from Bataille] for this writing must assure us of nothing, must give us no certitude, no result, no profit. It is absolutely adventurous, is a chance and not a technique (Derrida 1978i: 272).

This Bataillean writing reminds one of Artaud's 'writing of the body' ('l'écriture du corps'). Both thinkers wish to assert the freedom of the body, of breath, but they are also wary of Hegelian immediacy. Thus, by *writing* the body, 'without certitude', they seek to affirm embodiment in a nondialectical way.

The last sub-section of the essay follows immediately from this and is entitled by Derrida 'the transgression of the neutral and the displacement of the *Aufhebung*' (Derrida 1978i: 273). It is clear that Derrida and Bataille's thinking are in close proximity here, that Derrida's discussion of Bataille might serve (with some provisos) as a discussion of deconstruction itself. It is reminiscent of Derrida's constant refrains (especially in interviews from *Positions*, Derrida 1972a) onwards that deconstruction is not a method, that deconstruction involves no overall mastery. Otherwise, it would of course be Hegelian, and as seeking mastery it would become merely servile as a discourse. Deconstruction would be 'neither this nor that' (Derrida 1978i: 273). In this it would indeed be akin to the 'writing of sovereignty...which can enounce nothing, except in the form of a neither this nor that'(Derrida 1978i: 273). Derrida then draws the connection with Blanchot; 'is this not one of the affinities between the thought of Bataille and that of Blanchot' (Derrida 1978i: 273).

With regard to Derrida's conclusion, however, it should not be seen (despite all the proximities and affinities just mentioned) as an unconditional affirmation of

Bataille's work. Much as with the Artaud essay which precedes it, if these essays can be seen as seeking to develop a 'grammatological opening' and seeking to provide a 'nonphilosophical site' from which to question philosophy, they can only be seen in the context of the meta-reading which Derrida gives of both Bataille and Artaud. Both thinkers enage in an 'adventure' of thought, which affirms 'chance'. In the case of Artaud, we are left with an 'enigma of flesh'. In the case of Bataille, with the 'sketch of an opening'. Both risk returning us to metaphysics, into a complicity with dualism and with Hegelianism and philosophy. Nonetheless, both are also exemplary in their desire for the other of philosophy, in their sketching of the gaping chasm 'between desire and fulfillment'. This sketching can only take place through Artaud's 'writing of the body' and Bataille's 'glissement' which is always moving in opposite directions at once.

The 'Unhappy Consciousness' Between Derrida and Bataille

In his seminal text, *French Hegel: From Surrealism to Postmodernism* (Baugh 2005), Bruce Baugh develops an argument which can help us to understand the close connection between Derrida and Bataille, which develops from *Writing and Difference* onwards, and also specifically in terms of the thematic of 'a writing of the body' which we have been attempting to follow in Derrida's writings. While Artaud and Bataille are both keen to overcome a traditional philosophical dualism between mind and body or form and matter, nonetheless they are also conscious of the pitfalls of a naïve realism or materialism which would seek to posit an immediate access to embodiment. If the early Artaud dreams of such immediacy (or 'presence'), the later Artaud affirms the necessity of a detour through the graphism of a new kind of body-writing (Derrida 1998a/ 2002). Similarly, Bataille's texts demonstrate simultaneously a 'base materialism' and a highly sophisticated philosophical and literary 'operation' which seeks to enact the transgression of dualism through writing (Derrida 1967k), in effect another kind of (Bataillean) 'l'écriture du corps'.

Hegel in France Before Kojève

Baugh provides some very helpful historical contextualisation of this problematic and begins by complicating 'the notion that Kojève's lectures brought Hegel to France' (Baugh 2005: 1). This argument with regard to Kojève underestimates the influence of surrealism, Marxism and also Jean Wahl, whose book on the 'unhappy consciousness' in Hegel precedes Kojève by a decade, being published in 1929. We have already cited the significance of surrealism for both Bataille and Artaud (Ades et al. 2006, Mundy 2006). Although surrealism is often presented, philosophically speaking, as some kind of vulgarised offshoot of psychoanalysis (a kind of sub-Freudianism), the early surrealists were comparatively well read in philosophy, including specific works of Hegel.

As Baugh outlines (Baugh 2005: 5), the neo-Kierkegaardian Wahl also developed early a penetrating analysis (via a negative reading of Hegel) of 'a self divided against itself, an internally divided and self-alienated subject; a subject that strives vainly for synthesis but instead oscillates between self and non-self, being and nothingness' (Baugh 2005: 5). For Baugh, the theorists of the 1920s and 1930s, although finding Hegel a useful 'diagnostic tool', mostly refused the synthesis of a Hegelian solution, which would seek to reconcile difference in a higher unity. Different groupings disagreed with the Hegelian synthesis in different ways. The Marxists (Henri Lefebvre foremost amongst them), for example, asserted that the moment of synthesis was possible but not under present economic and social conditions. It could only be brought about by social revolution.

The mainstream surrealists, with their hybrid mix of Marx and Rimbaud (Trebitsch 1991), more or less concurred (Mundy 2006), rendering them too 'idealistic' from Bataille's point of view (Richardson 2006). Paradigmatic here is the conflict over the interpretation of eros between Bataille and Breton; it is clear in this context that Breton is far closer to Hegel than Bataille (Richardson 2006: 24ff.). Others, in a perhaps more radical way, refuse the moment of synthesis altogether, 'seeing the divisions that render consciousness unhappy inescapable' (Baugh 2005: 5). Here, we have as our prime examples Bataille and Artaud and of course it is these figures who exert such a significant influence on Derrida's work. In both cases, synthesis (at least in Hegelian terms, if not in any sense) is seen as impossible. In Baugh's phrase, there can thus only be 'antithetics'; 'the play of opposed terms that negate and pass into each other; without ever coinciding into a meaningful whole' (Baugh 2005: 6). We can see how significant this influence on the whole generation of French thinkers was when we consider that existentialism too, and Sartre most especially perhaps, came under the sway of this radicalisation of Hegel (Sartre 1947). As Baugh notes:

> it is not difficult to see that the early forms of existentialism, as a philosophy of the absurd, follow from a refusal of synthesis that makes the unhappy consciousness a condition from which there is no escape, the necessity and inescapability of internal division, the impossibility of synthesis and dialectics (Baugh 2005: 6).

And, of course, these are also precisely the hallmarks of postmodernity, 'an anti-finalism', the denial of an ultimate *telos* rather than an anti-foundationalism (Drolet 2003).

It is only with Deleuze and Foucault, on Baugh's interpretation, that we actually get away from Hegel's extraordinary lure. With both these thinkers, there is at least an attempt to reject Wahl's 'unhappy consciousness' with all its attendant suffering. This, then, would be the story of the effects of the theme of the unhappy consciousness on French philosophy, which does call for a radical rewriting of the history of twentieth century French thought. It brings to the foreground figures who are usually relegated to secondary roles, focusing on the emergence in the 1920s of a dominant 'anthropological reading of Hegel'. This anthropological turn predates Kojève's interventions and was decisive, as it allowed Hegel (or at least a certain Hegel), to be brought within the ambit of movements such as surrealism, Marxism and existentialism. Wahl's focus on the unhappy consciousness is perhaps more important in this regard than Kojève's more famous exegesis. For our purposes, Baugh's reading is also significant to the extent that, unlike Foucault and Deleuze, Baugh reads Derrida's own work as still under the sway of Hegel and especially Wahl's reading of Hegel: 'the persistence of Hegelian negativity in Derrida' (Baugh 2005: 20).

In the last section, we spoke of the rather surprising emphasis which Derrida places on Bataille's reading of Hegel, as opposed to those elements of Bataille's work which might be more well known. For example, his emphasis on eroticism, his literary work, etc. However, given Baugh's reading of French philosophy and the twentieth century reception of Hegel, it is perhaps easier to understand the importance of Hegel to a reading of Bataille. What Baugh is stressing (perhaps overstressing) is the overwhelming influence which Hegel had on succeeding French thought, and he sees Bataille and Derrida as crucially under Hegel's sway. While Kojève's reading of Hegel was also important for Bataille, to the extent that he attended the lectures and wrote several texts in explicit response and several others which implicitly refer to Kojève, Baugh understands Bataille as in conflict with Kojève, at least in some crucial instances. One of the problems of interpretation here is that there is no consistent Bataillean approach to Hegel (Bataille's reading of Hegel, as with all of his readings of whomever, have various phases, inversions, and counter-inversions). Nonetheless, on Baugh's terms, according to Bataille, or at least the Bataille of the first letter to Kojève (Bataille 1988c), 'the Kojèvian-Hegelian saga leaves out of account humanity's desire for dissatisfaction and disharmony; a desire for incompleteness; in the self and in commensurability with the world; humanity is tension…' (quoted Baugh 2005: 81).

This becomes especially clear in Bataille's text *Le Coupable* [hereafter *Guilty*] (Bataille 1988b), which seeks to transgress the Hegelian boundary of sense and reason. 'I think of my life – or better yet, its abortive condition, the open wound that my life is – as itself constituting a refutation of Hegel's closed system' (Bataille 1988b: 123). Indeed, this last phrase comes from Bataille's direct 'Letter to Instructor of a Class on Hegel' (Bataille 1988c), who, of course, is Kojève. Speaking of Kojève's reading of Hegel, Bataille says that 'negativity isn't recognised…it's introduced into a system that nullifies it, and only the affirmation is recognised' (Bataille 1988c: 124).

Unlike Kojève, who still sees Hegel's dialectic as a dialectic of desire which can be recuperated and ultimately meaningful, for Bataille:

> self-consciousness is achieved then, only when the mind renounces action and becomes 'indefinite desire', negativity in revolt against itself, without any transcendence towards ends, a freedom for which nothing matters anymore; signifying nothing (Baugh 2005: 83).

Bataille thus pits Nietzsche against Hegel and we will return to the continuing (and persisitently underplayed) Nietzschean dimension in Derrida's work below. 'I refuse to be happy' (quoted Baugh 2005: 8), Bataille tells us in *Inner Experience*. For Baugh, there is in Bataille not simply an emphasis on a subjectivity which is 'under erasure' but also a reality which is similarly exposed: 'Bataille's fusion of an irrational and indeterminate subject with an irrational and indeterminate reality; nonknowledge is an endless movement of questioning...an ecstatic annihilaton of self and universe' (Baugh 2005: 84). But this movement of Bataille's discourse should not be seen as wholly negative, as we have earlier seen Sartre misrepresent it. Baugh also refers to Sartre's misreading of Bataille and counters (with Derrida) that 'Bataille describes a position that is not so much lacking in a system but which exceeds the system and resists being incorporated into it' (Baugh 2005: 86).

Bataille thus resists Hegel in a way that perhaps Sartre's work is unable to. But Baugh also refers interestingly here to Derrida's cautionary 'insistence that we must interpret Bataille against Bataille' (Baugh 2005: 91). The whole question of how to interpret Bataille's discourse is thus fraught with the tensions between the surface level reading of his discourse and the more attuned reading which takes into account the 'sliding' ('glissement') of the concepts and what Klossowski calls the 'simulacrum' of the text (Klossowski 1991). These problems of interpretation are consistently foregrounded by Derrida but they are also attempts at self-reading which pinpoint the same or similar difficulties in being able to interpret Derrida's own textual 'operations'. These questions also bring us back to Derrida's interviews where he constantly cites these problems of finding 'another site' (Derrida 1986c). In these early 1960s texts, Derrida is certainly engaging with these issues. It is also arguable that as his work develops into the 1970s most especially, that there develops a more direct 'enactment' of these issues in an extraordinary radicalisation of style across several texts (most notably in *Glas* [Derrida 1974a], but also in *Signéponge* [Derrida 1988], 'Tympan' [Derrida 1972c], *Dissemination* [Derrida 1972h], where, as one commentator has observed, Derrida 'self-implicates' himself and his work, in a way that is perhaps unique or unprecedented, at least in the history of philosophy [Derrida 1995a]).

This discussion takes place in the dialogue entitled 'Between Brackets' (Derrida 1995a). The interviewer suggests that Derrida's are 'texts which are unclassifiable according to normal standards and in which you implicate yourself, along with your body, your desire, your phantasms, in a way that perhaps no philosopher has ever done until now' (Derrida 1995a). The interlocutor goes on to delineate two stages of this process identifiable in Derrida's work. First, this process was already in Derrida's writing and themes, as it were, from the beginning in the Husserl texts. But second, 'now it has been extended in its multiplicity more explicitly' (Derrida 1995a). I very much concur with this reading of the evolution of Derrida's work and style of philosophising, and it is this interpretation which has guided the structure of my own work. Of course, outside conventional philosophy, the 'self-implication' of which the interviewer speaks here has analogous instances in literature, although not in all literature.

Rather in literature 'with a small l', as Derrida puts it, with Artaud, Bataille, Blanchot and Mallarmé, amongst others.

In the chapter which he devotes to Derrida, Baugh emphasises what he sees as the 'persistence of the unhappy consciousness' in deconstruction. In the first instance, there is of course Derrida's own critique of structuralism, the latter which Derrida distances himself from, even before he does the same with phenomenology. It is already happening in the early text 'Force and Signification' (Derrida 1967d), which is the earliest of the *Writing and Difference* texts, but it certainly happens most famously in 'Structure, Sign and Play' (1967l), and Derrida's comments in response to the questions on this paper in the infamous John Hopkins symposium (organised by René Girard) make this unequivocally clear (Macksey 2007). For Derrida, it is the case (albeit rather exaggeratedly) that 'the search for structures was totalitarian' (quoted Macksey 2007: 119). For Baugh, Derrida's response to Hegel would be to deepen the Hegelian dialectic, calling for a 'Hegelianism without Reserve', in which 'negations and differences could proliferate endlessly without being recuperated into a positive and totalising synthesis' (Baugh 2005).

As we have already argued here and as Baugh also argues, one of Derrida's main inspirations was Bataille's notion of 'expenditure without return'. Baugh also cites Jean Wahl's championing of irreconcilable divisions and differences as very significant for Derrida and it is well known that Derrida worked with Wahl closely at the ENS. On Baugh's terms, 'Derrida offers a Hegelian critique of Levinas; the other is always my other; but just when he comes closest to Hegel, he takes his distance' (Baugh 2005: 126). This, on our terms, is precisely the connection to Bataille; we follow Hegel so far, but only so far. For Derrida, as for Bataille, Hegel only recognises alterity in terms of an appeasement. Derrida, therefore, seeks another way; 'if there is an outside of thought, it must be thought in a different way' (Baugh 2005: 126). Here, we have seen how 'From Restricted to General Economy' seeks to posit just such an alternative approach to philosophy, what Derrida calls elsewhere a 'grammatological opening', what Bataille might have called the 'accursed share'.

Conclusion: Bataille Beyond *Writing and Difference*

We have seen in this chapter how Derrida seems happier to remain closer to Bataille than he does to Hegel, but ultimately there is also distance. There must always be difference, disagreement, alterity between the one and the other. We will return to this theme of Derrida and Bataille later, especially in Chapter 7 when we look at Derrida's more overt political thinking. Bataille's writings are significant in a number of other places in Derrida's work. Indeed, Bataille remains a constant reference for Derrida in his work, early, middle and late. He reappears in *Glas* (Derrida 1986b) in relation to the reading of Jean Genet, he is present in the 'Double Session' (Derrida 1972k) in terms of to 'die laughing', he appears at several key junctures in *Margins*, for example in contrast to Lacan (in the essay 'Différance': Derrida 1972d) who makes 'the hole a transcendental principle' (Derrida 1982c: 6).

In contrast, Bataille follows 'Nietzsche…a critique of philosophy as an active indifference' (Derrida 1982c: 7), and there is also a rare reference to Gilles Deleuze here. Bataille, *contra* Lacan, succeeds in the 'displacement and reinscription' (Derrida 1982c: 19) of 'philosophy/Hegelianism' (Derrida 1982c: 19). The famous final flourish of this essay which affirms with Nietzsche 'a certain laughter and a certain dance' (Derrida 1982c: 27) also has obvious resonances with Bataille (and Derrida's discussion of Bataille in *Writing and Difference*). As already mentioned, Bataille reappears at a crucial juncture in the later Levinas essay. Indeed he is already (back in 1964) referred to (alongside Nietzsche) as both close and far from Levinas in 'Violence and Metaphysics' (Derrida 1967f). Without wishing to be reductionistic, I think that the convergence between Derrida and Levinas in this essay has been highly exaggerated. Aside from issues of double reading, that is always reading for and against the relevant author (which are integral to all of Derrida's readings), it has always baffled me how the Derrida-Levinas relation is seen as so convergent (for example, in Critchley 1999, although at least he recognises the differences). The 'ethicisation' of Derrida's later work stems, it seems to me, from an overestimation of the Levinasian influence which is very much at odds with the letter (but also, I would argue more importantly, with the spirit [*l'esprit*] of Derrida's work).

As Derrida says in 'Violence and Metaphysics' (Derrida 1967f), 'The other cannot be what it is, infinitely other, except in finitude and mortality (mine and its)' (Derrida 1978d: 124). In other words, there can be no pure exteriority. It is also worth mentioning that there is a strong influence of Nietzsche in these early texts; a critique of morality *per se* and ethics and religion *per se*. The Levinas and Bataille relation returns in 1980 in 'At this moment in this work here I am' (Derrida 1994a). In many ways a more positive reading of the experience of bodily situatedness ('here I am') in Levinas's phenomenology than Derrida had given in his earlier essay 'Violence and Metaphysics', nonetheless ultimately there is a strong critique of Levinas's interpretation of difference, which Derrida reads as having been pre-determined by a masculine ('il') before the binary opposition 'il/elle' is instituted (Derrida 1997c/1994a). Crucially, for our purposes, the moment where Levinas's philosophy suffers a breakdown is marked by Derrida with an invocation, not to another phenomenologist, but to Bataille.

> His [i.e. Levinas'] 'text' (and I would even say *the* text, without wishing to efface an irreplaceable idiom) is always that heterogeneous tissue…and whoever…ventures to plot the absolute tear, absolutely tears his own tissue, once again become solid and servile in once more giving itself to be read (Derrida 1994a: 63).

With the publication of Bataille's *Oeuvres Complètes* in the 1980s (edited by Denis Hollier), Derrida seems to return to certain themes in Bataille. Bataille becomes central here to the rereading of philosophy's current situation; 'to be read right to left or left to right' (Derrida 1967k). Aside from the Levinas references, Bataille is also notably mentioned as highly significant in many of the later interviews and he also reappears in relation to Derrida's encounter with feminism. And, we see this also most recently in regard to the late texts on Jean-Luc Nancy (who is significantly influenced by Bataille as well as by Derrida) (Derrida 2005). I will return to some of these texts later. In the next chapter, I want to take up Derrida's complex development of the relation between deconstruction, the *avant-garde* and 'the writing of the body' through his readings in *Dissemination*. There, the main 'pre-texts' are Stephane Mallarmé's *Mimique* and Plato's enigmatic dialogues, the *Phaedrus* (Plato 1961) and the *Philebus* (Plato 1961). Once more, Derrida seems interested in the relation between philosophy and its other, which, as we shall see, is a relationship which is played out not simply in Mallarmé but also in Plato's dialogues. As the epigraph to the 'Double Session' makes clear, this would be a case of 'between [inter-] Plato and Mallarmé' (Derrida 1972k), which does not necessarily amount to 'between philosophy and nonphilosophy'. The question of the border between philosophy or nonphilosophy would, Derrida argues, be much more complex than this.

Chapter 3

From the 'Outwork' to 'Plato's Pharmacy': On Derrida, Plato and Pickstock

Introduction

This chapter will look at how Derrida's work develops the thematics already described in his early 1970s work, most especially in his enigmatic 'book', *Dissemination* (Derrida 1972h). Once more, the *avant-garde* influence is prominent with two of the key three pre-texts being those of Stéphane Mallarmé and Philippe Sollers. However, there is also a powerful encounter with the supposed founder of the Western philosophical tradition, Plato (Plato 1961). In the first main text of *Dissemination*, after the enigmatic 'Hors Livre: Préfaces' [hereafter 'Outwork, prefacing'] (Derrida 1972i, 1981b), 'La Pharmacie de Platon' [hereafter 'Plato's Pharmacy'] (Derrida 1972j, 1981c) takes up a reading of Plato which has been central to the reception of Derrida's work, most especially as it relates to his supposed critique of phonocentrism. Derrida, so the argument goes, is out to provide a critique of Plato and Platonism which sees the latter as instituting a radical privileging of the voice over writing, which is highly influential on succeeding thought and which continues to the present.

In this reading, Derrida's essay 'Plato's Pharmacy' (Derrida 1981c) attacks the dominant interpretation of Plato and the function of the reading of the *avant-garde* authors which follows is to institute the 'grammatological opening' (quoted Bass 1978: x). However, I want to argue against this reading here. On my interpretation, Derrida's reading of Plato is not a simple externalist critique. Rather, Derrida is keen to stress the internal complexity of the Platonic text, which in its 'doubling' strategies, already performs a kind of deconstruction on philosophy. Thus, for Derrida, Plato is at least in some important respects a precursor of the *avant-garde*. The philosophical status of Plato's text is not univocal. To a great extent, Plato already plays out the questioning of philosophy from a nonphilosophical site. Plato would thus be both inside and outside philosophy. In this measure, Plato would not be unlike Mallarmé, and not unlike Derrida and the very movement of deconstruction itself. Such a reading also complicates the understanding of Derrida's critique of phonocentrism. 'Plato's Pharmacy' (Derrida 1981c) cannot be seen as demonstrating the dominance of Platonic speech over writing or even some relative privileging there. Throughout the text, Derrida is keen to stress how Plato also asserts the significance of writing. Moreover, Derrida complicates the simple opposition between Platonism and sophistics,[1] which more traditional commentaries see as constitutive of what Platonism represents philosophically. For Derrida, the borderline between sophistics and Platonism, and thus between the supposed paradigm of philosophy and its other, would be not so easily drawn or maintained.

Dissemination begins with the disclaimer 'this will not then have been a book' ['ceci (donc) n'aura pas été un livre'] (Derrida 1972i: 9). It has a complex structure, which begins with an 'outwork', or 'hors livre' (Derrida 1972i), which rather than prefacing the text with a résumé of its contents and thus 'finalising' or 'synthesising' the text, seems to have the very opposite effect. As with many of Derrida's prefaces to individual essays in the earlier collections of work, such as *Writing and Difference* (Derrida 1967c), where the beginning of the essays serve to disorient the reader, so too with this 'Outwork'. Except, in this case, the effect is exacerbated by the preface being more lengthy and also more obscure. Thus, I will devote the first section of this chapter to looking at how Derrida complicates the overall status of *Dissemination* in his 'Outwork'. I will then look at how Derrida addresses the complex issue of Plato's understanding of philosophy, embodiment and meaning in the following section, through an analysis of the text which immediately follows the 'Outwork' in *Dissemination*, 'Plato's Pharmacy' (Derrida 1981c).

This text has received widely differing interpretations and I will next look at Catherine Pickstock's influential critique of Derrida from a Radical Orthodoxy standpoint, which she elaborates in her text *After Writing: On the Liturgical Consummation of Philosophy* (Pickstock 2000). I will then put forward my own reading of 'Plato's Pharmacy' in offering significant criticisms of what I see as Pickstock's rather simplifying and reductionistic interpretation of Derrida's work. I will develop this reading into the next chapter through looking at how Derrida reintroduces the problematic of the *avant-garde* which we have seen in the earlier chapters, in his essay which follows 'Plato's Pharmacy', 'La Double Séance' [hereafter 'the Double Session'] (Derrida 1972k, 1981d) which takes up an original and radical reading of Stéphane Mallarmé. Here, Derrida develops the thematic of 'between Mallarmé and Plato' (Derrida 1981d).

'Hors Livre': Out of Work

In her preface to *Dissemination*, Barbara Johnson (Johnson 1981) begins with a definition of grammatology, of the 'science of grammatology' (Johnson 1981) whose arrival Derrida had announced in his 1967 text *Of Grammatology* (Derrida 1967a): 'a science of writing which would study the effects of difference...which Western metaphysics has repressed in its search for self-present truth' (Johnson 1981: ix). What this definition foregrounds for Johnson is the double bind in which deconstruction is now situated: 'how to account for an error with the tools

---

1   'Sophistics' refers to the Sophist movement, an early school of thinkers who emphasised rhetoric rather than truth and which opposed Socrates.

which the tradition has made an error with; this is the task of deconstruction' (Johnson 1981: ix). Derrida employs a complex scheme of textual devices and stratagems to complexify his reading in *Dissemination*, and in many respects, this text represents the transition from the earlier formal paradigm shift towards the *avant-garde* (and away from phenomenology) to an increasingly radical stylistic shift towards *avant-garde* poetics which reaches its culmination in *Glas* (Derrida 1974a), published in 1974.

It is perhaps no coincidence that it is Mallarmé (Mallarmé 2008) who is Derrida's chosen interlocutor from the *avant-garde* in *Dissemination* (alongside contemporary novelist and writer Philippe Sollers). For it is Mallarmé who above all others is credited with bringing the 'crisis' of French literature to its apex. Elizabeth McCombie notes Mallarme's 'extraordinary reinvention of poetic expression' (quoted McCombie 2008: xi). This reinvention had been noted both positively and negatively by Mallarmé's contemporaries. While Paul Valéry referred affirmatively to the irresolvable tension in Mallarmé's work between 'structural coherence and fragmentation' and J.K. Huysmans developed Mallarmé as a character in his paradigmatic decadent novel *Against Nature*, Marcel Proust was less interested or forgiving. But Mallarmé also had an answer for Proust and his other prominent critics: he retorts that they cannot read, except perhaps newspapers (quoted McCombie 2008: x). This is Mallarmé's break with the emphasis on semantics, or the monopolisation of poetry by semantics which represents Mallarmé's greatest achievement and his most revolutionary gesture. McCombie also speaks of this as Mallarmé's emphasis on 'non-meaning', not as 'an absence of meaning but a potentiality of meaning which no specific meaning can exhaust' (McCombie 2008: xii). He also sought to eradicate the distinction between poetry and prose and to create a new genre of writings called 'anecdotes', which combined travel writing with autobiography and impressionistic images.

'This Will Therefore Not Have Been a Book'

With all of these elements, it is clear that Mallarmé has been a powerful influence on Derrida. Johnson refers to Derrida's numerous textual strategies, the use of 'syntax, allusions, fading in and out, multiple coherences' (Johnson 1981: xvi), translation as undecidable, the 'anagrammatical texture', 'lateral association' 'myth', etc. and she speaks very accurately of Derrida's myriad styles as 'mime[ing] the movement of desire rather than its fulfilment' (Johnson 1981: xvi). The 'pretexts for Derrida's inquiry will be Plato's *Phaedrus*, Mallarmé's *Mimique*, and Soller's *Nombres*' (Johnson 1981: xvi), but here in the preface it is perhaps the *avant-garde* authors who get the most prominence. Plato's turn will have to wait until 'Plato's Pharmacy'.

Derrida begins the 'Outwork' (and *Dissemination*) as he means to go on; 'this will therefore not have been a book' (Derrida 1981b: 3). Playing with and subverting the Hegelian dialectic, much as we have already seen him speak of Bataille miming the dialectic in 'From Restricted to General Economy' (Derrida

1967k), Derrida invokes yet another paradigm-shift, this time from the number three to the number four, away then from triangular synthesis and towards the 'add-on' (Derrida 1981b: 25), the 'always one more'. It is not so much that four would be the final number or the definitive term but more that it would signify the subversion of the triadic synthesis. It will always now be '3+n'. No more synthesis, just dispersal and dissemination after the failure of Hegel's philosophy. This is what Derrida means to demonstrate by denying the book its very identity at the beginning, both a rejection of the (total) book and a rejection of the idea of an absolute beginning or origin.

The preface for Hegel represented precisely this cumulative origin and directing normativity for the book to follow. But Derrida's work is an 'outwork', an 'out of book', in a sense then a book which is not a book, a non-book. This brings us back to Derrida's repeated insistence that he is seeking a site of nonphilosophy. *Dissemination* would be 'out of the book', out of philosophy, 'out of its head', or as Derrida plays on later, 'mine de rien' (Derrida 1972k: 244), a mine of nothing, a 'never min(e)d', as Johnson translates it. It was precisely the move from the paradigm of three to four which also represented Mallarmé 's great 'crisis of verse'. Alongside the figure of Mallarmé, the outwork also accumulates and intensifies the referencing of the *avant-garde*. It is reminiscent of Rimbaud's 'systematic derangement of the senses' (Rimbaud 1962), it is not arbitrary (but 'systematic') and yet it is a generalised disorientation. It is not surprising to find Derrida invoke the Comte de Lautréamont (Lautréamont 1978) quite substantially in the preface. He also appears in an epigraph to the essay 'La mythologie blanche' [hereafter 'White Mythology'] (Derrida 1972f, 1982e), written around the same period. Invoking Lautréamont's famous text *Les Chants de Maldoror* (Lautréamont 1978), perhaps *the* example of an *avant-garde* 'outwork', Derrida plays on the very same emphasis which Lautréamont gave his preface ('la preface hybride', Derrida 1972i: 46).

Once more, as with Bataille and Klossowski, it is a question of 'simulacrum' ('simulacre'). Unlike Hegel, who emphasised the preface so as to finalise the work and complete and totalise the meaning, with Lautréamont we once again have a parodying satire on totalised meaning, where the preface which is supposed to help support the work, ends up taking the very ground from under it. Lautréamont, as with Plato, is obsessed with caves ('ma chère caverne', quoted Derrida 1972i: 46) and alongside Mallarmé, is obsessed with mirrors. We will return to this question of the cave and the mirror, and the affinity of the *antre* (cave) and the *entre* (between) below. But here Derrida is stressing 'the preface of *Maldoror*' (Derrida 1981b: 36). There, Lautréamont satirises the usual comprehensive overview as well as the ethical defence of the writer's intentions. Moreover, from a Derridean perspective, what is perhaps most striking is that the prefaces in *Maldoror* seem to multiply, until they almost take over the whole book. The very book itself becomes a preface to a book which never arrives, a non-book. As Derrida observes, this is 'Lautréamont's departure from the book' (Derrida 1981b: 43) and we have already seen how Derrida seems to mime this strategy in *Dissemination*. This also will have implications for the whole 'ontology of the cave' which will become a theme through the analysis of Plato. For Maldoror, the cave is 'beloved', 'the depths of my beloved cave' (quoted Derrida 1981b: 39) rather than something which one wishes to get out of into the light. There is also the issue of the relationship between the shadows (or images/mirror) as derivative and the location of reality, as outside the cave. What, Derrida asks, 'if the mirrors could no longer be comprehended within the ontology of the cave, but would rather envelop it totally?' (Derrida 1981b: 41). This will become a paradigmatic issue in 'Plato's Pharmacy', in relation to Plato's designation of the difference or border between 'good and bad mimesis' (Derrida 1981c), which begins from Socrates' descriptions of the various kinds of bed in Plato's *Republic* Book 10 (Plato 1961).

As with all of Derrida's books, there are constant inter-references to earlier Derridean texts, and here in the 'Outwork', at the supposed 'beginning' of the text, they are especially significant. While Mallarmé appears as an interlocutor in a number of texts in *Writing and Difference* (Derrida 1978a), it is often forgotten that the epigraph to the text 'as a whole', which is cited at the very 'beginning', in fact before the beginning (in lieu of a preface, one might say) is from Mallarmé. It is not coincidental that it also appears in the Outwork here; 'the whole without newness except a spacing out of reading' (Derrida 1981b). This introduces the important Mallarméan notion of 'espacement' which is related to Derrida's very notion of 'différance' as a spacing of time and a temporalisation of space (Derrida 1981b: 57). Derrida also speaks of 'Mallarmé's *lustre* for Plato's *sun*' (Derrida 1981b: 53).

Paradigms of the Imagination

Richard Kearney has provided in his text *Wake of the Imagination* (Kearney 1988) a very lucid genealogy of the concept of 'lustre', which shows its distinctiveness in marking a 'post-modern' epoch. It also demonstrates the innovativeness and revolutionariness of Mallarmé's approach which is here being put to work by Derrida. Kearney distinguishes between three epochs and three paradigms of imagination, culminating in the paradigm of the 'lustre'. There is no univocal semantics of imagination but rather what we mean by imagination has evolved through a rather conflictual historical genealogy. In the first case, we have the paradigm of the *mirror* (Kearney 1988: 253ff.), and this broadly reflects the perspectives of the ancient and medieval worlds on imagination. The paradigm of the *mirror* exemplifies how imagination merely re-presented an image of a pre-existing and superior reality. In this sense, imagination and the products of imagination in art were always seen as secondary and derivative. The second and more modern paradigm for imagination, precisely the paradigm of modernity, is the image of the *lamp* (Kearney 1988: 253ff.). Here, imagination no longer merely reflects but lights up or draws attention to reality. Imagination and creativity reveal the world in new ways.

The third paradigm which Kearney invokes is that of the postmodern epoch and here he borrows explicitly from Mallarmé, the image of the 'lustre' (Kearney 1988: 253ff.). In Kearney's words, the lustre is a:

chandelier with multiple glass pendants endlessly reflecting each other. With this trope of the multi-faceted *lustre* which is nothing beyond its own intra-fragmenting light, we discover that there is no essential distinction between 'the image and thing, the empty signifier and the full signified, the imitator and the imitated' (Kearney 1988: 255).

At least according to this image, postmodernism refers to the breakdown in the surety of the modern 'lamp'. No longer so sure of our light and power to discern reality, no longer convinced that we can indeed create new worlds or even words, postmodernism starts from an acute sense of dizziness and vertigo. And so the 'lustre' suggests itself as an appropriate image. But this is no longer an image amongst images. It is rather an image, which in presenting an inter-nihilistic plays of image-to-image, calls a halt to imaging *per se* and the capacities of imagination and creativity.

Or so one might think. But what *Dissemination* demonstrates is the very affirmation of this play of chance and disinterred imagery and conceptuality. Once again, Derrida looks to the *avant-garde* for guidance. He tells us that 'dissemination places philosophy on stage and its book at stake' ['remet la philosophie en scène et son livre en jeu'] (Derrida 1972k: 61, 1981b: 53). Another rendering of this phrase might see Derrida as placing philosophy in 'the game'. There is a direct reference here to Artaud and his conception of 'forces' ['des forces'] (Derrida 1972k: 61) and once more we have a connection back to the earlier texts and the reiteration of the paradigm shift away from phenomenology to the *avant-garde*. There is a castigation of 'l'impuissance d'une forme' (Derrida 1972k: 61), the 'impotence of form'. Derrida says that this will be 'pyrotechnical as well as metaphysical' (Derrida 1972k: 62), surely a further (implicit) reference to Artaud and his plea 'to be done with forms when we should be signalling from the flames'. Pierre Klossowski's work, and its complex notion of doubling is also invoked here, in a reference to the 'simulacrum' (Klossowski 1997), and taking into account Klossowki's recently published work on Nietzsche, we can see that the laughter and excess of the latter is not far away either.

Against all this, it would seem that Plato 'must block his ears' ['se bouche les oreilles'] (Derrida 1972k: 196). The theme of noise (*klang*) and music are foregrounded in a number of texts of this time, not least 'Tympan' (Derrida 1972c) in *Margins of Philosophy* (Derrida 1972b) and also *Spurs: Nietzsche's Styles* (Derrida 1979), and of course *Glas* (Derrida 1974a). But if Plato must block his ears, what does this signify? If the 'Outwork' represents the necessary deconstruction of the work and the book, and the latter's dialectical dream of totalisation, surely the attendant excessive noise must be listened to? Surely philosophy must be attentive to its other? At this point of the text, Plato would seem certainly to be entering as an opponent of all this otherness, as someone who instigated the very tradition which attempted to bring such otherness and excess back inside, to either destroy or repress the outside. As always with Derrida, however, nothing is ever quite as obvious as it might appear to be. In concluding the 'Outwork', Derrida states 'the conscious lacks' ['le conscient manque'] (Derrida 1972k 66, 1981b: 58). He suggests we can take either word as noun. And so, in the first case, consciousness as a noun or thing would lack (with lack as a verb). This would be reminiscent of Jacques Lacan's claims regarding the unconscious. In the second instance, where 'lacks' would be the noun, he would be delineating the lack which we are conscious of. Philosophy would be conscious of its own lack. Derrida plays on the ambiguity between these two meanings and we see that the 'Outwork', as with so many of Derrida's prefaces, has served less to introduce and more to disorient.

Leading into the Plato/Derrida Encounter: From Artaud's 'en Jeu' to Pickstock

In Chapter 1, we spoke of Artaud's 'physical language' (Derrida 1967k), his 'corps à corps' and emphasis on life, breath and *a writing of the body* ('l'écriture du corps'). These were all seen as pivotal to Derrida's conception of a 'a nonphilosophical practice' (Derrida 1986b) and his radicalisation of style. On my interpretation, this emphasis on *avant-garde* poetics, which we looked at in Chapter 2 through the prism of Bataille's work (and Derrida's interpretation of Bataille), can be seen as opening up to desire for the other of philosophy and thus contesting philosophy and its limits. I have in Chapters 1 and 2 been interpreting this Derridean approach as a positive phenomenon. I have read deconstruction affirmatively as seeking to develop a way out of the impasse of dualist metaphysics. Not all commentators, of course, agree with this affirmative reading of Derrida. I have also suggested in the last section that the 'Outwork' to *Dissemination* seems to construct a critique of philosophy's traditional attempt to limit the play of meaning. Drawing on a number of *avant-garde* authors, including Artaud, Lautréamont and Mallarmé, *Dissemination* seems to set the stage for a theatrical encounter (as Derrida himself uses the Artaudian reference). He tells us that 'dissemination places philosophy on stage and its book at stake' ['remet la philosophie…en jeu'] (Derrida 1972k: 61, 1981d: 53). The scene would seem to be set for the appearance of Plato, the great custodian of the book and meaning and the truth of philosophy, as an apparent opponent on the stage of all these *avant-gardists*. This will certainly be the way that many interpret the logic of *Dissemination* (Derrida 1981a).

Let us recapitulate slightly. The Artaudian reference is helpful here and it is another example of how despite all the chance, all the play and simulacrum, there is also a 'play of necessity' in Derrida's texts. As Peggy Kamuf has made clear, one must respect a certain chronology in Derrida's work, or at least it helps to do so (Kamuf 1991). There are significant patterns here, certain movements, not linear ones but nonetheless ones which as Barbara Johnson suggest, mimic the play of desire (Johnson 1981). And while desire may not be linear, it does have its patterns, its tendencies. So too with Derrida's writing. Let us return, then, briefly to Artaud before we begin to look at the way Pickstock reads the Platonic text. If Artaud helps us to put philosophy on stage, then what exactly is at stake here?

For Derrida, as for Artaud, there is obviously a question of writing *per se*, as we will see (linked to the much vaunted but debatable critique of phonocentrism in Derrida's work) as well as more specifically and more interestingly, a 'writing of the body'. Artaud introduces, as Susan Sontag reminds us, *a theatre of the senses* (Sontag 2001): 'a physical language, a corps à corps, a life, a breath' (Derrida 1967h). And crucially what draws Derrida to Artaud, on this thematic, is that it is (if not quite exactly) then at least close to what he terms 'a nonphilosophical practice' (Derrida 1986b).

But why is this the case? Why is the discourse or writing which gets closest to the body and to the physical by definition 'nonphilosophical'? This, in Artaud's case, relates to his whole critique of the Western tradition, with the philosophical endeavour as key to this architectonic. The history of metaphysics in the West has been the history of dualism, of the separation of the mind and body, of the sensible and the intelligible and the stealing and alienation of what Artaud refers to as the 'breath' ('le souffle') and the 'life-force'. So this is the indictment which has been set against the Western philosophical tradition. We have already seen some of its criticisms being levelled at Hegel in the chapter on Bataille. There, Bataille criticises Hegel for seeking to exclude and reduce the 'forces' of existence, which exceed meaning and the dialectic. We saw Derrida in his early work make a similar criticism of Husserl's phenomenology, for example with regard to the distinction between expression and indication or between meaning and supposed nonsense. Indeed, we can also cite the distinction between 'speech and writing' as Derrida seems to suggest in *Of Grammatology* and *Speech and Phenomena* or between the 'origin and history', as Derrida has suggested in his *Introduction to Husserl's Origin of Geometry*, and the list goes on. So, the stage would indeed seem to be set, after the *avant-gardism* of the 'Outwork', for the further indictment of Plato and Platonism in 'Plato's Pharmacy'.

A Liturgical Reading of Derrida

Before looking at how one might read Derrida otherwise here, I will first look at perhaps the most eloquent example of such a more traditional reading, and critique of Derrida. This highly influential reading is that of Catherine Pickstock in her text *After Writing: On the Liturgical Consummation of Philosophy* (Pickstock 1998). Pickstock interprets Derrida and deconstruction as evolving a deficient and dangerous philosophy of 'nihilism' (Pickstock 1998: 64ff.) an accusation which is here labelled at Derrida from the vantage point of so-called 'Radical Orthodoxy' (Pickstock 1998: xiiff.). For our purposes, what is significant in this context is that the accusation of nihilism is associated by Pickstock with the very emphases which we have looked at in Derrida's analyses of Artaud and Bataille, the attempt to move beyond the dialectic of Hegel and to cite the irreducibility of difference and existence. Pickstock is claiming that the postmodern era represents a renewed possibility for the religious and for theology, a possibility which deconstruction is incapable of fulfilling. For Pickstock, it is postmodern theology which is alone capable of retrieving the premodern roots of religious and philosophical truth. These roots are grounded in 'doxology' or 'praise of the divine' (Pickstock 1998: xii), as exemplified by the metaphysics of Platonism and fully realised in Christianity. This is also a key element in the disagreement between Pickstock and Derrida, their varying interpretations of Platonism. As Pickstock observes:

> This essay completes and surpasses philosophy in the direction, not of nihilism, but of doxology. It shows how philosophy itself, in its Platonic guise, did not assume, as has been thought, a primacy of metaphysical presence, but rather, a primacy of liturgical theory and practice. This same primacy, it claims, was developed, and more consistently realised, in mediaeval Christendom (Pickstock 1998: xii).

For Pickstock, then, Derrida's supposed interpretation of Platonism as a 'metaphysics of presence' is simply wrong. But more than this, Pickstock's thesis represents a powerful challenge to the very presuppositions of Derrida's thinking. Nonetheless, I will argue that, despite its subtlety, Pickstock's thesis represents a serious oversimplification of the development of deconstruction. That is, I will claim that Derrida's philosophy cannot be simply equated with nihilism. And, moreover, this disagreement will go even deeper to the extent that I will question Pickstock's understanding of Plato's own texts. With regard to her reading of Derrida specifically, Pickstock's reading of deconstruction is premised on a reading of the entire philosophical tradition. She is at odds with what she interprets as Derrida's own meta-reading of philosophy as being entirely based on a fixation upon 'presence' and the 'myth of transcendence': 'The entire postmodern historical and philosophical perspective is called drastically into question. No longer are we legatees of a Western logocentrism, fixated upon presence, and a domineering gaze secured by myths of transcendence' (Pickstock 1998: 48). Derrida's diagnosis of a logocentric and a phonocentric bias is thus seen by Pickstock as severely misguided. Pickstock directs her attention here specifically to Derrida's reading of Platonism in 'Plato's Pharmacy' (Derrida 1981c).

Misunderstanding Phonocentrism

On Pickstock's interpretation, Derrida's reading presents Plato as advocating a 'metaphysical suppression of temporality, supplementarity and difference (Pickstock 1998: 4). Again, this ties in with the reading of the *avant-garde* being precisely in opposition to Platonism. Here, Artaud, Bataille and Mallarmé would line up (as advocates of difference) in opposition to Plato and the Platonic heritage. The paradigm text in question here is the *Phaedrus* (Plato 1961) which, according to Pickstock, is radically misrepresented by Derrida. This misrepresentation has two main aspects:

1. Derrida, according to Pickstock, accuses Plato of 'phonocentrism', a privileging of speech over writing. Whereas speech involves presence to self and presence to another, writing is capable of subsisting in the

absence of the original author. For this reason, the activity of speech is more amenable to the maintenance of clarity and identity and becomes the philosophical medium *par excellence*. In contrast, the possible absence of the author of the written word leaves open the danger of an alienation and misunderstanding of meaning. Writing, in contrast to speech, therefore becomes, for Plato, the great threat to philosophical clarity and truth. Again, the contrast with the *avant-garde* couldn't be more acute. For Artaud, for example, (despite all the anti-graphematic rhetoric) it is precisely the '*writing* of the body' which is being sought. For Bataille, it is precisely the 'sliding' ('glissement') which writing allows which enables an exceeding of Hegelian dialectic. And in the case of Mallarmé, again it is writing, which in its very 'non-meaning', provides the basis for meaning itself. Writing for these *avant-gardists* is thus not simply positive but perhaps more fundamental to meaning than even speech itself.

2. Second, on Pickstock's terms, Derrida's analysis of the Platonic Form of the Good misconceives the 'transcendence' (Pickstock 1998: 11) of such an ultimate ontological source. According to Pickstock, Derrida paralyses Plato's text by pointing to an apparent contradiction within the description of the Form of the Good. For Derrida, the Good is 'at once radical absence *and* original presence' (Pickstock 1998: 11). On the one hand, Plato requires the presence of the Good to act as a foundation for morality and existence in general, but, on the other hand, it is radically inaccessible: 'the Good beyond Being'. For Derrida, such contradiction in Plato's dialectic then leads to irresolvable conflict and the failure of the quest for truth. As we shall see below, this is a rather limited conception of Derrida's reading of the Theory of Forms.

However, what is clear is that in terms of both these analyses, that of the relation between speech and writing and that of transcendence, Pickstock accuses Derrida of misunderstanding Platonism. In the first case, Pickstock re-reads Plato (and specifically the *Phaedrus* [Plato 1961]) with regard to its supposed phonocentrism. Pickstock does not deny that Plato privileges speech over writing but she vehemently rejects Derrida's conclusion that this privileging seeks to repress difference, temporality, supplementarity, etc. Rather, the Platonic privileging of orality has a different focus: it is designed to liberate difference from its suppression within the sophists' privileging of writing. As Pickstock notes:

> It is precisely a sophistic suppression of genuine difference in favour of commercial and manipulative interests – through the instrumentalisation of language – which Socrates attacks for being inimical to the practice of dialectical differentiation. For both rhetoric and writing can be characterised by their assimilability to any cause and usefulness in any situation: a kind of saturation of difference which, Socrates implies, reduces to the closure of difference or sheer indifference (Pickstock 1998: 6).

Plato is thus a 'phonocentrist' in that he does privilege orality over writing but he is not a phonocentrist as Derrida understands the term. Indeed, quite the contrary. The especial status given the voice in the *Phaedrus* (Plato 1961) is directed towards the very possibility of increased differentiation and temporality. But there is worse to come for Derrida in this context. Not only has Derrida misrepresented Platonism as a 'metaphysics of presence' (Pickstock 1998: 47). Additionally, his own method of deconstruction turns out to be the very opposite of what he claims for it. Whereas Derrida presents deconstruction as opening up difference, temporality, etc., in reality it suppresses these very possibilities in a way akin to the writings of the sophists:

> Both Derrida and the sophists paradoxically hypostasise writing so that it becomes an ideal science which, like Lysias' scroll, both mystified and appropriated beneath Phaedrus' cloak, can be transferred equivalently to any place and is unaltered by the passage of time (Pickstock 1998: 8).

Pickstock's reading of Derrida's work, therefore, sees itself as turning Derrida's own analysis back against itself. The supposed charges Derrida makes against Platonism (with regard to phonocentrism) become the very charges which Pickstock addresses to deconstruction. This also will have serious implications for the postmodern meta-reading of the history of philosophy. In the last analysis, Pickstock will accuse Derrida of simply developing the errors of Cartesianism: 'it also appears that Derrida remains within a post-Cartesian set of assumptions whose ancestry lies in sophistry and not Platonic dialectics' (Pickstock 1998: 48). Pickstock's second main criticism of Derrida concerns the problem of 'transcendence': specifically, the interpretation of the Form of the Good/the Good beyond Being [*epekeina tes ousias*] (Pickstock 1998: 12). In line with a more recent school of Platonic interpretation (Ferrari 1987), Pickstock argues against the traditional reading of the Platonic Forms as completely 'separate' from the empirical world. But she is also keen to question what she refers to as Derrida's 'immanentist' (Pickstock 1998: 12) interpretation:

> Derrida's approximation of the good to capital betrays a reading of the forms as scientific postulations verifiable by the immediacy of facts – as ontic rather than ontological – whereas, in this dialogue, Socrates is concerned to expose the dangerous dishonesty of such an epistemology…this [Derrida's] explanation… overlooks its transcendent nature, which makes immanent propositions concerning its content impossible (Pickstock 1998: 11).

This interpretation leads to what Pickstock refers to as 'the contagion of the Good' (Pickstock 1998: 11). Here, one is steering a middle course between the conception of the Forms as completely separate from the empirical world and a reading of the Forms as immanent. As transcendent, the Forms (and, in particular, the Form of the Good) are said to 'participate' in the empirical. This is a development of Plato's own concept of *methexis* or 'participation' (Plato 1961) and this is exemplified by the discourse of the *Phaedrus*. As Pickstock observes: 'Indeed, in the *Phaedrus*, Plato portrays the transcendence of the good, its beyond presence-and-absence, as a kind of contagion, for its plenitude spills over into immanence, in such a way that the good is revealed in the beauty of physical particulars' (Pickstock 1998: 12).

Derrida's reading of a 'contradiction' in Plato's concept of Form, according to Pickstock, thus only holds if one subscribes to an 'immanentist' categorisation of philosophy. On these lines, as exemplified by Derrida, the Form is both 'present' in the sense of being participatory within the world, and 'absent' in the sense of being ultimately inaccessible. Defined in immanent terms, this undoubtedly leads to contradiction and an apparent impasse in the Platonic philosophy. But such an interpretation, according to Pickstock, can be superceded if one moves to the reading of the 'contagion' of the Form. Here, the Form is interpreted as 'an inaccessible and inexhaustible plenitude' (Pickstock 1998: 11), which is never completely absent insofar as it participates in the finite. Plato's icon of the sun in the *Republic* is another relevant metaphor:

> As source of all light, the sun is more difficult to see than anything else, but it is a beneficent mystery which lets things be seen in their true nature, while itself remaining but obliquely visible. As well as letting things be seen, the sun gives things to be seen, for although it is beyond being, it is the ground of all being(s) (Pickstock 1998: 11).

Pickstock presents Derrida's reading of such a Form as sophistic: 'we cannot grasp or appropriate the good, but it is only a sophistic consciousness which would interpret this as a compromise' (Pickstock 1998: 14). Pickstock's interpretation of Derrida as a sophist demonstrates that there is more at stake in her reading than simply a critique of deconstruction. For Pickstock, Derrida (as a paradigm postmodern 'nihilist', Pickstock 1998: 64), is repeating an age-old gesture which can be traced to the early sophists, i.e. the suppression of difference and temporality (Pickstock 1998: 8). Far from instituting the metaphysics of presence, Plato is thus presented as resisting this very metaphysics through his critique of sophistry. In attacking Platonism, Derrida is thus reinstituting a postmodern sophism, which contrary to its supposed emphasis on difference, is paradoxically merely affirming a metaphysics of presence: 'In presenting a new sophism, Derrida himself is exposed to all Socrates' criticisms. He is himself culpably "metaphysical" insofar as he celebrates sophistry and writing' (Pickstock 1998: 46). This extraordinary reading of the Derrida-Plato relation is certainly striking in its originality. But in its effort to itself present a meta-reading of the whole history of philosophy, it occludes some significant complicating factors in Derrida's reading of Plato in 'Plato's Pharmacy'.

Apophasis or Nihilism of the *Pharmakon*?

In this section, I will put forward a critique of Pickstock's reading of Derrida as a postmodern nihilist. Pickstock's analysis adopts an overly literalist approach and I will foreground the ambiguity and openness of Derrida's reading of Platonism. Far from reducing Platonism to a 'metaphysics of presence', Derrida rather presents Platonism as itself self-deconstructive, a precursor of Derrida's own thinking. In effect, Derrida's reading of Platonism is very close to that of Pickstock, in its emphasis on temporality, supplementarity and difference. The disagreement stems from different readings of the relation between Platonism and doxology. Whereas Pickstock sees Platonic philosophy fulfilled and superceded in Christian dialectics, Derrida rather holds out for an ultimate philosophical 'apophasis'. Before addressing the meaning of such 'apophasis', I will first analyse Derrida's interpretation of Platonism. The obvious text to foreground in this context is 'Plato's Pharmacy' (Derrida 1981c), insofar as this essay remains Pickstock's primacy focus. Below, however, I will extend this analysis to related Derridean texts which can shed light on Pickstock's narrow critique. Derrida's analysis in this essay has as one of its primary loci the relationship between Plato and sophistics (Derrida 1972j: 120–36, 1981c: 105–19). Initially, Derrida makes the following blunt statement:

> men of writing appear before the eye of God not as wise men (*sophoi*) but in truth as fake or self-proclaimed wise men (*doxosophoi*). This is Plato's definition of the sophist. For it is above all against sophistics that this diatribe against writing is directed: it can be inscribed within the interminable trial instituted by Plato, under the name of philosophy, against the sophists [*on peut l'inscrire dans l'interminable procès entamé par Platon, sur le nom de philosophie contre les sophistes*] (Derrida 1972j: 120/21, 1981c: 105/6).

Just two pages on, however, Derrida adopts a rather different tone: 'Contrary to what we have indicated earlier, there are also good reasons for thinking that the diatribe against writing is not aimed first and foremost at the sophists. On the contrary: sometimes it seems to proceed *from* them (*il semble parfois en procéder*)' [Derrida's emphasis] (Derrida 1972j: 123, 1981c: 108). The negative, rejoining aspect of this second statement is clear – Derrida twice uses the term 'contrary' alongside a single use of 'not'. But the more affirming, extending sense of this passage is easier to miss. It is encapsulated in the 'also' – 'there are *also* good reasons for thinking'. Once again, Derrida is not so much arguing against himself as *adding* a second (apparently contradictory) proposition to a prior premise. Plato would be *both* against sophistics *and* for sophistics. This logic of both/and is developed by Derrida in the succeeding discussion.

Socrates' and Plato's original criticism of the sophists is presented by Derrida (see above) as being linked to writing. The diatribe against writing is primarily a diatribe against sophistics (Derrida 1972j: 120/21, 1981c: 105/6). In the *Sophist*

(Plato 1961), Socrates gives a definition of the character of the title – the sophist is 'the imitator of him who knows' (*mimëtës tou sophou*). This status of 'imitation' is grounded in the privileging of speech over writing – writing can only imitate speech. But now Derrida points to a discussion of writing in the *Laws* (Plato 1961) where Plato seems to adopt a more affirmative attitude:

> In this instance, the immutable, petrified identity of writing is not simply added to the signified law or prescribed rule like a mute, stupid simulacrum: it assures the law's permanence and identity with the vigilance of a guardian [*elle en assure la permanence et l'identité avec la vigilance d'un gardien*] (quoted Derrida 1972j: 128, 1981c: 113).

Derrida quotes from two passages in the *Laws*, the first (891a) where the putting into writing (*en grammasi tethenta*) is interpreted as being both a challenge to posterity and a safeguard against people's tendency to miss the point at first hearing – 'since even the dull student may return to them for reiterated scrutiny' (Plato 1961: *Laws* 891a). The second passage concerns the need to procure books (*grammata*) as a condition for being a righteously equal judge. Such a judge 'must keep these matters before his eyes', a possibility underivable from speech but intrinsic to the permanence of writing. The final sentence of the passage leaves one in no doubt that here at least Plato is *privileging writing over speech*:'There is, in truth, no study whatsoever so potent as this of law, if the law be what it should be, to make a better man of its student' (Plato 1961: *Laws* 957c).

Already, Derrida states, there has been a 'reversal' [*renversement*; also 'overthrow'] (Derrida 1972j: 128, 1981c: 112) of Plato's original position of a distancing from writing and sophistics, understood as interdependent, to an endorsement of writing, as *the most potent* method of studying law and moreover, the best means to make *a better man of its student*. Writing is thus now tied, positively, to morality and civil ethics. But this is only the first of the apparent inversions which Derrida will describe. These inversions are not limited to the Platonic side of the 'border' [*frontière*] (Derrida 1972j: 123, 1981c: 108), but are equally engaged in by sophistics. Isocrates, sophist *par excellence*, is the next thinker foregrounded in 'Plato's Pharmacy':

> Inversely, symmetrically, the rhetors had not waited around for Plato in order to *translate writing into judgement*. For Isocrates, for Alcidamas, *logos* was also a living thing (*zoon*) whose vigor, richness, agility and flexibility were limited and constrained by the cadaverous rigidity of the written sign (Derrida 1972j: 129, 1981c: 114).

'Inversely, Symmetrically'

'Inversely, symmetrically' [*Inversement, symétriquément*] – before discussing the details of the Isocrates case, it is useful to once again move towards what might be called the meta-level, towards Derrida's motif of *closure*. *On the one hand*, there is inversion here ('inversely'). Plato inverts a privileging of speech over writing into a privileging of writing over speech. Isocrates inverts a (conventionally) sophistic privileging of writing over speech into a privileging of speech over writing. *On the other hand*, there is simultaneously an undeniable symmetry ('symmetrically') at work. If the opposition between Plato and sophistics is premised on their maintaining their stereotypical positions, the above inversions problematise such a fundamental opposition, such a fundamental assymmetry. They thus, by definition, point towards the possibility of symmetry. But, of course, one is not here (*chez* Derrida) dealing with a dialectic of thesis, antithesis, synthesis. Symmetry would not constitute the final term of a series. Rather it would now be added as a supplemental term to the previous binary opposition between Plato and sophistics. Thus:

1. Plato and sophistics would be symmetrical.
2. Plato and sophistics would be assymmetrical.

This enigmatic series of simultaneous inversion, symmetry and assymmetry is eloquently described by Derrida in 'Plato's Pharmacy' in the following, revealing passage:

> The front line that is violently inscribed between Platonism and its closest other, in the form of sophistics, is far from being unified, continuous [*est loin d'être unie, continue*] as if stretched between two homogeneous areas. Its design is such that, through a systematic indecision, the parties and the party lines frequently exchange [*echangent*] their respective places, imitating the forms and borrowing the paths of the opponent. These permutations are therefore possible, and if they are obliged to inscribe themselves within some common territory [*sur un terrain commun*], the dissension no doubt remains internal and casts into absolute shadow some entirely-other [*tout-autre*] of *both* sophistics *and* Platonism, some resistance having no common denominator [*sans commune mesure*] with this whole commutation (Derrida 1972j: 123, 1981c: 108).

Derrida's suggestion appears to be that any clear demarcating line between philosophy on the one hand, and sophistry on the other, is an impossibility. Instead, there is just the ever increasing process of blurring and complicity, of *doubling*. And this argument is intensified in the final pages of Part I of 'Plato's Pharmacy' (Derrida 1972j: 129–36, 1981c: 114–19). In the first case, Derrida outlines the content of Isocrates' critique of writing and his eulogy to speech. The rigidity of writing is a result of the fact that no matter how many republishings take place, the texts must obey the 'preestablished pattern' (Derrida 1972j: 130, 1981c: 114) of what was written down originally:

writing, in that it repeats itself and remains identical in the type, cannot flex itself [*ne se ploie*] in all senses, cannot bend [*plie*] with all the differences among presents, with all the variable, fluid, furtive necessities of psychagogy. He who speaks [*Celui qui parle*], in contrast, is not controlled by any preestablished pattern [*ne se soumet a aucun scheme préetabli*]; he is better able to conduct his signs; he is there to accentuate them, to inflect them, retain them, or set them loose [*les lâcher*] according to the demands of the moment, the nature of the desired effect, the hold [*la prise*] he has on the listener (Derrida 1972: 129, 1981c:114).

This is a crucial passage in terms of Derrida interpretation. Critics and defenders of deconstruction alike have focused on a much vaunted Derridean critique of phonocentrism (for example, Norris' *Derrida*) [Norris 1987], the privileging by metaphysics of the voice over the written word, to which deconstruction would then be an inversion, i.e. a privileging of writing over speech. But what I have tried to show through this analysis of 'Plato's Pharmacy' is the constant interplay between opposing inversions in Derrida's work – an opposition is inverted only to be later re-inverted or de-inverted. This reading of Platonism, which far from presenting it as a univocal 'metaphysics of presence', reads it as interminably dual and ambiguous is supported by a later text of Derrida's, 'Comment ne pas parler: Dénégations' (Derrida 1997f) or 'How to avoid speaking: Denials' (Derrida 1992c). Here Derrida is interested in distinguishing between what he calls '*two* movements or *two* tropics of negativity…in the Platonic text' (Derrida 1992c: 101). He refers to these structures as being 'radically heterogeneous' (Derrida 1992c: 101). In the first case, Derrida identifies 'the idea of the Good' which, for Plato, 'has its place beyond being or essence' (Derrida 1992c: 101). This conception is found primarily in the *Republic* (509b ff.):

One of them [i.e. one of the movements of negativity] finds both its principle and its exemplification in the *Republic* (509b ff.). The idea of the Good (*idea tou agathou*) has its place beyond Being or essence…whatever may be the discontinuity marked by this beyond (*epekeina*) in relation to Being, in relation to the Being of beings or beingness (nevertheless, three distinct hypotheses), this singular limit does not give place to simply neutral or negative determinations, but to a hyperbolism of that, beyond which the Good gives rise to thinking, to knowing, and to Being. Negativity serves the *hyper* movement that produces, attracts or guides it. The Good is not of course in the sense that it is not Being or beings, and on this subject every ontological grammar must take on a negative form. But this negative form is not neutral. It does not oscillate between the *ni ceci-ni cela* (the neither/nor). It first of all obeys a logic of the *sur*, of the *hyper*, over and beyond, which heralds all the hyperessentialisms of Christian apophases (Derrida 1992c: 102).

Derrida's point here is that this first negative moment in Platonism remains metaphysical – in denying the predicate of 'being' to the Good, Plato is not putting the Good in suspension or doubting its existence in Derridean fashion. Rather 'the idea of the Good beyond Being' suggests that the Good has an Existence greater than empirical being. Plato therefore subverts essentialism with this conception (and, in this, he is a deconstructionist) but only to replace this prior essentialism with what Derrida calls a '*hyper*essentialism' (Derrida 1992c: 102). At this point, Derrida refers specifically to the 'hyperessentialisms of Christian apophases' (Derrida 1992c: 102), and the suggestion is that while Christian negative theology (or apophasis) involves something of deconstruction it, nonetheless, supersedes this deconstruction with a hyper-positive predication. In 'Denials', Derrida is identifying a more radical deconstructivism in Plato. The second 'tropic of negativity' (Derrida 1992c: 101) which Derrida describes can be found in the *Timaeus*: 'I will distinguish the tropics of negativity, which I have just outlined in such a schematic manner, from another manner of treating what is beyond (*epekeina*) the border, the third species, and the place. This place is here called *khora*; I am, of course, alluding to the *Timaeus*' (Derrida 1992c: 104).

The 'khora', for Derrida, represents the most radical aspect of Plato's thought insofar as it avoids the hyperessentialism which is present in 'the idea of the Good beyond Being' and in the so-called 'Christian apophases' (Derrida 1992c: 102). Or, rather, the 'khora' avoids this hyperessentialism in its second moment which Derrida is careful to distinguish from a first more metaphysical aspect:

> To be sure, one of these languages [in the *Timaeus*] multiplies the negations, the warnings, the evasions, the detours, the tropes, but *with a view* to reappropriating the thinking of the *khora* for ontology and for Platonic dialectic in its most dominant schemas. If the *khora* – place, spacing, receptacle (*hypodokhe*) – is neither sensible nor intelligible, it seems to *participate* in the intelligible in an enigmatic way (51a). Since it 'receives all', it makes possible the formation of the cosmos. As it is neither this nor that (neither intelligible nor sensible), one may speak as *if* it were a joint participant in both. *Neither/nor* easily becomes *both...and*, both this and that (Derrida 1992c: 105).

Derrida sees this first exposition of the 'khora' (in the *Timaeus*) [Plato 1961] as still a form of 'hyperessentialism' – the *neither/nor* of deconstruction becomes the *both/and* of metaphysics. To this extent, this first exposition of the 'khora' is, for Derrida, analogous to the structure of the 'Good beyond being' in the *Republic* (509b ff.). In 'Denials' (Derrida 1992c), Derrida describes how this first metaphysical 'khora' has come to define the readings of the *Timaeus* in the history of philosophy, most notably inaugurated by Aristotle:

> Aristotle provided the matrix for many of the readings of the *Timaeus* and, since his *Physics* (bk.4), one has always interpreted this passage on the *khora* as being *at the interior* of philosophy, in a consistently anachronistic way, as if it prefigured, on the one hand, the philosophies of space as *extensio* (Descartes) or as pure sensible form (Kant); or on the other hand, the materialist philosophies

of the substratum or of substance which stands, like the *hypodokhè*, beneath the qualities or the phenomena (Derrida's emphasis, Derrida 1992c: 105).

Having outlined the first moment of the 'khora' as being still too metaphysical, he now describes the second section of the *Timaeus* as being appropriately deconstructive:

> The other language and the other interpretive decision interest me more...This other gesture would inscribe an irreducible spacing interior to (but hence also exterior to, once the interior is placed outside) Platonism, that is, interior to ontology, to dialectic, and perhaps to philosophy in general.

This 'other gesture', for Derrida, is developed by Plato precisely against the previous reading of 'khora'. This is, in effect, a *doubling* of 'khora', a 'khora' *contra* khora:

> Under the name of *khora*, the place belongs neither to the sensible nor to the intelligible, neither to becoming, nor to non-being (the *khora* is never described as a void), nor to Being...All the aporias, which Plato makes no effort to hide, would signify that *there is* something that is neither a being nor a nothingness; something that no dialectic, participatory schema, or analogy would allow one to rearticulate together with any philosopheme whatsoever, neither 'in' Plato's works nor in the history that Platonism inaugurates and dominates. The *neither/ nor* may no longer be reconverted into *both...and* (Derrida 1992c: 105/6).

The second moment of the 'khora' in the *Timaeus* is affirmed by Derrida to the extent that it no longer (in contrast with the first instance of 'khora') turns apophasis into hyperessentialism – in Derrida's words, the *neither/nor* no longer becomes a *both/and*. It is this instance of 'khora' which can be said radically to undermine Aristotle's reading of Platonism (*Physics* Book 4, quoted above), which later was employed to present Platonism as a harbinger of Cartesianism and Kantianism:

> This [i.e. the 'khora'] is neither an intelligible extension, in the Cartesian sense, a receptive subject, in the Kantian sense of *intuitus derivativus*, nor a pure sensible space, as a form of receptivity. Radically nonhuman and atheological, one cannot even say that it gives place or that *there is* the *khora*...It does not give place as one would give something, whatever it may be; it neither creates nor produces anything, not even an event in so far as it takes place.

Derrida now delineates how, for Plato, this 'khora' expresses a fundamental 'indifference', but not as negative:

> Plato insists on its necessary indifference; to receive all and allow itself to be marked or affected by what is inscribed in it, the *khora* must remain without form

and without proper determination. But if it is amorphous [*amorphon*; *Timaeus*,
50d], this signifies neither lack nor privation. *Khora* is nothing positive or negative.
It is impassive but it is neither passive nor active (Derrida 1992c: 107).

Derrida's reading of a duality in the history of philosophy is thus reinforced.
On the one side, one has the philosophies of essentialism such as Cartesianism
and Kantianism, and within this group there is also included the philosophies of
hyperessentialism (the examples in 'Denials' being the Platonic 'Good beyond
Being', the first description of the 'khora' and the 'Christian apophases'). On the
other side, one has the nonessentialist thinking of deconstruction which is practised
not simply by Derrida but often by the essentialist philosophies in their 'dual'
nature. In 'Denials' (Derrida 1992c), the obvious example is the dual thinking of
the 'khora' which, at separate instances of the *Timaeus*, is interpreted by Derrida as
being alternately hyperessentialist ('both/and', Derrida 1992c: 104; *Timaeus* 51a–
52b) and nonessentialist ('neither/nor', Derrida 1992c: 105; *Timaeus* 50b–d). What
marks the second instance of 'khora' as nonessentialist and deconstructionist is
precisely its *nondialectical* nature – it is *neither this nor that* (Derrida 1992c: 106).
And what marks the first instance of 'khora' (as well as the 'Good beyond Being'
and the 'Christian apophases') as essentialist/hyperessentialist or nondeconstructive
is exactly its *dialectical* aspect – the 'khora' becomes *both this and that*.

My claim is that Derrida's reading of 'khora' in 'How to avoid speaking:
Denials' (Derrida 1992c) is consistent with his interpretation of a dual structure to
Platonism in 'Plato's Pharmacy' (Derrida 1981c). But both of these readings run
counter to Pickstock's claim that Derrida is attempting to suppress difference and
ambiguity. Moreover, in locating 'apophasis' in Platonism and 'hyperessentialism'
in Christianity, Derrida's thinking calls into question Pickstock's presentation of
Platonism as a stepping stone to Christian doxology. Rather, on Derrida's reading,
Platonism (and thus deconstruction itself) would remain resistant to the attempt to
dialecticise apophasis into Christian truth and worship.

Conclusion: From *Doxology* to *Deconstruction*

Pickstock's interpretation of Derrida is grounded in an interpretation of Platonism
and, more generally, a reading of the history of philosophy. She reads Platonic
doxology as paving the way for the most adequate expression of theology in
Christianity. The highest moment of this latter theology would appear to be the
Thomistic synthesis as later medieval theology, in particular the Scotist form, is
already complicit with the modernist 'nihilism'. As Fergus Kerr has observed in
relation to an analogous argument from Phillip Blond (Blond 1997):

> The critical turn, according to Blond, was when theology surrendered to secular
> reason's account of nature – perhaps not so much in France, with Descartes, but in
> England, between the time of Henry of Ghent and Duns Scotus (Kerr 1998: 352).

The fateful innovation was that there could be an 'ontology without God' prior to theology – a 'simple elevation of an ontic understanding of Being over God as in Scotus' (Kerr 1998: 353). Pickstock's thesis can be seen as reinforcing this conception of the history of thought: 'Pickstock's book also depends a good deal on a certain anti-Scotism' (Kerr 1998: 354). The deterioration which sets in with Scotus is exacerbated by such early modern figures as Ramus and Descartes (Pickstock 1998: 47–100) and reinforced by the postmodern nihilism of Derrida, Foucault et al. Consequently, from a theological perspective, one must seek to retrieve something like the Thomistic synthesis and, from a philosophical perspective, one can affirm the embryonics of this synthesis in Platonic doxology.

I have attempted in this chapter to demonstrate how this thesis, however eloquent and intellectually masterful, remains unconvincing. First, Pickstock's reading of Derrida is too literal; he does not seek to critique Plato as a 'metaphysician of presence' but rather outlines the dual movement of Plato's text between dialectical closedness (the hyperessential Good beyond Being) and apophatic openness (the second movement of *khora*). In effect, Platonism is presented as the first self-deconstructive philosophical system. Far from being nihilistic, such duality (in Plato and Derrida) represents a genuine philosophical openness to Pickstock's much vaunted difference, temporality and supplementarity (Pickstock 1998: 4). But this apophasis also spells danger for Pickstock's attempt to supercede philosophy with theological doxology. Against Pickstock's reading of deconstructon as nihilistic, one might rather present it as the subversion of the possibility of converting philosophy into theology. Such a subversion is shared rather than opposed by Platonism. In the last analysis, the real contemporary threat of sophism appears to be identifiable with the movement of Radical Orthodoxy.

In the next chapter, I want to look at how we might see Derrida's complex presentation of the relation between Plato and Mallarmé (Mallarmé 2008), in the text which follows 'Plato's Pharmacy' in *Dissemination*, 'The Double Session' (Derrida 1972k). As Derrida notes, in his title page to the essay, 'Inter Plato et Mallarmé'. This 'between' is also of course once more the between of philosophy and nonphilosophy. Although 'The Double Session' is often read as specifically an essay on Mallarmé, it is also crucially concerned with the relationship between Mallarmé and the philosophical tradition, most especially in terms of whether the desire for the other of philosophy is repressed or affirmed by that tradition. In re-reading Mallarmé against conventional interpretation (which has sought, despite all the warnings, to present an argument for the 'essence' of Mallarmé's work), so too Derrida will caution against reading an essential Plato or Platonism. 'The Double Session' then rereads against the grain not simply the *avant-garde* and Mallarmé, but also Plato and Platonism. As we will see, this problematic primarily focuses on the relationship between the Forms and the sensible world, or, in our recurrent terms, the problematic of desire, embodiment and the 'l'écriture du corps'.

Chapter 4

Mallarmé After Plato: On Derrida and 'La Double Séance'

Introduction

In this chapter, I want to take up the reading of *Dissemination* where 'Plato's Pharmacy' ends and where Derrida reintroduces the problematic of the *avant-garde* which was so central to the 'Outwork' and his earlier essays in *Writing and Difference*, which we looked at in Chapters 1 and 2. First, we might ask, how we are to think about the relationship between the various parts of *Dissemination* (Derrida 1972h, 1981a)? As we saw in the last chapter, Derrida in the 'Outwork' makes clear that this is not to be understood as a totalised book project; 'this will therefore not have been a book' (Derrida 1981b: 3). The 'Outwork' rather vehemently deconstructs the pretensions to unity which the superficial appearances of the book might suggest. But this still leaves the question of the relation between the various parts of the text, in some kind of abeyance. Much as we can see, alongside Peggy Kamuf (Kamuf 1991), that the development of Derrida's work, despite appearances, is in no way arbitrary, so too we can say the same of the structure of *Dissemination*. While it may not be a totalised book, that does not amount to saying that there is no pattern to its organisation.

We have seen the argument put forward by Pickstock that Derrida's work is nihilistic but we have also seen that this does not bear up to close scrutiny of the texts concerned. On our terms, Pickstock (Pickstock 1998) is wrong on two counts; she is wrong in terms of her intrepretation of Derrida but she is also wrong in her interpretation of Plato. Both these thinkers (i.e. Plato and Derrida) may be closer to each other in philosophy than one might be led to expect. If Derrida has always sought a nonphilosophical site from which to question philosophy, it is clear that Plato's dialogical form and its emphasis on *elenchus* or refutation (Plato 1961) is clearly a strategy in the same direction. It seeks to inscribe philosophy in a space which questions and contests philosophy's own right to authority and legitimacy. In this sense, it is arguable that the Platonic dialogue comes close to being an extra-philosophical space and in this we can argue that Plato is a precursor of deconstruction, a kind of proto-deconstructionist. This in effect is the argument which Derrida makes suggestively in 'Plato's Pharmacy'. It also counts against the argument made by Pickstock (which underlies and biases her reading of Derrida) that Platonic apophasis should make way for Christian dialectic and liturgy. This giving way or supercession of philosophy by religion is hardly in keeping with the very precise philosophical engagement in both the Platonic and Derridean text.

If we look at this new found affinity between Derrida and Plato, we can locate it on different levels of their thought. First, there is the question of Plato's theory of Forms which, as one topic itself, allows other significant philosophical issues to be addressed and mediated through it. If the Forms are no longer seen as 'separated', then the whole relationship of the sensible to the intelligible needs to be readdressed. Derrida's reading affirms the Platonic dialogue form as, against all appearances, a 'writing of the body'. But moving beyond this, there are additional connections in terms of the question of a philosophical methodology, most especially as this relates to the question of the relation between *mythos* and *logos*, the relationship between philosophy and literature, the question of the status of writing and its relation to the so-called phonetic prejudice (which I think has been much misunderstood). As with so much of Derrida's work, however, this is a complex intertextuality, and, as well as the *Phaedrus*, a number of other Platonic dialogues become relevant here.

We can cite the *Meno*, most especially the discussion of paradox and aporia, the *Republic* for its discussion of the Forms, mimesis and the Allegory of the Cave, the *Symposium* for its discussion of Eros and the later dialogues such as the *Sophist* and the *Parmenides* for their critique of the notion of 'separate Forms'.[1] In this chapter, I want to tackle these related questions. I will first look to some of the tensions within the Platonic texts which we have seen (and will see) foregrounded in the essays 'Plato's Pharmacy' and 'The Double Session'. I will then provide an analysis of 'The Double Session' and how it understands the 'between' (entre), the 'intercourse' between Mallarmé and Plato. We will see this topic directly continued in Chapters 5 and 6 through a reading of *Spurs: Nietzsche's Styles* (Derrida 1979) and Nietzsche and finally through a reading of Derrida and feminism in the later texts which more directly address issues of embodiment and the senses, such as 'Geschlecht: Différence Sexuelle, Différence Ontologique' [hereafter 'Geschlecht: Sexual Difference, Ontological Difference'] (Derrida 1997d, 1991d) and 'Choréographies' [hereafter 'Choreographies'] (Derrida 1992b, 1991c).

Reading Plato before Mallarmé

We have already spoken of the importance of the dialogues the *Phaedrus* and the *Meno* to 'Plato's Pharmacy'. Perhaps even more important than those two dialogues, for Derrida, is the access which the *Phaedrus* and the *Meno* give to a whole problematic in Plato, what we might term the relation between philosophy and non-philosophy, or philosophy and its other. From a Derridean perspective, while difference depends upon identity, identity depends upon difference. Thus, the positing of a unity independent of difference becomes highly problematic, indeed impossible. Derrida's reading of Plato in 'Plato's Pharmacy' points to this impossibility, through the irreducibility of *doubling*. Derrida locates points of stress

---

1   All the Platonic dialogues mentioned here are translated into English in Plato 1961.

within the Platonic text and this is not so much a deconstructive critique of Plato as a recognition that Plato is already engaged in self-deconstruction. Derrida's reading is very subtle here. But 'Plato's Pharmacy' also recognises a prevalent *metaphysical* movement in Plato's work. At one point, for example, Derrida refers to 'Platonism' (Derrida 1981c: 76) as 'setting up the whole of Western metaphysics in its conceptuality' (Derrida 1981c: 76). An overly simple reading of Derrida might identify this statement as a *critique* of Platonism, and by implication of metaphysics as such. However, 'Plato's Pharmacy' makes clear at several points that, from a Derridean perspective, there is no one Plato, no one interpretation of Platonism: 'we do not believe that there exists, in all rigor, a Platonic text, closed upon itself, complete with its inside and its outside' (Derrida 1981c: 130).

The metaphysical moment of Plato's text is interpreted as provisional, contextual and therefore subject to always possible re-contextualisation. Far from repressing Plato, a deconstructive reading thus opens up the Platonic text to an endless *dissemination* of possibilities. Plato would not merely be a metaphysician, but potentially a thinker of the anti-metaphysical, the transmetaphysical, the nonmetaphysical, the premetaphysical and the postmetaphysical. Indeed, strictly speaking, there would be no closed metaphysics to transgress. 'Metaphysics' would 'itself' be far more complex than has often been supposed. These developments of Derrida's logic are in no way meant as ironical. Rather they point to a relentless drive towards nonfinalisation at the heart of deconstruction, a wellspring of futural possibility.

Interpreting Plato

The dialogues of Plato themselves manifest extraordinary procedures of reversal, doubling, apparent contradiction and impasse. At stake here is the very status of Plato's discourse, a fact not lost even on Plato's most traditionalist interpreters. W.K.C. Guthrie, for example, in the Introduction to his translations of the *Protagoras* and *Meno*, outlines some of the difficulties which any interpreter of Plato must face:

> When a philosopher expounds his thoughts in the more usual form of a systematic treatise, it may be profound and difficult, but at least the reader's task is limited to finding out what it means on the assumption that the writer was doing his best to communicate his own views in as clear and orderly a manner as possible. But in dealing with something that so far from being a treatise, is a unique amalgam of philosophical discussion with dramatic art, humorous irony, and poetic myth, a number of prior questions must arise (Guthrie 1956: 8).

Edward Zeller, on the other hand, while recognising the (Platonic) complexity which Derrida describes, nonetheless wants to claim that a unity in Plato's philosophy can still be, as it were, rescued:

> Although Plato's philosophy is nowhere transmitted as a systematic whole
> and in the dialogues we can only observe from afar its gradual growth and
> development, it is only in the form of a system that any account of it can be
> given. The justification for this is the incontestable fact that in the dialogues
> we see circles spreading wider and wider until they finally embrace the whole
> universe (Zeller 1980: 126).

While one might admire Zeller's confidence in positing a unity or a Platonic
system based on 'circles spreading wider and wider', a close analysis of the
dialogues concerned reveals significant and rather recalcitrant complexity. Taking
the *Meno* first, we can see that the tone is set abruptly at the very beginning of
the dialogue with *Meno* immediately asking, 'Can you tell me, Socrates, whether
virtue can be taught, or is acquired by practice, not teaching?' (Plato 1961: *Meno*
70a; *ekheis moi eipein, ho Socrates, ara didakton he arete; he ou didakton all
asketon*). Plato avoids the articulation of dramatic context he so ably elaborated in
the prior *Protagoras* (Plato 1961). This enables him (via Socrates) to focus on the
philosophical issues more clearly and the introduction of the topic of virtue (*arete*)
provokes Socrates into a question concerning the nature of virtue itself.

Far from being able to offer an answer to whether virtue is acquired by teaching
(*didakton*) or practice (*asketon*), Socrates cannot even elaborate what virtue is in
the first place:

> a drought of wisdom has come on (*aukhmos tis tes sophias gegonen*)…so far am
> I from knowing (*eidenai*) whether it can be taught or not (*eite didakton eite me
> didakton)* that I actually do not even know (*host oude auto eidos*) what the thing
> itself, virtue (*arete*) is at all (Plato 1961: *Meno* 71a).

Under the experience of Socrates' dialectical questioning, Meno's state is
transformed from that of eristic *tharraleos* (over-confidence) to what he himself
will refer to as *aporien* (utter perplexity). This transformation and Meno's insuing
indignation reaches a climax at the famous passage where Meno accuses Socrates
of being akin to a torpedo-fish:

> I consider that both in your appearance and in other respects you are extremely
> like the flat torpedo sea-fish; for it benumbs (*narkon*) anyone who approaches and
> touches it, and something of the sort is what I find you have done to me now. For
> in truth I feel my soul (*ten psukhen*) and my tongue quite benumbed (*narko*), and I
> am at a loss what answer to give you. And yet on countless occasions I have made
> abundant speeches on virtue (*aretees pampollous logous*) to various people – and
> very good speeches they were, so I thought – but now I cannot say one word as to
> what it is (*nun de oud ho ti esti to parapan ekho eipein*) (Plato 1961: *Meno* 80b).

This is then the result of the way of dialectic. While eristic leads to the making of
abundant speeches on virtue (*aretees pampollous logous*) dialectic leads rather to

a drought of wisdom, a state of being benumbed (*narko*). This situation is repeated in the example of the slave-boy (Plato 1961: *Meno* 84a) where Socrates trys to prove a mathematical truth to the slave of Meno. Initially, the boy is confident but this confidence is shown by Socrates to be over-confidence (*tharraleos*) and he is reduced to a state of perplexity (*aporein*). In effect, the *Meno* represents the *doubling* strategy of deconstruction in its implication that Socratic knowledge can only be nonknowledge, Socratic objectivity only the lack of an object. If the *Meno* seems to deconstruct epistemology and the will-to-knowledge, the *Phaedrus* (Plato 1961) addresses what appears to be a very different issue; the relationship between the sensible world (the world of the senses) and the Forms and also the mediation of this problematic through the dynamic of eros (or love).With regard to the Forms, we can say that, in Plato's work, this project has a rather tortured history. The early and middle dialogues clearly outline a metaphysics of *separation* – in the *Republic*, for example, the Good is 'beyond Being'. But by the time Plato came to write the *Timaeus*, he had realised the difficulty of surmounting this philosophical chasm – how was the individual subject to access the Forms? Kenneth M. Sayre in *Plato's Late Ontology* (Sayre 1983*)* makes the point that the brevity of the *Critias* (Plato 1961) might be seen as the last gasp of Plato's 'two-world' ontology:

> Plato's abrupt termination of Socrates' conversation with Timaeus and his companions only a few pages into the *Critias*, in fact, might possibly signal his ultimate disaffection with the 'two world' ontology upon which these dialogues are explicitly based (Sayre 1983: 14).

The Phaedrus*: Plato's Writing of the Body?*

Depending upon how one dates the *Phaedrus*, it is either a late middle (or 'intermediate') dialogue or a very late work. Rowe (Rowe 1986), for example, sees only the *Laws* and the *Philebus* as later. Whatever view one takes, the *Phaedrus* is placed right at the nexus of the difficulties concerning Plato's interpretation of the Forms. On Sayre's view, the later Plato begins to develop a more dialectical view of the relation between subjectivity and the Forms. The *Parmenides* (Plato 1961) is the crucial deconstructive text in this regard. *Parmenides II*, in particular (Sayre 1983: 16), represents a 'massive and formally conclusive refutation' of the two-world ontology. It is the *Philebus* (Plato 1961) which then builds on this deconstruction a new sense of the ontology of the Forms:

> The ontology of the *Philebus* is entirely different…in the *Philebus* the Forms are ontologically derivative…whereas sensible objects are composed of Forms and the Unlimited, Forms themselves are composed from the same Unlimited in combination with the principle of Limit (Sayre 1983: 14)

Previously (for example, in the *Republic*), the Forms were said to be ontologically separated from the sensible world. This separateness, of course, is the basis of

Aristotle's famous accusation against the Platonic Forms in the *Metaphysics* (Aristotle 2004): how can philosophy continue if it has no connection to truth? The later Plato appears to take this accusation on board and the *Phaedrus* and *Philebus*, in particular, can be seen as attempts to bridge the chasm between the sensible and the intelligible. However, before this constructive project is undertaken, Plato unequivocally undoes the logic of his prior two-world ontology. This two-world ontology has precisely also maintained a dualism of soul and body. At stake here then is once more the possibility of a 'writing of the body', but this time in the rather unlikely surroundings of the Platonic text.

G.R.F. Ferrari (Ferrari 1992), for example, contrasts the *Phaedrus* on precisely this level with the *Symposium*:

> the place of Beauty in the two dialogues is different. Diotima's initiate comes to see Beauty just in itself; he comes to see, I suggested, that there *is* such a thing as Beauty, independent of what we find beautiful. The experience of the inspired lover in the *Phaedrus*, by contrast, is to shuttle in memory between the bodily beauty of the boy and the Beautiful itself. It is to be awoken by an exemplar of Beauty to the conviction that there is such a thing as Beauty (The boy, too, comes to have this experience, seeing the lover's face transformed by love, made beautiful by the sight of beauty; 255b7–d3) (Ferrari 1992 : 268).

It would, however, be misguided to portray the later Plato as resolving all the questions concerning the Forms in a clear and distinct manner. The *Phaedrus* manifests such ambiguity and reversal of argument (e.g. Socrates gives one speech which he then completely recants in a succeeding speech) that it has been interpreted throughout history as either a work of an immature (Diogenes Laertius) or senile (H. Raeder) Plato. Derrida notes this history of a 'badly composed' dialogue in 'Plato's Pharmacy'. Before analysing the details of the *Phaedrus*, I will first outline some of the ontological tenets of the roughly contemporary (or slightly later) *Philebus* as this dialogue seems to make explicit much of the metaphysics which remains implicit in the structure of the *Phaedrus*. The *Philebus* (Plato 1961) is Plato's most explicit attempt to offer an alternative view of the Forms to the two-world ontology. The difficulty of trying to link subjectivity or the sensible world with the Forms, given the latter's ontological 'separation', is overcome through the interpretation of the Forms and the sensible world as 'ontologically homogeneous' (Sayre 1983: 15).

The Forms are no longer described as ultimate but rather as 'ontologically derivative' (Sayre 1983: 14) to the extent that they (like the sensible world) partake of the principle of the Unlimited. While the *Philebus* offers no clear account of how the sensible world or its individual subjects relate to the Forms, it nonetheless has now provided the philosophical framework within which such communication is at least possible. This increased possibility has not been effected by making the subject more knowledgeable but rather by conceiving of the Forms as more participant in the sensible world. In other words, the resolution lies in an increased emphasis on the object rather than on the subject. Hackforth refers to this objective emphasis as being particularly a feature of the *Phaedrus:* 'a susceptibility to the influence of external Nature felt as a power lifting him (Socrates) out of his normal rational self into a state of "possession" (*enthousiasmos*)' (Hackforth 1952: 14). This is precisely Ferrari's point in the essay 'Platonic Love' (Ferrari 1992). There Ferrari describes Plato as building a 'bridge' (Ferrari 1992: 248) in the *Phaedrus* 'between love and philosophy' (Ferrari 1992: 248). If love is still a Form for Plato it is now at least an incarnate Form, a Form which manifests itself in the sensible world. In the *Phaedrus*, this incarnation is exemplified by the beauty of the Ilissus (which is an exemplar of Beauty as such). There is also a sense in which Phaedrus himself represents an empirical incarnation of Beauty, leading Socrates outside the city with his seductive power.

But the thematic of the incarnate beauty in the *Phaedrus* is not simply an issue concerning the Forms. It also foregrounds the whole question of philosophical methodology in Plato, as well as the question of the relation between philosophy and eros. Again, a traditional reading of Plato presents his texts as 'rationalist', as seeking to outlaw and prohibit (for example in the *Republic*) [Plato 1961] any examples of irrationality, which he, in the *Republic*, associates with the negative influences of art and *mimesis*.

Here, in the *Phaedrus* however, Socrates will reject the basis of Lysias' very arguments concerning the preferability of a non-lover over a lover (Plato 1961: *Phaedrus* 230e–234c), or strictly speaking the superiority of rationalism over love. Socrates' initial speech agrees with Lysias' fundamental point while disagreeing with his method, but the second Socratic speech is a complete refutation of the principle that 'the rational must always be praiseworthy and the irrational always deserve censure' (Plato 1961: *Phaedrus* 235e and Hackforth 1952: 36). Ferrari's distinction between the *Symposium* and the *Phaedrus* (see above) is crucial here. In the latter dialogue the conception of the Forms as 'separated' becomes developed into a sense of the Forms (particularly the Form of Love) as 'shuttling' between the sensible and intelligible worlds. This is manifested, for example, in Socrates' eulogy to the banks of the Ilissus and in the erotic play between Socrates and Phaedrus which is a continuing feature of the dialogue. Here, we see how the question of the Forms is interconnected in our reading of Plato with the question of desire and embodiment as well as with the question of the very status of philosophy itself.

The Socratic ideal of wisdom as a 'divine madness' or 'love' is most explicitly stated in Socrates' second speech, the third and final speech of the *Phaedrus* (after Lysias' and Socrates' first speech). However, the essence of this wisdom is already articulated by Socrates directly after Lysias' speech. At 242b–c (Plato 1961: *Phaedrus*), Socrates declares that he has been visited by a 'divine sign' which now necessitates him to recant his original speech:

> all at once I seemed to hear a voice, forbidding me to leave the spot until I had made atonement for some offence to heaven. Now, you must know, I am a seer;

not a very good one, it is true, but, like a poor scholar, good enough for my own purposes (Plato 1961: *Phaedrus* 242b–c).

At this point of the dialogue, Socrates is just about to introduce his second speech which will be a complete recantation of both the initial speech of Lysias (recounted by Phaedrus) and Socrates' own first speech. 'I am a seer' – it is crucial that at this juncture in the dialogue Socrates once again reiterates his nonrational paradigm. It is Socrates' second speech which constitutes the centre-point of the dialogue, at least in terms of its underlying philosophy, if not its 'formal structure' (Hackforth 1952: 136). On this point, Hackforth claims that there is an apparent 'formal defect' (Hackforth 1952: 137) in the *Phaedrus* to the extent that the formal structure of the dialogue, which appears to be guided by the importance of 'dialectic' as a new philosophical methodology (of 'collection and division'; Plato 1961: *Phaedrus* 264e–266b), is undermined by the nonrational excess of the second speech. Hackforth nonetheless sees this 'formal defect' as purposeful on Plato's part – the *Phaedrus* is really about philosophy as love and this underlying basis of the dialogue is perfectly exemplified by the extremism of the second speech. Formalism, despite initial appearances, plays only a small part in the *Phaedrus*.

There is also a point to be made here concerning the nature of Plato's formalism. The distinction which Hackforth maintains between the second Socratic speech and the formal emphasis on dialectic assumes that the latter is exclusively rational. But Hackforth himself clearly shows that even the formal aspects of the *Phaedrus* are far from being rationalist in a simple sense of the term. While Socrates sets very high standards for dialectical procedure in general his own employment of this technique in the *Phaedrus* is undermined by inconsistency and a lack of precisely the clear definition which the new methodology is intended to inaugurate. Commenting for example on the passage 265e–266b, Hackforth states the following: 'It must therefore be admitted that Socrates' account of the dialectical procedure followed in his speeches is far from exact' (Hackforth 1952: 133).

On this interpretation, the extremism of the second speech (i.e. its complete refutation of rationalism) is no longer diametrically opposed to the formalism concerning dialectic. The emphasis on dialectic now becomes at least compatible with the stress on eros so pronounced in the second speech, insofar as the new Socratic dialectic is itself far from being completely rational (or as Hackforth observes, 'far from exact'). This affinity between eros and dialectic seems hardly surprising. The Platonic dialectic is after all a dialectic grounded in 'love' – at 266b, for example, Socrates describes himself as a 'lover' (*erastes*) of these divisions and collections (Plato 1961: *Phaedrus* 266b). It seems possible to therefore read Hackforth's so-called 'formal defect' in the Platonic dialectic as being purposeful on Plato's part.

If dialectic is driven by a love of wisdom rather than wisdom itself (which Socrates describes as being accessible to God alone; 'God alone knows'; Plato 1961: Phaedrus 266b) then one can refer its nonfinalisation back to, for example, the Heraclitean model of striving (or *orexaito*) for an unattainable truth. In Epistle

VII, surveying a life lived as a seeker after truth, Plato himself states that he has never outlined a manual of his doctrine (Plato 1961: Epistle VII 341c; Hackforth 1952: 163), thus conclusively vindicating the sense of philosophy as an open-ended project. In other words, the failure of the Platonic dialectic in the *Phaedrus* to live up to its stated intentions is not a specific failure due to error which might be superceded by a better methodology. Rather this is the failure which is intrinsic to the philosophical project as such – as Socrates himself so frequently observes, one can know only that one doesn't know.

Understood from this perspective, the emphasis on dialectic no longer seems disproportionate with the radical invocation to 'mania' in Socrates' second speech. The second speech itself is Plato's most eloquent invocation of philosophy as an activity of the erotic. Socrates outlines the thrust of the speech in the interlude prior to the speech when he locates the defect of the previous two speeches in their conviction that Love could involve any kind of evil. Is not love a god, Socrates asks Phaedrus rhetorically, and insofar as it is, the two early speeches in their attribution of evil to it have been guilty of gross blasphemy:

> Socrates: Well, do you not hold Love to be a god, the child of Aphrodite?
> Phaedrus: He is certainly said to be.
>
> (Plato 1961: *Phaedrus* 242ff.)

The Preferability of Eros

Socrates' second speech is basically a spirited development of the logic of this interlude. In the first case, Socrates makes clear that the primary reason for the preferability of a lover over a nonlover derives not from the former's rationality but rather from an affirmation of his/her very *mania* ('in reality, the greatest blessings come by way of madness, indeed of madness that is heaven-sent', Plato 1961: *Phaedrus* 244a–b). Socrates then delineates three types of 'divine madness' of which the manic 'love' of the philosopher is posited as a fourth possibility. The three initial types of divine madness described are prophecy (Plato 1961: *Phaedrus* 244d), the mania of rites of purification (Plato 1961: *Phaedrus* 244e) and the poetic madness for which the Muses are the source (Plato 1961: *Phaedrus* 244e). This analysis is intended as a revaluation of madness against those who would wish to subordinate it to sanity or rationalism:

> this sort of madness is a gift of the gods, fraught with the highest bliss. And our proof assuredly will prevail with the wise, though not with the learned (Plato 1961: *Phaedrus* 245b–c).

The final point deserves reiteration – 'our proof assuredly will prevail with the wise, though not with the learned'. Socrates is reemphasising his distance from the rationalists. If madness is indeed a gift from the gods, a divine blessing, this is not something which can be understood by what he has earlier referred to as the 'over-clever' and 'laborious' explanations of science. Socrates initially describes his projected analysis of soul as a 'proof' (Plato 1961: *Phaedrus* 245c), but again this turns out to be no rationalist proof but rather an enigmatic myth. Frutiger classifies this particular myth as *parascientific* and his explanation of this type of myth in general is instructive with regard to the difference between rationalism and the nature of Platonic dialectic:

> To complete the results of *logos*, to extend them beyond the limits of pure reason, to take the place, by way of *deuteros plous*, of dialectic when it comes up against some inpenetrable mystery – that is the function of those myths which, for want of a better epithet, we have called parascientific (Frutiger 1930: 223).

It is this extra-rational function which Frutiger (and Hackforth: 'I would agree that our myth belongs to this class': Hackforth 1952: 76) believes the Myth of the Soul (Plato 1961: *Phaedrus* 246a–247c) performs in the *Phaedrus*. When one considers that Socrates has introduced the analysis of the soul as being the philosophical basis of the invocation of divinity (or 'divine madness'), it is clear that this invocation of 'divine madness' does not rest on a rational foundation. Following Frutiger and Hackforth, one might say that the *Phaedrus* rests on a *parascientific* basis – extending philosophy 'beyond the limits of pure reason' into the realm of 'inpenetrable mystery'. It would seem then that Derrida's reading of Plato in *Dissemination* (Derrida 1981a) is hardly distorting. Here, lining up alongside Frutiger and Hackforth, the Derridean Plato remains enigmatic and proto-deconstructionist. In the next section, I want to look at how Derrida intensifies this vision of Plato through his engagement 'between Plato and Mallarmé' in 'The Double Session' (Derrida 1972k, 1981d).

Reintroducing the *Avant-Garde*: Between Plato and Mallarmé in 'The Double Session'

As Barbara Johnson makes clear in her introduction to *Dissemination*, 'the pretexts for Derrida's inquiry are Plato's *Phaedrus*, Mallarmé's *Mimique* and Soller's *Nombres*' (Johnson 1981: xxiv). We have just looked at the complex question of how to interpret the *Phaedrus* specifically and also its relation to the Platonic corpus as a whole. In this section, I want to look at how Derrida's reintroduction of the *avant-garde* problematic and the figure of Mallarmé in 'The Double Session' can be seen to relate to the question of the Platonic text. At issue here is one key concept of our guiding theme – that of 'l'écriture', writing. Derrida, in being concerned with *mimesis*, is also thinking about the status of writing. Already in the 'Outwork', Mallarmé has a significant role as announcing 'the crisis of verse', as well as subverting through his writings and reorganisation of poetry the notion of Hegelian or overall philosophical synthesis. Derrida refers to this as a move from the figure of three to the figure of four: 'three to four' (Derrida 1981b: 25).

The original version of 'The Double Session' had been delivered (in two sessions, unsurprisingly) in 1969 and the finished work was published in 1970 in two issues of the seminal journal, *Tel Quel* (edited by Sollers). The epigraphs to 'The Double Session' tell their own story, as Derrida uses quotations from Hegel, Sade and Artaud, again demonstrating this intimacy (and/or duality) between philosophy and the *avant-garde*. The Parisian room where the lectures took place was lit by a 'lustre', which invokes the paradigmatic image of Mallarmé's and which designates a revolution in aesthetics and the concept of perception in his work.

Derrida tells us that this 'this double session will find its corner between literature and truth' ['ENTRE la literature et la vérité'] (Derrida 1972k: 203, 1981d: 177). The 'entre' is capitalised by Derrida, and we will see why below. While Derrida is often seen as valuing literature over philosophy, as in the case of Habermas' 'levelling of the genre distinction between philosophy and literature' (Habermas 1990), it is clear from Derrida's texts (and interviews most especially) that he has always sought to precisely resist such a supposed 'levelling' (Derrida 1986b). Doubling, we might say does not involve levelling, but quite the contrary. It avoids such reductionism and further complicates and intensifies the relationship between philosophy and literature. Derrida is always interested in the 'resituation' (Derrida 1986b) of philosophy rather than its levelling or annihilation and his constant invoking of the 'relation' between philosophy and literature also resituates the genre distinction itself. Moreover, in the case of a writer like Mallarmé, Derrida refuses the category distinction between literature and philosophy. These figures do not stand apart from the philosophical tradition completely. There is no pure 'outside' of philosophy. Derrida's search for a supposedly nonphilosophical site is thus always idealised. It must negotiate with the more complex realities of the interplay and intertextual connections of philosophy and literature.

This is what Derrida means to imply when he tells us that Mallarmé had led deconstruction by his work 'to indecision; to a suspension of the question' (Derrida 1981d). In other words, Mallarmé's work (Mallarmé 2008) interrogates the philosophical basis of the question or even we might say the very *raison d'être* of philosophy itself, often in ways which philosophy itself is incapable of. 'The Double Session' would thus truly be 'between Mallarmé and Plato'. One term Derrida introduces in *Dissemination*, already in 'Plato's Pharmacy', but especially in 'The Double Session', is the concept of 'hymen'. This can be translated either as hymen in the sense of a membrane or in the (Latin) sense of marriage. 'Voice donc la production apparente du spasme et, disons déjà, de l'hymen' (Derrida 1972k: 228). This is a term which Mallarmé constantly returns to and, for Derrida, it is indicative of the ambiguity at the heart of his work. But what does 'hymen' mean or what does it signify? The sexual dimension of this concept should not be lost. When Derrida uses the term 'inter' to signify the between of Plato and Mallarmé, he is also playing with the notion of 'intercourse' between Plato and Mallarmé ('la production du spasme', Derrida 1972k: 228), of a sexual relationship between philosophy and its recalcitrant otherness, philosophy and its desire for the other, but also its desire to repress the other.

Related to this problematic, Derrida introduces the thematic of *mimesis* which has also been present in the essay 'Plato's Pharmacy' and which becomes crucial in 'The Double Session'. Derrida tells us that, for Plato, there is 'always more than one kind of mimesis' ['y a-t-il donc toujours plus qu'une seule mimesis'] (Derrida 1972k: 217, 1981d: 191). In effect, what Plato seems to be telling us is that there is a 'good' kind of *mimesis* and a 'bad' kind of *mimesis.* Here, we get to a 'crisis' stage in the philosophical discourse, Derrida would seem to be suggesting, a little like Mallarmé has warned us of the 'crisis in verse'.

This will not be a simple matter of inversion however. Derrida here responds to an accusation which some critics have already employed against him. That is, on the basis of *Of Grammatology* (Derrida 1974b) and other earlier texts which seemed to suggest a bias against the voice, the accusation of seeking to privilege writing over speech or graphocentrism over phonocentrism (Derrida 1981d: 182). Rather something more foundational, something more authentically revolutionary rather than simply inversion must happen, if deconstruction is to properly take place; 'the values of *arche* and *telos*, along with the history and transcendentality that are dependent upon them, constitute precisely the principal objects of the deconstructive critique' (Derrida 1981d: 182). In other words, we can't simply replace the *telos* of speech, a pure and present to self speech with the *telos* of writing. Rather, the very value of *telos* and teleology (and with it of the *arche* and the origin), as we have seen in the readings of Husserl most especially, must be radically questioned.

We have seen, in the last chapter, how Derrida resists the reading of deconstruction (put forward by Pickstock and many others) which would oppose it to Platonism or which would seek to present the readings in *Dissemination* as simply oppositional. With regard to the supposed opposition between sophistics and philosophy, so apparently crucial to an understanding of philosophy's border (and thus to the identification of philosophy's other), we saw how Derrida complicates this border. Derrida says there, '*Inversely, symmetrically*' [*Inversement, symétriquément*]. Thus:

1. Plato and sophistics would be symmetrical.
2. Plato and sophistics would be assymmetrical.

This enigmatic series of simultaneous inversion, symmetry and assymmetry has, as we have seen, been eloquently described by Derrida in 'Plato's Pharmacy'. Derrida's suggestion appears to be that any clear demarcating line between philosophy on the one hand and sophistry on the other is an impossibility. Instead there is just the ever increasing process of blurring and complicity, of *doubling.* Here, we must remember that the double is also another name for the 'image' which comes to stand in (as a double) for the original. The double thus always comes after. There is thus the one and the two, the simple and the double. 'The double comes after the simple; it multiplies it as a follow-up' ['il le multiplie par suite'] (Derrida 1972k: 217, 1981d: 191). But having looked at how this doubling works in relation to sophistics and Platonism, how will this doubling-effect work in terms of the relationship between Mallarmé and Plato, between or 'inter' Plato and Mallarmé? This is the theme which is developed provocatively in 'The Double Session'.

In English translation, this discussion of *mimesis* will begin with 'The "Into" of Mallarmé', the 'inter' of Mallarmé, the 'antre' of Mallarmé, the 'in-two' of Mallarmé (Derrida 1981d: 81). Here, we have a complex web of signification being spun by Derrida. In the first case, the 'into' of Mallarmé signifies the difficulty in reading what is really going on with Mallarmé and Derrida's reading as a complex reorganisation of the traditional hermeneutics of Mallarmé's work. How can one get 'into' Mallarmé? What does it take? Second, the 'inter' of Mallarmé. Here the Latin is used on purpose, as Johnson explains:

> in using Latin, we thus inadvertently but perhaps inevitably find ourselves caught in one of the crucial hinges of Western philosophy; the textual rifts and drifts produced by the process of translation of the Greek philosophers; precisely into Latin (Johnson 1981: 182 trans. note).

At stake then in 'The Double Session' is not simply the relation between Mallarmé and Plato but the relation between Platonism and the West and thus the relationship between philosophy and its other.

We might take this notion of transition from Greek to Latin a stage further. What happens when Plato is translated into the context of Mallarmé, or indeed of Derrida and *Tel Quel*? The comment concerning the relation between the Greek and the Latin texts suggests that we should be wary of the idea that the Plato we know is Plato as he is in himself. There is always textual drift here; rifts and shifts, a process of translation. So how do we translate between Plato and Mallarmé?

The final two epigraphs concerning Mallarmé give us the clue: 'the antre of Mallarmé', 'l'entre-deux Mallarmé', 'the in-two of Mallarmé' or 'the between-two Mallarmés' (Derrida 1981a: 181). The *antre* is a reference to the imagery concerning the 'cave' which Mallarmé frequently uses. Again, the analogy to Plato's Allegory of the Cave (from the *Republic*) will be significant in 'The Double Session'. Are Plato and Mallarmé's metaphors of the cave the same? Do they represent the same dialectic? If not, what are the differences between their caves? We will return to this important question, which also touches on the whole problematic on *mimesis* below. And Derrida finishes his epigraphing title; 'the in-two of Mallarmé'. Again, in what sense would Mallarmé's corpus be in two? There is a reference here certainly to the doubling effect which we have spoken about before. Perhaps also we can say that one interpretation of Mallarmé might bring Mallarmé close to Plato and one further away? As Derrida notes with regard to the subtitle: 'Hymen: Inter Platonem et Mallarmatum' (Derrida 1981a: 181), hymen can indicate a membrane which stands between a consummation but it can also (in Latin) indicate a marriage; a marriage between Plato and Mallarmé. As Johnson notes, 'the Latin makes it clear that the word hymen is to be read both as "membrane" and as "marriage"' (Johnson 1981: 182 trans. note).

A Double Parricide

In 'The Double Session', although the *Phaedrus* and the *Meno* are never far away, the *Philebus* (Plato 1961) takes centre stage, a dialogue which is not without significance in terms of paradigm-shifts in the Platonic *oeuvre*. Derrida had, in the original performance of the text in Paris, distributed a sheet with a specific passage from the *Philebus* and also a short text by Mallarmé, *Mimique*. Derrida says with reference to the choice of the *Philebus*: 'without actually naming mimesis, [the *Philebus*] illustrates the mimetic system and even defines it, let us say in anticipation, as a system of illustration' (Derrida 1981d: 183). Derrida proceeds to invoke what seems to be his main question in the essay, 'what goes on or doesn't go on between [entre] literature and truth' (Derrida 1981d) and we again see the wordplay which will become significant later; *antre* (cave) and *entre* (between) are homonyms. While warning us that these texts before us 'will definitely escape any exhaustive treatment' (Derrida 1981d: 183), Derrida assures us that nonetheless we will be able to 'begin, to mark out, in a few rough strokes, a certain number of motifs' (Derrida 1981d: 183). The very relationship between literature and truth, which will become the central issue of this essay, is organised in its history by 'a certain interpretation of *mimesis*' (Derrida 1981d). And the key players in this reading of *mimesis* will be Plato and Mallarmé.

I mentioned, in the last chapter, how one reading of the development of the theme of imagination, but also of the relationship between the image and reality, posits an evolution from the paradigm of the mirror to the paradigm of the lamp to that of the lustre. In traditional terms, for example those of Catherine Pickstock which we elaborated in the last chaper, it is customary to interpret Plato as invoking the paradigm of the 'mirror' and Mallarmé that of the 'lustre'. It is clear, however, that 'The Double Session' is intent on complicating this scene of interpretation of the positioning around *mimesis* and to blur some of these hard and fast distinctions, boundaries and oppositions, much as we have seen Derrida do the same in 'Plato's Pharamacy'. On first inspection, Plato's text appears to give us a very clear demarcation of the precise paradigm of the mirror and the image which we have just spoken of. There is a clear line of succession here from the original and true *logos* to the imitative; '*logos* must indeed be shaped according to the *eidos*; the book then reproduces the *logos*, and the whole is organised by this relation of repetition, resemblance, doubling, duplication, this sort of specular process and play of reflections where things, speech and writing, come to repeat and mirror each other' ['la parole et l'écriture viennent se réfléchir les unes les autres'] (Derrida 1972k: 214, 1981d: 188). The *Philebus* develops this structure very clearly in four steps outlined by Derrida (Derrida 1981d: 190ff.):

1. The book is a substitute for the original dialogue of the soul with itself; i.e. writing is a substitute for a lost speech;
2. The book or writing must be judged by the standard of truth, of how close to the original truth they are;

3. Writing, in general, is of no value in itself, it is only useful as a double, a duplicate, a kind of necessary evil which can never match up to the original;

4. Finally, Plato transfers this notion of the book as an example of representation to the whole structure of representation and *mimesis* in itself (Derrida 1981d: 188ff.).

So far, the structure in the *Philebus* would seem to repeat the famous outline of the three levels of reality in *The Republic* Book 10 (Plato 1961), where Socrates speaks about the Form of the bed, and then the carpenter's bed as a secondary image and, thirdly, of the painter's representation of the bed as at yet another remove from reality. The structure which is elaborated in these passages of the *Philebus* and the *Republic*, at least on a surface level, seems very unambiguous: 'according to logic itself, according to a profound synonymy, what is imitated is more real, more essential, more true, etc. than what imitates. It is anterior and superior to it. One should constantly bear in mind, henceforth, the clinical paradigm of *mimesis*, the order of the three beds in the Republic Book X (596a ff.): the painter's, the carpenters', and god's' (Derrida 1981d: 192). God's Form here would be a reference to the Ultimate Form, in this case the ultimate Form of the bed. Of course, given Plato's notorious sense of humour (it is rumoured that he died with a copy of Aristophanes' collected works under his pillow), one can wonder at his choice of example here. A bed! And of course with the bed, we are not too far from sleep, the unconscious, never mind desire and sex. But for now Derrida leaves all this ambiguity aside: 'it is at bottom this order of appearance, the pre-cedence [pre-séance] of the imitated, that governs the philosophical or critical interpretation of "literature"' (Derrida 1981d: 192).

It is worth recalling here that the epigraph to the essay also spoke of the possibility of a 'marriage between Plato and Mallarmé'. How would such a marriage be possible? Derrida tells us that Plato's system of *mimesis* is 'extremely complex' (Derrida 1981b: 186). The first example he gives is of an apparent contradiction in the dialogue most famous for its critique of representation, *The Republic*. There, the poets, not just the bad ones, but even the most revered ones, beings who are in the very same dialogue cited and praised as 'holy and wondrous', these self-same beings are asked to censor themselves, to take out the dangerous political passages, although they cannot decide themselves what should or should not be censored; that would a job for the guardians. But along with this humiliating censorship, these poets must endure something much more shameful. Homer, like all the poets, good and bad alike, 'must be cast out of the city' (Derrida 1981d: 186); 'Homer, the blind old father, is condemned because he practices *mimesis*'.

This then is a parricide in the name of philosophy, against art, against poetry and literature, against all forms of representation. Should one mention here another fact: that the *Republic* is itself a representation? Should one mention that the famous Allegory of the Cave which would seem to structure the whole of *The Republic* and all its tenets, is itself the very thing being condemned? What kind of self-deconstruction is at work here? We will come back to this below in the discussion of the difference between Plato's and Mallarmé's caves, and the difference between the *antre* and the *entre*, the cave and the between. But matters get more complicated ever before we move onto the Allegory of the Cave. Already, Derrida tells us that this parricide of the mimetic father is double. It is a double parricide but also the double of the parricide. It is not a parracide in a normal sense. Why? The original parricide against Homer was already curious to the extent that the old poet is simultaneously revered and expulsed from the city. This makes even Homer's parricide somewhat double or dualistic. But in the case of Parmenides, there is once again a duality in relation to his own treatment and, second, there is a duality between his parricide and that of Homer.

First, of all, in his own case, Parmenides is the father of philosophy. Coxon, for example, sees Parmenides as a key figure in the transition from 'polytheism to philosophy' (Coxon 1986). He also cites Parmenides as a very significant influence on Plato. Plato's philosophy, for Coxon, represents 'a pluralistic development of Parmenides' monism' (Coxon 1986). But Parmenides' monism has always been highly contested as a theory of what Parmenides actually believed. In what sense is Parmenides a monist? This strikes to the very heart of the philosophical project itself, right at its origin, which of course is why Derrida dwells here for a while. This would be a kind of paradigmatic scene, but rather than Parmenides constituting the father, we would seem to have a parracide on our hands. What can be happening here? How is this distortion possible? One of the issues concerns the actual status of Parmenides' original poem, or rather the relation between the first part of the poem and the second part of the poem. There has been much philosophical controversy over this. It also bears on the relationship beween Heraclitus and Parmenides, which again is often simplified into a relation of simple opposition. In traditional histories of Greek philosophy, Heraclitus and Parmenides are represented as diametrically opposed thinkers. W.K.C. Guthrie, for example, in *The Greek Philosophers: From Thales to Aristotle* (Guthrie 1967), groups their supposed mutual antagonism under the heading of the 'problem of motion' (Guthrie 1967: 43–50): 'He (Parmenides) was the exact reverse of Heraclitus. For Heraclitus, movement and change were the only realities; for Parmenides movement was impossible, and the whole of reality consisted of a single, motionless and unchanging substance (Guthrie 1967: 47). Nonetheless, Guthrie sees *both* Heraclitus and Parmenides as 'pioneers' (Guthrie 1967: 47) of philosophy, thinkers of both 'power' and 'limitation' (Guthrie 1967: 47).

Parmenides' concept of being (as One, changeless, timeless, etc. – fragment 8: 'that Being is ungenerated and imperishable, entire, unique, unmoved and perfect': *hos ageneton eon kai anolethron estin, houlon kai atremes mounogenes te hed ateleston*) is often seen as outruling the possibility of difference. However, in linking Parmenides with Plato, one can argue for a different interpretation of Parmenidean Being (*to eon*). As Coxon has noted: 'Parmenides' poem is dominated by his conviction that human beings can attain knowledge of reality or understanding (*noos*)' (Coxon 1986: 19). The traditional reading judges Part 1 of the poem, 'the Way of Truth', as if it were the poem as such, taking its tenets

(Being is One, etc.) as the essence of Parmenides' poem. This neglects the fact that the Prologue and Part 2 maintain an enigmatic and unclear relation to Part 1. Both of these points are linked to Parmenides' relation to Plato. The late Platonic dialogue, the *Parmenides*, for example has been described, by Millar (Millar 1986: 12) amongst others, as having 'surely proven itself the most enigmatic of all of Plato's dialogues' (Millar 1986: 3). One of the reasons for this enigma is Plato's placing of Parmenides in the position of questioner and Socrates in the position of interlocutor undergoing the trial of the *elenchus*. Moreover, it is not just any Socratic/Platonic position which is in question here, but precisely the Theory of Forms, perhaps *the* Platonic doctrine.

Even more surprisingly, Socrates seems unable to offer a defence of the Theory of Forms, and Parmenides' criticisms appear to be destructive of their very basis. This, once more, would seem to show the crucial importance of the relation between Parmenides and Plato, in the original scene of interpetation of philosophy. Thus, it is not coincidental that Derrida stresses it in this context. He has also of course already referred to the 'latin' translation of Greek texts. Here, we are re-entering a Greek world of early philosophy where the relationships between key thinkers (what Derrida might call their inter-texts) is rather convoluted and enigmatic. As Eric Voegelin notes:

> the effectiveness of Parmenides…would be unintelligible without the initial meaning of his work. This meaning was recovered, and magnificently enriched, in the work of Plato. The *Republic* is animated by the Parmenidean light-vision, giving the philosopher his grasp on the Truth of Being, and of the incarnation of the paradigmatic order in the work of the philosopher, that is, in the order of his Politeia. Philosophy in the strict sense, as the tree of speculation that grows from the heavenly root, is the creation of Parmenides and Plato (Voegelin 1982: 214).

Much would seem to be at stake then here in 'The Double Session', in the place where Derrida invokes a Platonic parricide of Parmenides, if it is really true, as Voegelin claims, that 'philosophy in the strict sense is the creation of Parmenides and Plato'. For this parricide of Parmenides ('l'autre père', Derrida 1972k: 212) would then be a parricide of philosophy per se, and the parricide would be carried out by Plato.

Against Parmenides: Plato's Reaffirmation of Writing

But why does such a parricide need to take place, if Homer has already been expulsed from the city? This is undoubtedly a later parricide, a second (as well as double) parricide. The first parricide would not have been enough. There would be need for another parricide. This failure of the first parricide is significant as it demonstrates the dangers of banning all representation or *mimesis* (including writing as a paradigmatic example), as had been suggested in Book 10 of the *Republic* to be the way forward. We have already mentioned how if this parricide was to be taken literally, and the prohibitions which it would supposedly institute in the new philosophical Republic were to be taken seriously, then there would be the ultimate paradox that Plato would himself have to be expulsed from the city. For the Platonic dialogues are nothing less than a series of representations, a series of highly complex creations which rely rather substantially on all kinds of representative devices (aside from the dialogical structure itself) such as myth, narrative, poetry and even in some cases (and not just any cases but key moments in dialogues such as the *Meno*, itself a central dialogue), on ellipsis. Not just writing, then, but a whole series of sub-genres of writing are at issue here. Truly then, given the complexity of the Plato and Parmenides relation, and the issue of philosophy itself being at stake, we can see that the stakes are high in the 'The Double Session'.

These issues make Plato's discussion of Parmenides in the *Sophist* (Plato 1961) and Derrida's references to it all the more intriguing: 'the other father, Parmenides, is condemned because he neglects *mimesis*. If violence must be done to him, it is because his *logos*, the paternal thesis, would prohibit (one from accounting for) the proliferation of doubles (idols, icons, likenesses, semblances)' ['la "thèse paternelle", interdirait (de render compte de) la proliferation des doubles ("idoles, icons, mimèmes, phantasmes")'] (Derrida 1972k: 212, 1981d: 186). Derrida then goes on; 'the necessity for this parricide ["la nécessité de ce parricide"], we are told in this very connection (*Sophist* 241d–e) ought to be plain enough for even the blind to see' (Derrida 1972k: 212, 1981d: 186). So it would seem that the killing of Parmenides as a philosophical authority was required to the extent that his *logos*, which was meant to found philosophy, 'cannot account for', that is cannot understand or cannot explain, what the 'double' really is about. In the *Sophist*, the Parmenides who is presented is in line with the more traditional reading of monism; the view that change is impossible. This rigidified metaphysics seems to be the very opposite of what Homer represented, who liked to play with the 'truth' in an imaginary realm. Parmenides' monism (as an ideal or *eidos*) is the culmination of the expulsion of the artist from the *Republic*. It leaves nothing except the One in its wake. But this eventuality, no less than the Homeric anarchy of the image, is a travesty for philosophy. It leaves philosophy without the resources for change and transformation. This would seem to be the philosophical subtext of Parmenides' treatment in the *Sophist* (Plato 1961).

But where does this leave Plato? If both Homer and Parmenides have been killed off, where does that leave the Platonic *logos*? It would seem that it can neither be an unequivocal advocate of the image but similarly it can neither be an unequivocal advocate of the One, or a strict conception of *mimesis*. Here we can see the possibility of a 'marriage' between Plato and Mallarmé. Nonetheless, this would be no simple marriage. Derrida tells us that 'Mallarmé must be read otherwise than as an idealist, Platonic or Hegelian, the mime follows no preestablished script' (Derrida 1981d: 194). The Mallarméan *mimesis* follows no pre-established script, it is free of the shackles set down in Book 10 of *The Republic*. But then surely in committing a parricide against Parmenides, the

Sophist also shows a paradigm-shift away from this more traditional concept of *mimesis*? Would the Mallarméan Mime and the Platonic *mimesis* really be all that distinct? The problem with Parmenides is that he '*neglects* mimesis' ['l'autre père, Parménide, est condamné parce qu'il *ignore* la *mimesis*'] (Derrida's emphasis, Derrida 1972k: 212).

This could certainly not be said of Mallarmé, who is preoccupied by nothing more than *mimesis*. It is his recurring theme. But just as we must be careful with our interpretations of Plato, so too Derrida warns us, we must be careful with our interpretations of Mallarmé:

> of course Mallarmé's text can be read this way and reduced to a brilliant literary idealism. The frequent use of the word idea – often enlarged and hypostatised by a capital letter – and the story of the author's supposed Hegelianism tend to invite such a reading (Derrida 1981d: 194).

Derrida however wishes to draw out a different reading of Mallarmé: 'one must reconstitute a chain in motion, the effects of a network and the text play of a syntax. In that case, *Mimique* can be read quite differently than as a neo-idealism or a neo-mimetologism. The system of illustration is altogether different there than in the *Philebus*. With the values that must be associated with it, the lustre is reinscribed in a completely other place' ['le lustre est réinscrit à une tout autre place'] (Derrida 1981d: 194).

Tickling, Hanging and the Mime of Death: Mallarmé After Plato

We spoke about the lustre above and how it seems to jettison the referent altogether. In 'The Double Session' (Derrida 1981d), Derrida traces this movement of the erasure of the referent through a foregrounding of Mallarmé's text *Mimique*. If the *Philebus* seems to follow the paradigm of the mirror then this cannot be said for *Mimique*. Although, as we have seen, the Platonic text is complicated here insofar as the *Sophist* [Plato 1961] (amongst other dialogues, especially the later ones) actually seems to outrule the possibility of the paradigmatic 'mirror' through the parricide of Parmenides. Through all the inversions and crossings present in the different Platonic texts, one could then argue that the paradigm guiding the Platonic text was itself no longer the mirror, but rather the lustre. But let us return to Mallarmé. In *Mimique*, Mallarmé refers to a 'mimodrama' which follows 'no preestablished script', a gestural mime which was performed by 'M. Paul Marguerite…Pierrot Murderer of His Wife' (Derrida 1981d: 197). However, the mimodrama can only describe the mime after the fact and again there is no set script for the mime as it never actually happened, at least as described. The writer picks up on certain themes and occludes others. It is not clear whether Mallarmé actually saw the Mime or not but the different versions of *Mimique* in his notes, some of which are untitled, differ in content, and so Derrida surmises that we are dealing here with a 'Mallarméan fiction'. Thus, Mallarmé has invented the ruse of a mime which took place as he describes it, except that it never took place and, second, his description is not a strict textual one but itself an enigmatic and meandering poetic description of the mime which never took place:

> thus in the apparent present of his writing, the author of the booklet, who is none other than the mime, describes in words the past-present of a mimodrama which itself, in its apparent present, silently mimed an event – the crime – in the past-present but of which the present has never occupied the stage, has never been perceived by anyone, nor even, as we shall see, ever been really committed. Never, anywhere, not even in the theatrical fiction (Derrida 1981d: 200).

As Derrida observes, it is a 'simulacrum of a citation' (Derrida 1981d: 200). In Mallarmé's words, 'the scene illustrates but the idea, not any actual action' (quoted Derrida 1981d: 194ff.). 'Silence, sole luxury after rhymes, an orchestra only marking with its gold, its brushes with thought and dusk, the detail of its signification on a par with a stilled ode and which it is up to the poet, roused by a dare, to translate! The silence of an afternoon of music…the ever original reappearence of Pierrot' (Derrida 1981d: 175). Here, we see precisely the 'crisis in verse' which cuts across all Mallarmé's poetry but which, according to Derrida, is especially pronounced, paradigmatically pronounced in *Mimique*. It is this complexity of verse which drew derision from Proust and many of Mallarmé's contemporaries who, on his terms, were better off 'reading newspapers'. Derrida also explores the content of the mimodrama. It tells the tale, or rather gestures the tale, of a man who murders his wife.

But this is no ordinary murder. Pierrot plans to kill his wife for stealing his gold and wine. Initially considering various methods of killing her, he thinks of hanging her ('no, the tongue hanging out, the horrible face'), a knife in the heart ('yes, but the blood flows out in torrents'), a poison ('yes but then the cramps, the runs…and it would be discovered') [all quoted Derrida 1981d: 201]. Pierrot trips and hurts his foot but in holding his injury he begins to feel ticklish; 'haha that's funny; it makes me laugh; he slaps himself on the head. I've got it. I'm going to tickle my wife to death' (quoted Derrida 1981d: 201). To make matters more complicated, the Mime plays the roles of both Pierrot and his wife Columbine alternately.

The crucial question here becomes one of what separates Plato from Mallarmé? Certainly, in terms of the Plato of *The Republic*, there is a wide chasm, i.e. the Plato of the first parricide against Homer and the expulsion of the poets from the city. But with regard to the Plato of the second parricide against Parmenides, the Plato of the *Sophist* (who might also be more closely aligned with the writer of the *Phaedrus*, the *Symposium*, maybe even the *Meno*, and certainly the *Parmenides*), we can say there is little here 'between' Plato and Mallarmé. Both can be said to have moved well beyond the 'neglect of *mimesis*' which called for the sacrifice of Parmenides. But there would of course also be tensions between these two thinker-artists. Derrida tells us that 'Mallarmé is neither a Platonist or a Hegelian;

his work comprehends philosophy' (Derrida 1981d: 207). That is, once again, Derrida is marking the possibility of a nonphilosophical site from which to question philosophy. Here, that would be Mallarmé's site, although not, it would seem, Plato's. But 'who, Plato?' As we have seen in this chapter, the 'between' of Mallarmé and Plato is often a shared space.

One of the most famous Platonic metaphors is, of course, the Allegory of the Cave. As we have seen, Derrida's discussion of Mallarmé in 'the Double Session' weaves together the motifs of the threshold, the in-between and the double (especially Derrida 1981d: 181ff.). The French language provides a symptomatic confusion here in the word '*entre*', meaning 'between' and closely connected etymologically to 'entrer', meaning 'to enter', something Derrida has loved to play with. But in the background is undoubtedly the whole thematic of the cave, first encountered in Plato's *Republic* but also significantly present as a recurrent motif in Mallarmé poetry. It also appears as a motif in Lautréamont's *Maldoror* (Lautréamont 1978), perhaps the quintessential *avant-garde* text, and one which was to have such a huge effect on the aesthetics of surrealism and its inheritors. In the case, of Lautréamont, as Derrida discusses in the 'Outwork' to *Dissemination*, the motif of the cave seems to be linked to the whole extension of the notion of the preface. Just as the preface comes before the truth of the main text or book, so too the cave is meant to be a passage to the truth. But this is a passage which leads nowhere, at least for Maldoror. Derrida also plays on the homonymns antre and entre, so that the cave is also a between rather than a passage beyond: 'one cannot get out of Mallarmé's *antre* as one can get out of Plato's cave. A mine full of nothing [*mine de rien*]' (translation modified) (Derrida 1972k: 244, 1981d: 216).

Derrida has carefully woven many different issues into this condensed declaration. Firstly, *antre* is the French word for 'cave'. Throughout 'The Double Session', Derrida plays on the fact that 'antre' and 'entre' are homonyms. The latter means 'between' or 'through'. Mallarmé's 'cave' [*antre*] is a cave which one cannot get through, it is in effect a 'between' [*entre*], a kind of limbo state. Derrida is here turning 'entre' into a noun, while 'antre' becomes a preposition. Significantly, there is an English phrase which can capture this ambiguity. The word 'passage' could possibly translate 'antre' or 'entre'. 'Passage' is also advantageous because it allows one to refer back to Plato's 'passage' or 'cave'. For Derrida, Plato's cave is a *passage without passage* – it is the preposition which becomes a noun. There is no exit from Plato's cave to an outside of light and truthfulness. Plato's philosophy is always *à travers* – in passage. This, on my interpretation, is also the implication of the *Meno*: Meno exemplifies the *in-betweenness* of Socrates' questioning, the fact that it is in-between knowledge and nonknowledge, objectivity and nonobjectivity.

This is also linked to Derrida's discussion of *aporia* in *Dissemination*. As we have seen in the discussion of Plato, although this conception of 'aporia' is often seen as a postmodern notion *par excellence*, it actually derives in philosophical terms from Plato's discussion of Meno's paradox in the dialogue, the *Meno*, where the concept of 'aporia' is first introduced. Significantly, Derrida notes (Derrida

1981d: 186ff.) how the concept of 'aporia' recurs in the *Sophist*, precisely during the discussion of the concept of *mimesis*. We have seen how the *Sophist* stages the second parricide, the other side of the double parricide, the killing of that 'other father Parmenides', who is condemned because he 'neglects *mimesis*' (Derrida 1981d). As Derrida observes however, there is another doubling at work here *which* confuses matters even more and leads to a Platonic 'aporia'. This relates to what Derrida calls 'the double inscription of mimesis' (Derrida 1981d: 186), where there are two forms of the mimetic described, 'the making of likenesses (the eikastic) of faithful reproduction' and the 'making of semblances (the fantastic), which simulates the eikastic, pretending to simulate faithfully and deceiving the eye with a simulacrum (a phantasm)' (Derrida, 1972, 186).

Socrates seems to find an impossibility here in making a clear and hard and fast distinction between the two and comes up against an *aporia* (Plato 1961: *Sophist* 236e, Derrida 1981d: 186ff.). Derrida refers here to the *aporia* as being one for the 'philosophical hunter', while it is an 'endless escape route' ['échappée sans fin'; Derrida 1972k: 212] for the 'quarry' ('who is also a hunter') ['le chasseur philosophe…pour le gibier (qui est aussi chasseur)'] (Derrida 1972k: 212, 1981d: 186). Again, Derrida is playing on the reversal of roles ('inversely, symmetrically') between philosophy and its other, in this case between philosophy and art, but also, once more, on the blurred boundary of philosophy and sophistics. 'This mimodrama and the double science ['ce mimodrame et la double science'; Derrida 1972k: 212] arising from it will have concerned only a certain obliterated history of the relations between philosophy and sophistics' (Derrida 1972k: 212, 1981d: 186). Here, we have a clear connection between the reading of the *Sophist* in 'The Double Session' and the reading of the relation between Plato and sophistics in the text, 'Plato's Pharmacy'. There is something else also to note here. Derrida refers to the contorted text of the *Sophist* as a 'mimodrama' ('ce mimodrame'). In other words, we would not have to wait for Mallarmé to have a mimodrama or a *mimesis* witout a referent. Plato would already have been an *avant-gardist* in this respect, Derrida seems to be telling us, and in this case, most especially in his dialogue the *Sophist*.

But let us return in conclusion to the thematic of the cave. In 'The Double Session', Derrida introduces the thematic of the cave through the recurrring motif of the 'hymen', the ambiguous term which can mean either a female membrane or a marriage and which is consistently used to complexify the relationship between Mallarmé and Plato: 'it is an operation that both sows confusion between opposites and stands between the opposites at once. What counts here is the between, the in-between-ness of the hymen' ['ce qui compte ice, c'est l'entre, l'entre-deux de l'hymen'] (Derrida 1972k: 240, 1981d: 212). Again, for Derrida, it is also a matter of desire; 'the hymen "takes place" in the "inter-", in the spacing between desire and fulfilment, between perpetration and its recollection. But this medium of the entre has nothing to do with a centre' ['l'hymen "a lieu" dans l'entre, dans l'espacement entre le désir et l'accomplissement, entre la perpetration et son souvenir. Mais ce milieu de l'entre n'a rien à voir avec un centre'] (Derrida 1972k: 240, 1981d: 212). At this point, Derrida is marking a number of crucial issues which are raised throughout his work. First, we can note the emphasis on a term, 'hymen', with links both to a discourse on sexuality and the feminine which we look at, more explicitly, in Chapters 5 and 6, and also an emphasis on the 'between' ('l'entre'), the neither this nor that or both this and that, which we saw Derrida speak about in relation to Bataille and Blanchot in Chapter 2. This has also been a crucial issue for Plato, in terms of the relationship between the sensible and the intelligible, the image and the reality. This is an issue which we can take up in relation to the Platonic text very explicitly. The *Philebus*, which is a key dialogue for Derrida in 'The Double Session', is a dialogue which marks a much greater Platonic emphasis on the 'between'. There, Plato seems to move from a two-world ontology to a view that the Forms are ontologically homogeneous with the world. Thus, a 'between' (hymen) is now instituted from the Forms to the sensible world.

This marks a key difference from the earlier view which has the Forms as separate, for example the 'Good beyond Being' in the *Republic*. But it is not a view which arrives *ex nihilo*, or without some transition taking place. The mid-period dialogues, most especially the *Phaedrus* (which is Derrida's key dialogue in 'Plato's Pharmacy' [Derrida 1972j]) represents a transitional moment between the earlier view of separated Forms and the later view of Forms as ontologically homogeneous. Thus, Ferrari comments with regard to the sensible form of beauty and its relationship to the ideal Form of perfect beauty that the Symposium shows us 'a shuttling between the two worlds'; the *between* is key here. Thus we should not see this notion of the 'entre' as exclusively Derridean or Mallarméan and as oppositional to Platonic philosophy. Rather, it is arguable that there is an analogy to be drawn between this notion and the famous Platonic notion of the *metexis* (Plato 1961). Finally, on this point, one can also of course look to the Platonic idea of the *khora*, which becomes so important for Derrida in his later work, as another example of a 'neither this nor that' principle in Plato. We can also wonder at the impact of a different view of the Forms for the question of *mimesis*. Derrida points towards this when he speaks of the very different conception of *mimesis* which seems to be present in many of Plato's later dialogues, especially the *Sophist*, where we see the 'double parricide' of Parmenides, precisely because he 'neglects mimesis'. This would seem to be the result of a view which sees the sensible world and indeed the supposed world of imitation as having a much more integral role to play in philosophy. One cannot have a theory of Forms or a theory of art which sees the image as completely dependent or even in some cases nonexistent. This will also bear on the reading of the Allegory of the Cave (from the *Republic*) in 'The Double Session'.

We know also that, for Mallarmé, this question of the between, which is also an issue of the 'aporia', has been crucial. Derrida tells us that this been a question of desire, but of the 'spacing' [espacement] between desire and fulfillment. Again and again, deconstruction speaks of desire, but not a desire fulfilled ['l'accomplissement'], rather a desire in procees. As Johnson had commented, deconstruction mimics the movement of desire rather than its fulfilment (Johnson

1981). Finally, in this passage, Derrida has also delineated the difference regarding an emphasis on the 'between' and an emphasis on the 'centre'. This last philosophy of the centre 'has nothing to do' with a philosophy of the between ('ce milieu de l'entre'), and we see the connections between *Dissemination* and an earlier text where the issue of the centre was addressed more directly, 'Structure, Sign and Play' (Derrida 1978j) in *Writing and Difference*.

Conclusion: 'The Hymen Enters into the Antre'

Derrida has one key move left here; 'the hymen enters into the antre' ['l'hymen entre, dans l'antre'] (Derrida 1972k: 240, 1981d: 212). Aside from the sexualised connotations, one can note the crucial introduction of the problematic of the cave, but ambiguously. Thus, the cave is 'entered' and Derrida is playing on the homonymy between the French words 'entre' and 'antre' here. Then Derrida tells us that 'entre can just as easily be written with an a. Indeed, are these two (e)(a)ntres not really the same?' ['Entre peut aussi bien s'écrire avec un a. Les deux (e)(a)ntres ne sonts-ils pas le même?'] (Derrida 1972k: 240, 1981d: 212). Derrida refers to two Mallarméan texts which he has earlier cited in figures (figures II and IV, Derrida 1981d: 176), where Mallarmé explicitly mentions the 'antre':

> words...of themselves...projected on the walls of a cave...he has set foot in the antre...extracted the subtle remains...what inevitable treachery involved in the fact of an evening of our existence lost in that antre of cardboard or painted canvas or of genius; a Theatre (Derrida 1981d: 176).

So, the theatre would also be a kind of cave, which multiplies the resonances beyond Mallarmé and Plato, most notably to Artaud, for example. We can come back to this later. For now, I want to focus on the resonances between Mallarmé and Plato. The *Republic*'s (Plato 1961) first three words, 'I went down'[2] are said to signify a going down into the cave so that the whole dialogue is constructed in relation to an understanding of the cave analogy. The whole dialogue might thus be seen as an attempt to go back into the world of images, so as to come out into the light. Or so the idealist reading might surmise. Derrida is perhaps suggesting a different reading. The view which suggests that the cave is a place to leave from takes a rather negative view of this world down here below, and most especially of those who would mistake images for reality. Worst of all, these are the artists who lure us into a world of fiction.

But what if the 'I went down' was to signify more of an affirmation on Plato's part; what if the cave was itself to be affirmed, along with its images and its supposed deceptions? If such was the case, then the whole complex metaphysics of deception

---

2   I would like to acknowledge the lectures of the late Fr. Fergal O'Connor at University College Dublin for first complexifying this seemingly innocent Platonic phrase.

versus reality which Plato is supposed to be giving us would be complexifed. But there would also be the sense that we would now be able to see that Plato was not so naïve as not to realise his own performative contradiction here. Rather, the performative contradiction would be part of the plan. Unlike Parmenides who neglected *mimesis*, Plato paid his due respects to *mimesis*. And also to the sensible world and the world of change. The cave then would no longer signify a passage out of deception and a move towards the light. The cave would itself be the truth of life; as Derrida puts it; 'are these two (e)(a)ntres not really the same?' (Derrida 1981d: 212). Derrida develops the etymologies here, linking antre with a 'natural or man made deep dark cave' and also the Sanskrit *antara* which 'properly signifies interval; and thus is related to the latin preposition Inter; see entre…and the entry for Entrer [to enter] ends with the same etymological reference' (Derrida 1981d: 212). This is indeed a Derridean (but also Platonic) labyrinth.

Again, there are a number of points being suggested by Derrida here. If a cave is 'man made', then it is a *mimesis*. And so Plato's cave would be a *mimesis*, an imitation, rather than an original. To this extent, on the *Republic*'s terms, the Allegory of the Cave would constitute an art in line with Homer's corpus. Plato would implicitly be calling for his own parricide, or rather, in more extreme terms, the *Republic* would constitute a suicidal philosophical text, a text which seeks to destroy itself from within. The same would go for Derrida's reference to Socrates' *pharmakon* (in this case, the hemlock) as a 'poison deserved' (Derrida 1981c) in 'Plato's Pharmacy'. It would be a poison deserved insofar as the accusation of sophism and 'sorcery' made against Socrates would be a valid charge. And so, in a sense, it would be a *pharmakon* self-induced, brought on by Socrates himself and this is also a kind of suicide. The links back to 'interval' and 'inter' bring us full circle to the 'Latin' which began 'The Double Session' and which Derrida told us to look out for, as they signified a transition between Greek thought and the rest of history, the whole history of the West and its philosophy and conceptuality. There would be a cave between Plato and Mallarmé, but we should not always see a 'between' as something which comes to differentiate; it can also be what unites. Here, we have a different sense of Mallarmé and Plato, a kind of inter-course between Plato and Mallarmé. As Derrida observes, this etymology also links to 'entrer', to enter. Whom here would be entering whom? Once more, as ever, the problematic of desire, the body and sexuality would be not far away:

> the hymen, the consummation of differends, the continuity and confusion of the coitus, merges with what it seems to be derived from; the hymen as protective screen, the jewel box of virginity, the vaginal partition, the fine, invisible veil, which, in front of the hystera, stands between the inside and the outside of a woman, and consequently between desire and fulfillment. It is neither desire nor pleasure but in between the two (Derrida, 1981d: 213).

The hymen would then come to symbolise a certain kind of 'writing of the body' ('l'écriture du corps'). We might add that such a 'hymen' does not always have to constitute the invisible veil between the inside and outside of a woman. Here, Derrida might run the risk of feminising the hymen too much. Why should the hymen not be masculine also, the protective screen which shields one man from another, which hides one man's sex from another? In this case, Plato's sex might be hidden from Mallarmé until 'The Double Session'. One is reminded of Gilles Deleuze's desire to bugger the w(hole) history of philosophy.

Derrida reiterates the sexual reference; 'with all the undecidability of its meaning, the hymen only takes place when it doesn't take place; for example, when one is made to die laughing or come laughing' ['on fait mourir ou jouir de rire'] (Derrida 1972k: 241, 1981d: 213). Again, the references are multiplied by Derrida here. The first is to Mallarmé's *Mimique* where Pierrot kills his wife by tickling her to death, but in the measure to which the same actor plays the roles of the husband and wife alternately, the same person both kills and dies. Also, it is unclear as to whether Pierrot's last gasps of sexual pleasure are in fact leading to his death. Moreover, is all orgasm not a 'little death' ('le petit mort'), anyhow? Second, there is a clear reference to Bataille here, and his notion of a gay laughter, a laughter unto death. Finally, in relation to some of the comments we have seen Derrida make in the conclusions to his essays in *Writing and Difference* (Derrida 1978a) and in *Margins* (Derrida 1982a), we can say that there is an implicit Nietzschean reference.

So many connected thinkers and philosophies – Mallarmé, Plato, Bataille, Nietzsche. In the next chapter, we will look at how Derrida takes up the issue of his debt to Nietzsche more explicitly, in *Spurs: Nietzsche's Styles* (Derrida 1979). We can also say here – so many men, so many male philosophers, as if truth always had to be male, even when it was being deconstructed. But as we shall see, this is precisely Derrida's theme in *Spurs: Nietzsche's Styles* (Derrida 1979). What if truth were a woman? And in Chapter 6, I will take up this issue of Derrida's complex relation to feminism, but also to specific female philosophers. If we are going to speak of a writing of embodiment, then, we must also engage the themes of power, gender and the political. In the next chapter, we will see how, for Nietzsche, such a 'l'écriture du corps' must involve giving up some of our 'essentialising fetishes' concerning truth.

Chapter 5
What if Truth Were a Woman?
On *Spurs: Nietzsche's Styles*

Introduction

Much has been made in recent years of the relation between Derrida and Levinas and the supposed 'ethical' and 'religious' return of Derrida's work (e.g. Caputo 1997a/b). I would like to argue that this has been exaggerated. If we look at the detail of Derrida's work, and rather than simplify Derrida to justify our own presuppositions or to try to make him relevant for the latest philosophical 'fashion', it is clear that Derrida's work is firstly, far closer to Husserl than it is to Levinas. Here, I think that Leonard Lawlor's recent work on Derrida and Husserl has been instructive (Lawlor 2002). Second, that the Husserlian dimension of Derrida's work demonstrates his difference from both Levinas and Merleau-Ponty, as Derrida reiterates strongly in one of his last major works (Derrida 2000). But what the Levinasian emphasis also occludes, and perhaps far more importantly, is what might be termed 'the Nietzschean influence' on Derrida's work.

As we will see, this Nietzschean influence is significant with regard to Derrida's questioning of embodiment and desire, his 'writing of the body'. This latter also connects Derrida more clearly to *avant-garde* figures such as Bataille, Artaud and Klossowski, and indeed to surrealism, while also connecting Derrida more closely to his French compatriot thinkers, Deleuze, Foucault and more recently Jean-Luc Nancy and Hélène Cixous. In this chapter, I want to offer a corrective to what I see as the overestimation of the Levinasian influence on Derrida's work (also the Kierkegaardian)[1] by stressing this Nietzschean inheritance. Here, my main focus of attention will be on Derrida's seminal text on Nietzsche, *Spurs: Nietzsche's Styles* (Derrida 1979), but I will also refer, where necessary, to other significant texts where Derrida invokes Nietzsche. These are in his pre-*Spurs* work, for example in *Writing and Difference* ('Structure, Sign and Play', Derrida 1978j) and also in *Margins of Philosophy* (for example, in 'The Ends of Man' essay, Derrida 1982d). This will also enable me to foreground the key connections between Derrida's Nietzsche interpretation and his growing importance for the feminism debate, in relation to what *Spurs: Nietzsche's Styles* refers to as 'the question of woman'.

---

1   The issue of the Kierkegaardian influence is more complicated. Much would depend on how one reads the Nietzsche-Kierkegaard relation. See Dooley 2001 for an interesting example of a Kierkegaardian reading of Derrida.

Before looking at *Spurs* specifically, I would like to look at what Derrida says in a text from *Margins of Philosophy* (Derrida 1982a).

Here, my focus will be quite specific, developing themes from his crucial essay 'The Ends of Man' (originally 'Les Fins de l'homme'), dating from 1968 and published in France in 1972 (Derrida 1972e, 1982d). As with all of Derrida's work, the title of the essay gives a significant insight into the writer's intentions. Through the concept of 'end', Derrida is identifying the problem of teleology or purpose with regard to humanity. By discussing the 'ends' rather than the 'end' of humanity, Derrida is already problematising the vision of a unified *telos*. Derrida is already *pluralising* any notion of 'telos' – there is never any end as such, but only end(s).

Pluralising the Telos of Humanity

The second crucial concept in Derrida's title – that of 'man' – is also a heavily overladen and overdetermined notion. We will see the significance of this again in *Spurs*, when Derrida comes to ask the question; 'what if truth were a woman?' Derrida is ambiguously playing on a second meaning of the word 'end' (the paper was originally delivered in English rather than French) – that of something coming to a close, a finish. Derrida's question here asks: is the very notion of 'man' coming to an end? Is the supposed unity of this notion becoming fragmented? And is this very fragmentation itself plural, i.e. are these the 'ends' of man rather than simply the one, complete and discrete end? Again, it is interesting to think of this Derridean affirmation of fragmentation as against the attempt to maintain the unity of a specific tradition. Through the simultaneous fragmentation of 'end' and of 'man', Derrida would appear to be signalling the deconstruction of a monolithic tradition.

> The *we*...assures the proximity to itself of the fixed and central being for which this circular reappropriation is produced. The *we* is the unity of absolute knowledge and anthropology, of God and man, of onto-theo-teleology and humanism (Derrida 1982d: 121).

Taking his cue from the development of mid-twentieth century French philosophy, Derrida seeks to delineate an alternative philosophical conception:

> what is difficult to think today is an end of man which would not be organised by a dialectics of truth and negativity, an end of man which would not be a teleology in the first person plural (Derrida 1982d: 121).

Interestingly, however, Derrida is keen to distinguish his radical questioning of the 'we' of tradition from those approaches which would simply jettison tradition, or consider themselves to have done so, in one fell swoop. In an important and subtle analysis, Derrida identifies two types of revolutionary response to traditional philosophy and ethos. Here, the micro-reading is concerned with the warring aspects of French philosophy but the macro-implications of Derrida's reading extend very clearly to our own problematic (Derrida 1982d: 123ff.; especially 134–6). In the first case, there are those philosophers who seek to 'change terrain, in a discontinuous and irruptive fashion, by brutally placing oneself outside, and by affirming an absolute break and difference' (Derrida 1982d: 135). From the point of view of tradition, then, these are those who adopt a simply anti-traditional stance, who reject all aspects of the culture's inheritance. On the other side, notes Derrida, are those who:

> attempt an exit and a deconstruction without changing terrain, by repeating what is implicit in the founding concepts and the original problematic, by using against the edifice the instruments or stones available in the house (Derrida 1982d: 135).

The philosopher Derrida associates most especially with the first approach is Michel Foucault and with the second, Martin Heidegger. Derrida distinguishes his own philosophical approach, at the conclusion of this essay, from both these strands or rather problematises the choice between them: 'it goes without saying that the choice between these two forms of deconstruction cannot be simple and unique' (Derrida 1982d: 135). It is Nietzsche (Derrida 1982d: 135/6), it seems, who best encapsulates the dual strategy of *both these styles at once*, for Derrida, and most closely approximates to being a precursor of his own deconstructive method. As Derrida asks, 'But who, we?' (Derrida 1982d: 136). Any assumption of a tradition or univocal community, whether in a glorious past or projected into a re-unified future, is to be subjected to radical interrogation and, in effect, revolution. It is this revolution which the 'Ends of Man' announces or anticipates. It is arguable that the later 1970s texts, such as *Spurs* and *Glas* (Derrida 1974a), enact the very process of this revolution. But does this authentically develop a Nietzschean legacy? In the next section, I will look at how Nietzsche's work evolves a radical questioning of the philosophical tradition, particularly in terms of the relation between philosophy and art. This allows Nietzsche to subvert the 'will to knowledge' and to foreground the conception of a Dionysian 'truth as appearance', which will become so important for Derrida's reading in *Spurs* (Derrida 1979). I will then look, in the final two sections, at the specifics of Derrida's readings in *Spurs: Nietzsche's Styles* (Derrida 1979).

Setting the Scene: Nietzsche and the Question of Truth as Appearance

In *Spurs* (Derrida 1979), Derrida will take up a very particular reading of Nietzsche which emphasises a conception of 'truth as appearance', truth as the 'superficiality of existence' ['la superficialité de l'existence'] (Derrida 1979: 57). This will be linked specifically to what Derrida calls 'the question of woman' ['la femme'] (Derrida 1979: 81). That is, there will be a connection made between the theme of the feminine and the theme of truth as appearance in Nietzsche. But as with many of

Derrida's readings, it is arguable that Derrida is here focusing on a quite marginal aspect of Nietzsche's discourse. Nietzsche is consistently far more interested in the more general issue of truth as appearance than he is in the question of the feminine. This will be part of Derrida's strategy to in a sense read 'Nietzsche against Nietzsche' (as he read 'Bataille against Bataille') ['il nous faut interpréter Bataille *contre* Bataille'] (Derrida 1967k: 404, 1978i: 275), and to reorient some of the key Nietzschean insights away from his usual preoccupations so as to address the more contemporary issue [in 1972][2] of woman's rights. However, before looking at this provocative Derridean reorientation, it will be useful to look at the context of Nietzsche's own elaboration of the problematic of truth as appearance.

The most interesting texts in this context are the unpublished writings (during Nietzsche's lifetime) between 1872 and 1878. It is clear that one should be careful approaching Nietzsche's unpublished writings or *Nachlass* (Nietzsche 1990). As Daniel Breazeale has noted, however much importance we wish to ascribe to these writings, the fact remains that none of this material was published by Nietzsche himself and in the case of the early Notebooks which I will be looking at, it is also clear that Nietzsche could have revised these for publication during his lifetime but didn't (Breazeale 1990: xiv). Given this qualification, however, I think that we can put the early Notebooks to good use. The period after the publication of the *Die Geburt der Tragödie* [hereafter *Birth of Tragedy*] (Nietzsche 1967b) in 1872 and prior to the publication of *Menschliches, Allzumenschliches* [hereafter *Human All Too Human*] (Nietzsche 1986) in 1878 is a particularly significant one insofar as it can provide clues to Nietzsche's apparent turn away from his earlier style and content of thinking. Fink (Fink 2003), for example, sees *Human All Too Human* as representing the birth of a 'second period' of Nietzsche's thought (Fink 2003: 34) involving an 'inversion' of the philosophy of both the *Birth of Tragedy* and the four *Unzeitgemässe Betrachtungen* [hereafter *Untimely Meditations*] (Nietzsche 1997).

It is clear that this is a transformation not simply in how Nietzsche sees the status or vocation of philosophy but also and perhaps more crucially, a change in how he sees the relationship between philosophy and non-philosophy, most especially the triangular relation between what Nietzsche respectively identifies as philosophy, art and science. As we have seen throughout this book, the relation between philosophy and nonphilosophy is crucial also for Derrida and indeed Derrida has cited Nietzsche's method as paradigmatic in his move away from phenomenology and towards a more radical or *avant-garde* approach (Derrida 1986b). In many respects, we will see this movement played out in *Spurs* (Derrida 1979). Analysing the specifics of Nietzsche's own development in this respect can consequently be very helpful to us here. I want to especially focus on

---

2   Although only published as a complete, finalised text in French in 1978, and as a bilingual French-English text in 1979, *Spurs: Nietzsche's Styles* was originally delivered as a lecture in 1972.

Nietzsche's conception of art, understood initially as something quite independent of philosophy but at crucial textual moments in the Notebooks (Nietzsche 1990) as indissociable from philosophy. It is this conception of a philosophy of art which will allow Nietzsche to speak of 'truth as appearance', a notion which will become crucial for Derrida in *Spurs*.

Reflections on the Struggle between Art and Knowledge

My particular focus will be on the unpublished writings from 1872–1878, and most especially on Nietzsche's essay 'Der letzte Philosoph. Der Philosoph. Betrachtungen über den Kampf von Kunst und Erkenntniss' [hereafter 'The Last Philosopher. The Philosopher. Reflections on the Struggle between Art and Knowledge'] (Nietzsche 1990a). In this essay, Nietzsche focuses on the triangular relationship between art, science and philosophy. Nietzsche uses the terms 'science' (*wissenschaft*) and 'art' (*kunst*) in a broad rather than narrow sense; science refers to the discipline of theoretical enquiry and its will-to-knowledge, while art seems to be synonymous with creative activity and creative thought in general. 'The Philosopher' (Nietzsche 1990a) seeks to address similar issues through an emphasis on early Greek metaphysics, what Nietzsche refers to throughout as 'pre-Platonic philosophy'. Nietzsche wishes to bring the reader back to a time when, unlike now, culture and philosophy were not in opposition. This is the time of Greek thought between Homer and Plato. In another text of the 'Philosopher's Book', 'Der Philosoph als Arzt der Kultur' [hereafter 'The Philosopher as Cultural Physician'] (Nietzsche 1990b), Nietzsche makes clear that it is the arrival of Platonic philosophy which constitutes the moment of philosophical and cultural deterioration: 'overt hostility against culture – negation – begins with Plato. But I want to know how Philosophy behaves towards a presently existing or developing culture which is not the enemy' (Nietzsche 1990b: 74/5).

This reading of Plato and Platonism is central to Nietzsche's conception of the history of cultural decline in the West. In 'The Philosopher' (Nietzsche 1990a), Nietzsche also makes derogatory comments concerning Aristotle in this regard. In section 61, he asserts that 'the poorly demonstrated philosophy of Heraclitus possesses far more artistic value than do all the propositions of Aristotle' (Nietzsche 1990a: 23). What is crucial to understand here is that Nietzsche's evaluation of Heraclitus *contra* Aristotle is not simply an aesthetic as opposed to a philosophical evaluation, that Heraclitus would be the better artist while Aristotle would be the better philosopher. Rather, this claim foregrounds the primacy of the aesthetic for Nietzsche in any evaluative judgement. This brings us his important statement in section 41 that 'the only criterion which counts for us is the aesthetic criterion'. (Nietzsche 1990a: 13). Aesthetic philosophy, that is a philosophy which can embrace art in a radical sense, is superior to nonaesthetic philosophy.

The backdrop to this analysis is, for Nietzsche, the current state of modern culture and, in particular, German culture. 'Our age hates art...it desires no reconciliation' (Nietzsche 1990a: 21). The decadence of contemporary culture leads Nietzsche to seek for a source of cultural renewal. If, as Nietzsche says, 'culture is above all, the unity of artistic style in all the expressions of a people's life', then what contribution if any does philosophy have to make the possibility of a new reconciliation of modern culture? In developing this problematic, Nietzsche looks at what are the main barriers to cultural renewal in the contemporary era. He locates two significant obstacles: first, the egalitarianism of modern culture, its refusal of hierarchy and mastery which, for Nietzsche, obscures the necessity of what he terms a 'pathos of distance' in a thriving culture. Second, and most importantly for 'the Philosopher's Book', Nietzsche identifies the hegemony of 'science' or the scientific outlook as a central problem. The modern, enlightened man seeks to banish all illusion, error and vestiges of unconscious life in favour of a thoroughly rationalised knowledge and epistemological truth.

In 'The Philosopher', Nietzsche attempts to provide an explanation for the development of this 'will to truth'. In the first case:

> Man demands truth and fulfils this demand in moral intercourse with other men; this is the basis of all social life. One anticipates the unpleasant consequences of reciprocal lying. From this there arises *the duty of truth* (Nietzsche 1990a: 27).

Nietzsche provides a sophisticated deconstruction of the will-to-knowledge which operates on several different levels; one of his main criticisms relates to the question of science's effect on life (Nietzsche 1990a: 25). Underlying Nietzsche's analysis here is his assumption that all human life and culture depends upon a certain illusion and error, a certain art, and he looks here to the early Greek culture as a paradigm. This he contrasts with the scientific dominance of contemporary Teutonic culture:

> The Teuton uses the sciences to transfigure all of his limitations at the same time that he transmitted them; fidelity, modesty, self-restraint, diligence, cleanliness, love of order, the familial virtues. But also formlessness, the complete lack of any vivacity in life, and pettiness. His unlimited knowledge drive is the consequence of an impoverished life (Nietzsche 1990a: 25).

For Nietzsche, the hegemony of the will to truth is a sign that 'life has grown old' (Nietzsche 1990a: 7). The malaise of scientific culture is then Nietzsche's clear target. In attempting a renewal of this milieu, Nietzsche offers an ambiguous alternative, which involves contradictory evaluations of philosophy and its relationship to a vivacious artistic sensibility.

In Note 37 of 'The Philosopher' text, Nietzsche introduces an important distinction between what he terms the 'philosopher of desperate knowledge' and the 'philosopher of tragic knowledge' (Nietzsche 1990a: 12). It is the 'philosopher of desperate knowledge' who Nietzsche cautions against; he is, says Nietzsche, a philosopher who seeks knowledge at any price (Nietzsche 1990a: 12). What this seems to suggest is that while this philosopher is capable of offering a critique of science through an epistemological critique of knowledge, he/she nonetheless remains imprisoned at this negative, sceptical stage. Nietzsche distinguishes this intellectual and cultural paralysis from what he terms a 'mastery' of the knowledge drive which can be achieved through a 'philosophy of tragic knowledge'. The German term he uses here is *Bandigung*, which can mean to master or to restrain or to subdue. The philosopher of tragic knowledge is Nietzsche says 'never satisfied with the motley whirling game of the sciences' (Nietzsche 1990a: 12). He/she thus subdues or 'masters' science and its hold over culture. This cannot be achieved through epistemological means alone and this is the crucial difference between the philosophers of tragic knowledge and desperate knowledge. The philosopher of tragic knowledge can only master the knowledge-drive through a reconciliation with the aesthetic: 'he cultivates a new life; he returns to art its rights' (Nietzsche 1990a: 12).

It was the early Greeks' capacity to put such a philosophy of tragic knowledge into practice which enabled them to achieve the kind of cultural flourishing and harmony which Nietzsche himself seeks here. They, he says, 'mastered' (Nietzsche 1990a: 9) the knowledge drive, but lost their mastery after Socrates. At note 53, Nietzsche poses the question which all his readers have been asking themselves; is philosophy an art or a science? (Nietzsche 1990a: 19). Significantly here he doesn't ask is philosophy closer to art or to science, but is philosophy a species of one or the other?

> Great dilemma: is philosophy an art or a science? Both in its purposes and its results it is an art. But it uses the same means as science – conceptual representation. Philosophy is a form of artistic invention (Nietzsche 1990a: 19).

Here philosophy becomes part of art and also seems to play a more productive role in the renewal of culture. Again, unsurprisingly, Nietzsche looks back to early Greek philosophy as his inspiration: 'Heraclitus can never be obsolete. Philosophy is invention beyond the limits of experience; it is the continuation of the mythical drive' (Nietzsche 1990a: 19).

On my reading, this Nietzschean claim has two main implications. In the first case, it shows how philosophy can have a constructive and creative role in cultural formation. Second, it seems to blur the very distinction between philosophy and art. Philosophy *is* now art, albeit a specific form of art. And contrary to what Nietzsche says at the aforementioned Notes 38/39, where he seems to suggest that these were only possibilities available to early Greek philosophy, it is clear that here he is intent on holding this out as a possibility for contemporary philosophy, not least his own. It seems that as well as looking back and across to *The Birth of Tragedy* (Nietzsche 1967b) that this claim also looks forward, to *Also sprach Zarathustra* [hereafter *Thus Spake Zarathustra*] (Nietzsche 1987) perhaps and even to *Ecce Homo* (Nietzsche 1979). If Nietzsche's faith in Schopenhauer and Wagner as philosopher-artists in the *Notebooks* can be viewed as perhaps youthful naïvete which he will later disdain, it is nonetheless also the case that this early paradigm of the philosopher-artist remains consistently an ideal in his work. While he loses belief in these other possible exemplars, he perhaps never loses belief, however ironically expressed, in his own exemplarity as an 'artistic Socrates'. Notes 53 and 62 point beautifully towards what such an expression might involve: 'Philosophy is essentially pictorial...Here one can see the extraordinary productivity of the intellect. It is a life in images' (Nietzsche 1990a: 19/23).

With regard to Socrates' treatment in the *Notebooks*, there is the obvious background context of Nietzsche having already treated the issue of 'scientific Socratism' and 'the artistic Socrates' in the *Birth of Tragedy* (Nietzsche 1967b), published in 1872. While the concept of 'philosopher-artist' in Note 44 refers implicitly to a certain version of Socrates, the explicit reference to him at Note 31 is significant; 'This is the way in which the earlier Greek philosophers are to be understood: they master the knowledge drive. How did it happen that they gradually lost this mastery after Socrates? To begin with, Socrates and his school showed the same tendency: the knowledge drive should be restrained out of individual concern for living happily. This is a final, inferior phase. Previously, it was not a question of *individuals*, but of the *Hellenes*' (Nietzsche 1990a: 9). For Nietzsche, this Socrates thus represents a transitional phase before the final overt hostility of Plato. Again, this seems a rather one dimensional reading, which only serves as a means to a greater end.

But what of the 'artistic Socrates', the 'Socrates who plays music' invoked in *The Birth of Tragedy* (Nietzsche 1967b) and implicitly reinvoked in Nietzsche's reference in 'The Philosopher' (Note 44) to the philosopher-artist? The development of this concept by Nietzsche, in different texts, can I think help us to work towards some contextualisation of Nietzsche's views on philosophy and art in the *Notebooks*. In *Ecce Homo* (Nietzsche 1979: 271/2), Nietzsche refers to the 'offensive' Hegelianism and 'cadaverous perfume of Schopenhauer' which attends some of the formulas of *The Birth of Tragedy* (Nietzsche 1979: 271/2). In that text, the 'artistic Socrates' is still tied to an 'artist's metaphysics' which I think has been eschewed by the time Nietzsche wrote 'The Philosopher' text. There, Nietzsche is not concerned any more to defend art in the name of metaphysics but rather to defend art in the name of culture. This seems to me to constitute a radical difference and to highlight the importance of the *Notebooks* for an understanding of the development of Nietzsche's thought. Here, in a way that was not the case in *The Birth of Tragedy*, in Deleuze's words, Nietzsche comes to 'magnify the world as error, to sanctify the lie' (Deleuze 1986: 102). It is this aesthetic 'truth as appearance' and not the *Birth of Tragedy*'s 'artist's metaphysics' which Nietzsche will later call on in *The Genealogy of Morals* Book III (Nietzsche 1967a) to defeat the ascetic ideal.[3] And it is precisely this aesthetic 'truth as appearance' which will come to have such significance for Derrida in *Spurs: Nietzsche's Styles*.

---

3   However, this is no smooth narrative story. According to Fink, by 1878 and *Human-All-Too-Human*, Nietzsche seems to have turned away from art altogether. Indeed, he is unequivocal in his condemnation of the latter's ruses. As Fink notes: 'This ["second

Stefano Agosti and the Styles of *Spurs*

Having looked at how Nietzsche develops this thematic of truth as appearance, we now need to look at how Derrida elaborates this problematic in the text, *Spurs: Nietzsche's Styles* (Derrida 1979). Stefano Agosti in his enigmatic 'Coup upon Coup: An Introduction to *Spurs*' (Agosti 1979: 3), foregrounds some of the key textual strategies employed by Derrida in *Spurs*: 'there is a coup de don which silently resounds out of these pages; there are many possibilities for meaning in the abyss of this coup' (Agosti 1979: 3). Certainly, when faced with *Spurs*, the reader is struck by not simply an ambiguity, or even a polysemy of meaning, but a genuine dissemination. The feminist authors, who become so preoccupied with *Spurs* a decade later, consistently comment on this difficulty, on this very elusiveness of the text which nonetheless draws so many diverse readers into its ambit. Given our previous two chapters, Agosti draws an interesting connection back to Derrida's readings in 'Plato's Pharmacy' and in *Dissemination* as a whole. 'There are coups du dehors (knocks from without) for example which are heard at the door of "Plato's Pharmacy", it is an incessant din…pharmakon means coup… Plato blocks his ears' (Agosti 1979: 5). The 'Plato blocks his ears' phrase is a direct quotation from Derrida's text. Here, Derrida has been keen to show how the Platonic text (on one reading) seeks to shut out otherness, and difference. This

---

period"] commences suddenly and appears to be a complete interruption of the original path of thought or even a radical turn' (Fink 2003: 34). Speaking of the poets for example in Section 148 of *Human-All-Too-Human*, Nietzsche says 'there are several things to be said against their means of alleviating life; they soothe and heal only provisionally, only for a moment' (quoted Fink 2003: 148). At section 220, he speaks of his 'profound sorrow' in contemplating the highest flights of artists. It is clear that a very different tone is being set here, but I think Fink is right to suggest that this is hardly completely discontinuous with what has gone before. Certainly if one focuses on the fundamental distinction between the primordial ground and the realm of appearance (Fink 2003: 36) present in the *Birth of Tragedy*, then we have indeed reached a completely discontinuous juncture. However, I have already suggested that within the early Notebooks, this view has been overridden by the philosopher-artist who simply affirms truth-as appearance. There is a sense in which this view can be seen as quite continuous with *Human-All-Too-Human*, even indeed with the latter's reinvocation of science, for now science is no longer based on the will-to-knowledge ideal but rather, as Fink has suggested, on a genealogical 'unmasking' which seeks to undo all forms of idealism (Fink 2003: 37/38).

> Nietzsche's second period is an inversion of the first in almost all respects; the former viewed the theoretical approach of science from the perspective of art. The latter views art from the perspective of science. However, in both cases, we find the perspective of life (Fink 2003: 41).

It is clear that this conception of 'life' and especially 'life as the cultural unity of a people' is thematised and developed most systematically prior to 1878 in the Notebooks.

is another example of Derrida's own inter-texts, or even intra-texts, the way that Derrida's work consistently self-refers, or refers back and forth.

Manipulating the Limit of the Concept

Here, I have agreed with Peggy Kamuf's reading that Derrida's work must be seen as systematic and that there is a chronological development (Kamuf 1991). We can also, for example, link this issue of noise, otherness and the ear for music, with the more or less contemporaneous essay, 'Tympan' (Derrida 1982b), which serves as a kind of extended preface to *Margins of Philosophy* (Derrida 1982a). Agosti makes this link explicitly, referring to this essay as 'manipulating the limit of the concept; and with several blows to knock it off its hinges' (Agosti 1979: 7). Once again, the subversive orientation of *Spurs* is being noted. Musical themes are also taken up in *Glas* [Derrida 1986a] (written during the similar period). *Glas* is itself a death-knell, sounding finitude. We can also refer back to Nietzsche's own work, for whom the problematic of music and sound was so crucial, in *The Birth of Tragedy* and beyond. For example, from an autobiographical note in the *Nachlass*:

> When I listened to the total sound of the early Greek philosophers, I thought that I perceived those tones which I was accustomed to hearing in Greek art, more precisely, in tragedy. I cannot yet say with certainty to what extent this lay in the Greeks and to what extent it only lay in my ears (the ears of a man with a great need for art) (quoted Breazeale 1990: xliii).

As with Bataille, there is in *Glas* the issue of whether Hegel can actually engage with the real excess of sounds. He always seems to want to keep the sounds repressed and silenced by the hegemony of meaning. Kamuf's description of 'Tympan' is helpful here. 'Tympan' is another example of Derrida's invocation of the *avant-garde*, 'with his employment of Michel Leiris's first volume of autobiographical memoirs, *Biffures* [1948] which Derrida uses as a long quotation which extends on the right hand side of the text throughout' (Kamuf 1991). Again, in typographic terms, this is Derrida's first flirtation with this new kind of 'style' which will be used more radically in *Glas*. As I've argued earlier, this radicalisation of style then seems from the beginning to be connected to a kind of paradigm-shift which Derrida makes to the *avant-garde* in the mid-to-late 1960s. In this case, Leiris is a very close associate of Bataille and Artaud, and also of surrealism.

Significantly, Derrida does not refer to the extended and continuous quotation at any stage in the left hand text and this is said by Kamuf to signify the space:

> where philosophy is configured as the apparatus of an ear, one that has learned to tune out everything but the sound of its own name…in the process, the question is repeatedly addressed of how to pierce this ear from outside without rendering it simply useless (Kamuf 1991: 147).

There is also the key issue of the feminine inscribed here. The original chapter which Derrida employs from Leiris is entitled 'Persephone', 'with which he associates all sorts of spirals and corkscrew figures, but particularly the French name of the insect known as an earwig; *perce-oreille*; literally ear-piercer' (Kamuf 1991: 147). As Kamuf notes, there is a paradigmatic issue of the feminine at stake here, and what happens to the feminine in the space of traditional philosophy. Thus, there is an implicit indictment of patriarchy occurring in these pages of 'Tympan': 'Leiris' apparently marginalised text thus displaces the centre of hearing while its spiralling words, its feminine names and sinuousities figure no longer the empty margin of philosophy but an inexhaustible reserve, the stereographic activity of an entirely other ear' (Kamuf 1991: 147). Agosti develops this thematic in 'Tympan': 'there is to be born some unheard-of musical score [tympanum]…putting the *loxos* (the obliquity of the tympanic membrane) to work in the *logos*; all the sonorities [the echoes of meaning] multiply' (Agosti 1979: 7). Agosti clarifies that there is an implicit reference to Mallarmé here, in terms of 'the tympanum's beats' (Agosti 1979: 7).

It is here that we can see the close connection between 'Tympan' and *Spurs* and the increasing sense of an emerging thematic in Derrida's work during this period: an emphasis on desire and the feminine which reaches its most explicit articulation in *Spurs*. If the 'writing of the body' has been thematised since the Artaud essay, it is now *operationalised*. Agosti sees the Mallarméan connection as not simply in 'Tympan' or *Dissemination* but also very much at the heart of *Spurs* itself; 'I wonder about this practice and whether it might not find a closely related model in an example; Mallarmé's example' (Agosti 1979: 13). Even taking aside Derrida's own direct consideration of Mallarmé's texts, Agosti here introduces an interpretation which relies on three 'levels of the practice of writing' 'the material, the notional and the meta-operational' (Agosti 1979: 13). According to Agosti, these three levels work together in Mallarmé and Derrida but this approach is quite singular insofar as with James Joyce, it is just the first level which is in operation, while with Bataille and Artaud, it is just the last two levels.

Whatever about the merits of this interpretation *in toto*, it does, I think, provide an interesting entry point into Derrida's work. In the first case, the material level, we are talking about the way language works in the Mallarméan and Derridean text. In other words, the very material construction of the text is significant. This relates both to the respective writing styles of Derrida and Mallarmé (and of course *style* itself will be one of Derrida's main themes in *Spurs*) and Johnson has described these very well in her preface to *Dissemination* but also the use the use of syntax and typography (Johnson 1981). This is what makes both Mallarmé and Derrida so difficult to translate in terms of an exclusive emphasis on meaning or semantics. Their texts also work materially in terms of the surface level of language and this is not so easy to translate across languages. The second level of the notional is synonymous with the philosophical; both thinkers employ concepts and ideas in their work. Again, however, this has been contentious in terms of both thinkers, where both have been seen as obscurantist and nonphilosophical. Finally, there is the meta-operational level. This is the level at which both thematise the very status of their work.

We have seen this consistently with Derrida when he speaks in interviews about trying to achieve a nonphilosophical space from which to question philosophy and in terms of issues concerning his own identity as a philosopher or writer. Similarly, in Mallarmé, the latter's work is metalevel insofar as it questions the very identity of poetry and refuses to accept the genre distinctions in literature between poetry and other kinds of discourse. For example, one can cite here his attempt to break down the distinction between poetry and prose and also his use of the so-called new genre of 'anecdotes' (McCombie 2008). But it is also arguable that Mallarmé seeks to break down the distinction between philosophy and poetry, and that this is what primarily links him to Derrida. These are useful levels of interpretation to have in mind when we come to read and seek to interpret the difficult and enigmatic text of *Spurs*.

On *Spurs: Nietzsche's Styles*

Spurs: Nietzsche's Styles (Derrida 1979: 35) begins with a letter from Nietzsche to one of his female friends or lovers, citing himself as being regarded as the most 'scabrous of present-day philologists', since the publication of his *Birth of Tragedy*. This foregrounding of the notion of scabrousness attaching to Nietzsche's public image is purposeful on Derrida's part. For Nietzsche's relations to the question of woman have a certain scabrousness attached to them: 'it is woman who will be my subject' ['la femme sera mon sujet'] (Derrida 1979: 37). Derrida is writing, originally giving his talk in July 1972 at Cerisy-la-Salle, alongside Pierre Klossowksi, Gilles Deleuze, Sarah Kofman and Jean-Francois Lyotard, etc. at a time when what Jane Gallop calls 'seventies feminism' was reaching its zenith (Gallop 1997). That feminism which called for the liberation of women from male shackles but which often did so in the name of a certain kind of 'essential woman'. This is the context in which we should see Derrida's emphasis on the 'question of woman' (Derrida 1979: 37) and of course Nietzsche was not regarded as an ally in such a task. It is significant that back in the early text on Levinas (published in 1964) Derrida has already said 'this could not have been written by a woman' (Derrida 1967f, 1978d). This is not meant as a compliment. And, by the 1970s, Derrida's work is radicalising some of the movements which were already implicit in his earlier work regarding patriarchy or what Derrida calls 'phallogocentrism' (Kamuf 1991). But in the choice of Nietzsche as his focus in this text and in employing Nietzsche in an affirmative way, as Gallop notes, Derrida is also doing something quite radical and controversial. A little like his earlier use of the *avant-garde*, this thinker would not be the feminist first choice. For many, he is seen as anti-feminist, vehemently so. Indeed, his comments often appear misogynistic and essentialising of woman in a negativising way. But, as Derrida will want to claim, he will present a Nietzsche who is neither anti-feminist nor feminist. And, for many feminists, this will be highly problematical. The problematicity does not simply concern Nietzsche's reading of woman which was already somewhat infamous. But now the problem extends to Derrida's own original reading of Nietzsche in 1972, published in a developed version in 1978 (the bilingual version was published in 1979). Now, Derrida will not be able to hide behind a reading of Nietzsche. Rightly, his work will be perceived also as a self-interpretation as much of his writings are. Thus, if one does not like *Spurs* (Derrida 1979), one can accuse not simply Nietzsche, but also Derrida, of misogyny and anti-feminism.

Neither Anti-Feminist nor Feminist

As Derrida suggests, this text will be more enigmatic than most. Some would argue that *Spurs* (Derrida 1979) is Derrida's most enigmatic text. As Derrida observes early on, the title for this lecture was to have been the 'question of style'. However, 'it is woman who will be my subject. Still, one might wonder whether that doesn't really amount to the same thing – or is it to the other?' ['la question du style…ou à l'autre'] (Derrida 1979: 34–7). Here, we see Derrida multiplying the interpretations: is this text about the subject, is it about woman, it is about style? Do these things mean the same? Or are we talking about the other? This playful mode is carried throughout and it can make for a frustrating read for those who wish to pin down Derrida on a specific argument. But, as with so much of Derrida's work, one cannot separate the form from the content. This is indeed what we have seen Derrida say about Bataille's work, against the Sartrean interpretation. These elements remain inseparable. Agosti has also pointed to how Mallarmé is a key reference for *Spurs*. So, in this sense, what Agosti calls the material level of the text is unsurprisingly contorted and complex. We can also see that Derrida is no longer working as a lone theorist. By the time of the critique of structuralism in 'Structure, Sign and Play' (Derrida 1978j), it is already clear that Derrida's reputation is becoming more well known (for example, in the ensuing questions at John Hopkins, Goldmann refers to his 'reputation in France and its power' (Macksey 2007).[4]

Derrida now is explicitly mentioning it in his text. He refers to 'a new phase of deconstructive affirmative criticism; they have opened up the problematic field to the very margin' ['ouvrant le champ problématique et jusqu'à la marge'] (Derrida 1979: 37). Here, we can think of Rodolphe Gasché and Sarah Kofman, amongst others, both of whom Derrida refers to in footnotes in *Spurs*. Thus, we are now dealing with something called 'deconstruction'. Another point to bear in mind here is the esteemed speakers who were also at this Cerisy-la-Salle conference on Nietzsche. In a sense, it is the culmination of a rebirth of interest in Nietzsche in France, which will have effects for the next thirty years. This process starts with Deleuze's text on Nietzsche and philosophy (Deleuze 1986), and also a little later,

---

4   I would like to thank Andrew O'Shea for the gift of the Macksey text and his subtle insights into the 'structuralist controversy' surrounding it.

Pierre Klossowski's *Nietzsche and the Vicious Circle* (Klossowski 1997), both of whom were also at Cerisy-Le-Salle. Moreover, it is also the case that the 'question of woman' is becoming a central question for what becomes known as French feminism, for example, Kristeva (Kristeva 1984) and Cixous (Cixous 1994), both of whom are already in dialogue with Derrida. Kristeva is one of the interviewers of Derrida in the *Positions* (Derrida 1972a) volume and she was also very involved with Derrida in *Tel Quel* (her husband Phillipe Sollers was the editor of the journal at this time). Luce Irigaray's text *Speculum* (Irigaray 1985), as another example, seems to criticise Derrida for keeping the question of woman under the register of a male understanding. But we should also note that the rebirth of interest in the 'question of woman' is part of a wider discourse on sexuality (what Derrida calls in 'Choreographies' 'the resexualisation of philosophy' [Derrida 1992b]).

Here, the key figures are also present at Cerisy-la-Salle, Deleuze whose *Anti-Oedipus* will be published with Felix Guattari (Deleuze and Guattari 2004) within a year and so too Jean-Francois Lyotard's text *Libidinal Economy* (Lyotard 2004), both under the influence (amongst others) of Nietzsche. So, while Derrida has singled out what is happening in deconstruction, we might say that something greater is happening beyond deconstruction in French philosophy and this is an extraordinary period of creativity and interest within this circle. Although Derrida is not seen as exactly in line with these other thinkers, he has in later interviews and texts made clear his connection to Deleuze, Lacan and Lyotard (and acknowledged that these affinities have often been occluded or overlooked). Finally, I haven't yet mentioned Foucault's *History of Sexuality* (Foucault 1997) which is also written during this period. An extraordinary convergence of thematics is thus to be noted here. One thinker who might be cited as anticipating all of this is Merleau-Ponty (Merleau-Ponty 2002) and certainly there are affinities here. However, as Derrida will show in *On Touching* (Derrida 2005) more recently, there is a distance between Merleau-Ponty's phenomenology of the flesh and the kind of philosophy of the erotic or sexuality which is being developed in the early 1970s.

Perhaps the key influences here are Georges Bataille (Bataille 2001) who we have spoken of most directly in Chapter 2, and also Pierre Klossowski who is mentioned several times in *Spurs*. Klossowksi was the French translator of Heidegger's *Nietzsche* (Heidegger 1991) volumes, while also being an excellent interpreter of Nietzsche in his own right. Derrida refers to Klossowski's *Nietzsche and the Vicious Circle* (Klossowski 1997) in *Spurs* and he has also been mentioned in Derrida's reading of Bataille in 'From a Restricted to a General Economy' (Derrida 1978i). Klossowski was a close friend of Bataille and a collaborator on numerous projects together. Derrida cites him several times in relation to the conception of the 'simulacrum', a key concept for Klossowksi.

To Spur, To Spurn, To Attack or To Defend

So what is the significance of Derrida's title; *Spurs: Nietzsche's Styles* (Derrida 1979)? Why the notion of 'spurs'? Derrida tells us that a spur can be 'a pointed object which could be used in a vicious attack ["attaquer cruellement"] against what philosophy appeals to' or as 'protection against the threat of such an attack' ['pour repousser une forme menacante'] (Derrida 1979: 36/37). Derrida also tells us that Mallarmé uses the term 'spur' to mean to spurn or to reject (Derrida 1979: 41). But to spurn or reject what? And what might philosophy be seeking to attack or defend itself from? Derrida uses the same word here in French, 'voile' (Derrida 1979: 38), as ambiguous in terms of its gender, as it can mean either 'veils or sails' (Derrida 1979: 39), either masculine or feminine. 'As one bends behind veils and sails; but let us leave this to float between the masculine and the feminine; Nietzsche must have been familiar with all genres' (Derrida 1979: 39). Again, we are clearly being told of Nietzsche's dexterity with style. Here, we might return to Agosti's three layers of interpretation. As with Derrida and Mallarmé, I think we can conclude that Nietzsche's texts also operate at the three levels which Agosti describes. On the material level, they constantly play with the structures, grammar and syntax. On the notional level, they are obviously philosophically complex and sophisticated. And finally, at the meta-operational level, they constantly interrogate their presuppositions. Perhaps the prime example of this is Nietzsche's last book, *Ecce Homo* (Nietzsche 1979), which is subtitled 'why I write such great books!'. Derrida tells us that 'style also uses a spur…[but] such an operation cannot be simplified' (Derrida 1979: 39). This is significant. If style is a 'spur' going on the previous definitions of 'spur', then style might be used to defend philosophy from its 'other' or to attack the other in the name of philosophy. Or indeed to defend the other from philosophy or attack philosophy in the name of the other. Again, we are brought back to Derrida's oft-repeated insistence that he is seeking a nonphilosophical site from which to question philosophy. Style might also be used to reject or to spurn in Mallarmé's sense. But reject or spurn what exactly? Would style in Nietzsche be used to spurn feminism? Or to spurn anti-feminism? Or both or neither?

Derrida reintroduces the problematic of woman here and links it intrinsically to the question of style and his motif of the spur: 'spur is what impresses the mark of style in the question of woman ["la question de la femme"]…between Nietzsche's style and Nietzsche's woman' ['entre le style et la femme de Nietzsche'] (Derrida 1979: 40/41). There is a link back to the theme of sound which we mentioned earlier especially in relation to the essay 'Tympan' (Derrida 1982b). 'Am I only ear…the labyrinth of an ear' ['le labyrinth d'une oreille'] (Derrida 1979: 42). Once more, this is a question of the capacity of philosophy to shut out voices or sounds that it doesn't want to hear, as in 'Plato's Pharmacy' where 'Plato blocks his ears' (Derrida 1981c). But Nietzsche in his work would have sought to intensify this sonorous assault on philosophy. This applies or is applied by Nietzsche to his own personhood; 'I too am an éperon; I too am a spur' (quoted Derrida 1979: 43). In this measure, the very concept of self or subject becomes implicated in the text, in a way which looks back to 'The Ends of Man' (1982d) essay and forward to the *Glas* (Derrida 1986a) text. Nietzsche is self-implicated in his texts in a way that few earlier philosophers were and as we have seen this is also something we can say about Derrida (this is commented on in the 'Between Brackets' interview) [Derrida 1995a]. Nietzsche says that 'the noise has made me a visionary' (quoted Derrida 1979: 45). His sense of being a seer is indicative of the complex notion of vision and truth in Nietzsche's discourse which sometimes borders on the prophetic. It also reminds one of Socrates' claim in the *Phaedrus* that 'I am a seer...but not a very good one' (Plato 1961).

Despite the great emphasis on woman in *Spurs*, Derrida seeks to clarify that for Nietzsche, there can be no essence of woman. There is here an implicit criticism of those feminisms (in Gallop's terms 'seventies feminism' [Gallop 1997]) which seek to posit an essence to woman. 'Perhaps woman is a non-figure; a simulacrum' ['peut-être est-elle, comme non-identité, non-figure, simulacra...'] (Derrida 1979 48/49), Derrida tells us, which connects powerfully with Klossowksi's reading of Nietzsche in *Nietzsche and the Vicious Circle* (Klossowski 1997) and also links back to Klossowski's reading of Bataille and the simulacrum, which Derrida cites approvingly in the essay, 'From Restricted to General Economy' (Derrida 1978i: 49). Nietzsche also invokes the conception of 'distance' here. One must keep one's distance from women insofar as they have no essence. As Derrida also states here, 'such might also be the advice of one man to another, keep one's distance from women' (Derrida 1979: 49). This is a significant statement which anticipates some of the feministic criticisms which will come later. This could be accused of being simply a matter 'between men'. This is Rosi Braidotti's criticism of *Spurs* and this is also Irigaray's (Irigaray 1985) critique: that this is intra-men, merely 'advice from one man to another'.

However, one can also look at this differently, that Nietzsche's de-essentialising of woman is an attempt to liberate woman from the essentials of feminism which, in effect, simply reduce woman to another thing. This latter would also connect feminism to exactly the kind of scientism which Nietzsche's project is seeking to usurp. Nietzsche had referred to this tendency in the *Nachlass* as 'the will to truth' (Nietzsche 1990a). The modern, enlightened man seeks to banish all illusion, error and vestiges of unconscious life in favour of a thoroughly rationalised knowledge and epistemological truth. But there is the real danger here for Nietzsche that feminists are seeking to become like the worst kinds of men. Is this any real route for feminism to take, to seek to become like the worst essentialists? Certainly, Derrida would seem to be attempting to provide a Nietzschean corrective to the 'fetishising essentialisms' of 1970s feminism. Key here, as Derrida acknowledges, is for Nietzsche the intrinsic relation between 'art and woman' (Derrida 1979: 47), drawing together all the aesthetic resources which we saw Nietzsche outline in his *Nachlass* (Nietzsche 1990a) essays. As with art, it would precisely be the ability of woman to usurp the metaphysics of truth which would enable her power: 'Perhaps woman is a non-figure; a simulacrum' (Derrida 1979: 48/49). And again: 'woman distorts all vestige of essentiality; woman is but one name for the untruth of truth' ['femme est un nom de cette non-vérité de la vérité'] (Derrida 1979: 50/51). This causes immense difficulties for feminist thinkers who wish to posit the truth of woman or even the truth of patriarchal exploitation. This has been the precise point made against Nietzsche/Derrida and *Spurs* by those feminists such as Rosi Braidotti and Luce Irigaray (nonetheless while recognising its relevance for the problem of woman and its immense influence as a text). This use of woman and art would also link with the consistent theme of life which we saw in the *Nachlass*; 'the greatest charm of life; that it puts a veil of lovely potentialities over itself' (Derrida 1979: 51). Life is thus full of artifice, this should not be criticised or resisted, this is precisely its enchantment and an enchantment which philosophers seem to constantly miss in their bids to objectify and classify. There would be a crucial reference back to the concept or figure of woman here for Derrida: 'supposing truth to be a woman; philosophers have had little understanding' (Derrida 1979: 55). The philosophers have had little understanding because of their dogmatism and their 'essentialising fetishes' ['les philosophes...ont mal compris les femmes'] (Derrida 1979: 54).

It would also be for Derrida a question of writing; 'Nietzsche's writing; a suspension of truth...indeed is the feminine operation' ['l'opération féminine'] (Derrida 1979: 56/57). The emphasis on Nietzsche's *writing* points us back to our theme of a 'writing of the body'. So art, woman, the feminine operation and the very process of writing itself would all be connected here in some kind of spider's web. And connected to all this or trapped in the web would be the very contradictions of Nietzsche's discourse, in this case, his 'apparently feminist and anti-feminist propositions' ['ces propositions d'apparence féministe...avec l'énorme corpus de l'anti-féminisme']. For Derrida is well aware of the accusations of 'phallocentrism in Nietzsche's discourse' (Derrida 1979: 61). Nietzsche was indeed unequivocal on a certain kind of feminism, a 'woman who aspires to be like a man; gone the style' ['la femme veut resembler à l'homme...Perd le style'] (Derrida 1979: 64/65). Here, another opposition would be being set up, between feminism (or at least a certain kind of feminism, a 1970s essentialising feminism in at least Gallop's terms) and the very notion of style which both Nietzsche and Derrida affirm so powerfully. There would not seem to be much possibility of rapprochement here. Braidotti refers to Derrida's approach dismissively as a 'negative feminism' (Braidotti 1991), a kind of feminism without any content.

In contrast to the aforementioned feminism, there is a valuation in Nietzsche of 'a pregnant woman and her unborn child' (Derrida 1979: 65). Authentic philosophy would also be a kind of pregnancy; this is precisely what an artist's philosophy would be, neither masculine nor feminine. But as Nietzsche was himself well aware, this whole discourse on woman, art, pregnancy and philosophy is 'itself divided' (Derrida 1979: 71). Derrida makes a reference to Klossowski's Nietzsche here, and one thinks of Klossowski's complex idea of the simulacrum. How to interpret this? 'The question of style must be measured against the question of interpretation itself' (Derrida 1979: 73). No easy solutions then, but it would still be a question of interpretation, however much under duress the philosophical status of the question would be put. But there would also be dangers in interpretation. Here, Derrida mentions both affirmatively and crucially Heidegger's Nietzsche texts; 'while Heidegger recognises that Nietzsche is seeking "something other

than simply inversion and a transformation of the value of hierarchy itself"
(Derrida 1979: 73), nonetheless Derrida seems to suggest that Heidegger is still
after a 'hermeneutic answer' eventually (Derrida 1979: 73). The problem with
such a hermeneutic approach for Derrida is that it would elide the issues of style,
woman, art, etc. which *Spurs* is so concerned with. To make his point, Derrida cites
the omissions in Heidegger's analysis: 'Heidegger analyses all the elements of
Nietzsche's text with the exception of truth become female' ['elle (l'Idée) deviant
femme'] (Derrida 1979: 85/87) but this truth become female, at least here now for
Derrida, would be the issue of all issues. What is thus lost in Heidegger's approach
and in feminism for different reasons is the very 'heterogeneity of Nietzsche's
text' ['l'hétérogénéité du texte'] (Derrida 1978: 95/97).

Nonetheless, despite this heterogeneity, one shouldn't give up on trying to read
or understand Nietzsche. Derrida himself offers three propositions but, we might
say, this would be an attempt at a provisional framework rather than a belief in a
definitive exhaustive analysis. We can outline, Derrida tells us, 'three propositions
concerning woman' (Derrida 1979: 97ff.) in the Nietzschean text. First, she was
despised as untruthful in the name of truth. Second, she is despised as truth, criticised
by the artists. Third, she affirms herself as a 'Dionysiac' power (Derrida 1979: 97).
Each of these propositions would need to be taken into account in going beyond
traditional feminism but it would the last which would be Nietzsche's legacy in
Spurs to be carried on by Derrida; 'woman affirms herself as a Dionysiac power'
['la femme est reconnue affirmée comme puissance affirmative, dissimulatrice,
artiste, dionysiaque'] (Derrida 1979: 96/97). In this context, Derrida reinvokes
the motif of the 'hymen's graphic' ['la graphique de l'hymen'] (Derrida 1979:
98/99) which has been so important for him in *Dissemination*. It is precisely this
'hymen' which 'describes a margin where the control over meaning is without
recourse' (Derrida 1979: 99). Nietzsche is mentioned alongside 'Lautréamont and
Mallarmé' (Derrida 1979: 101) in terms of 'a vertiginous nonmastery' ['le vertige
d'une non-maîtrise'] (Derrida 1979: 100/101). With all this discussion, we must
not lose sight of the radical anti-essentialism; 'there is no such thing as a woman;
as a truth in herself of woman in herself' (Derrida 1979: 101).

Derrida now develops the point he had made earlier concerning the need to
relate the question of style to the question of interpretation. First, he looks at how
Nietzsche himself seeks to address this question. There is initially an attempt at
defining the truth subjectively as 'these are only my truths' (Derrida 1979: 103)
and this is also connected to a notion that there is not just one truth but many
truths; 'truth is plural' ['la vérité est plurielle'] (Derrida 1979: 102/103). Here,
for the first time in the text, it is the notion of 'sexual difference' ('la difference
sexuelle') (Derrida 1979: 102) which becomes foregrounded. This is a notion
which becomes crucial from this time onwards. Up to this point, it is arguable that

feminism had sought to counter patriarchy with a notion of an essential female essence[5] which might be countered to the valuation of masculinity.

If Beauvoir (in *The Second Sex*) was the first to address the issue of sexual difference, she never named it so explicitly, and Derrida's discussion here sets the scene for a whole debate which will develop over the next thirty years. We will come back to the details of this debate, with a particular focus on feminist responses (in all their variation) in the next chapter. But here Derrida is clear that this invocation of sexual difference must not be seen in essentialist terms. In fact, this possibility of essentialisation would be the very lure which must be resisted: 'there is no truth in itself of the sexual difference' (Derrida 1979: 103). It is 'ontology [which] tries to hide this undecidability' ['indécidabilité'] (Derrida 1979: 105). Of course, traditional ontology has tried to hide this undecidability by valuing the masculine and setting up an essentialist hierarchy. In contrast, feminism also hides this undecidability or rather rejects it by trying to argue for equality. Nonetheless, there is a great danger here for Derrida as the accusations of negative feminism insinuate. If we keep speaking of undecidability, there is a danger that the status quo remains intact and we occlude the real sources of oppression and exploitation. Derrida here does not address this issue directly but he shows cognisance of it in his later 'Choreographies' (Derrida 1991c) interview where he makes clear that, although he opposes egalitarian feminism, nonetheless it must not be a matter of simply opposing it politically, as this can be used for more reactive purposes i.e. maintainence of the patriarchal status quo.

What Derrida is more interested in here, however, is the way that Heidegger, in his understanding of Nietzsche, has missed this crucial issue of sexual difference. What is at stake, then, is a whole interpretation of Nietzsche. The importance of this rereading of Nietzsche should not be overlooked. It is arguable that it this Nietzsche who also guides much of Derrida's interpretations of Bataille, Artaud, Leiris, etc. in his late 1960s work. All of these thinkers are compared to Nietzsche in Derrida's texts and he maintains an important if slightly marginal status in the essays. So Nietzsche would be pivotal. But which Nietzsche? 'For not having posed the sexual question...Heidegger's reading of Nietzsche has been idling offshore' (Derrida 1979: 109).

Here, we see the two pronged nature of Derrida's rereading of Nietzsche. Nietzsche would have been misread in the neglect of his emphasis on sexual difference which can have such a bearing, not simply on epistemological issues, but also political ones, what Derrida elsewhere calls the 'Hegelian-sexual' scene (Derrida 1995a). We have seen how, for Nietzsche, this is matter of the utmost importance for 'culture' itself. In the *Nachlass* (Nietzsche 1990), he wishes to make huge claims for philosophy but only insofar as philosophy engages with its other, with nonphilosophy and especially art. And thus the effects must be registered of this deconstruction of philosophy's borders or margins. For now

---

5   There is, however, no unilinear narrative here of historical feminism. Counterexamples to essentialist feminism would be Emma Goldman, referred to in Chapter 6, and Simone de Beauvoir.

truth must be put in quotation marks, in scare quotes. We must leave the artist's metaphysics behind and seek out instead truth as appearance. This is Derrida's task then but undoubtedly Derrida also reorients Nietzsche's discourse here away from the aesthetic emphasis. There is a move towards a more political discourse which will connect with the problematic of feminism but, also as we will see in Chapter 7, with a wider problematic of politics, which will lead Derrida into discussion with thinkers such as Habermas (Habermas 1990) in his later work. Second, however, the question of woman for Derrida will not be simply a regional question; 'the question of sexual difference was not at all a regional question in a larger order' (Derrida 1979: 109). It includes everything; everything is at stake in the question of woman, the relation between philosophy and its other, and the artist's philosophy. There is clear connection here between the macro and the micro; what Bataille would have called the 'general economy'.

Conclusion: Whither the Artist-Philosopher?

Nonetheless, we must not think ourselves to have somehow solved the riddles of philosophy now; 'there is no totality to Nietzsche's texts, not even a fragmentary one, there is evidence here to expose one to an enormous clap of laughter' (Derrida 1979: 135). Again, here, there would be an implicit reference to Bataille. So often Bataille seems to appear near the end of Derrida's essay, near the death so to speak, just when the Hegelian interepretation of the end and of death would raise its possibility. We might have had some conclusions here, but no, there would still be excess, laughter, and a death which cannot be understood. There would be no end as such, no death as such, just singular ends, pluralised deaths. As Derrida says elsewhere, we would not really know where we are going (Derrida 1986c) ultimately with this. But this is not to say that deconstruction is arbitrary. Rather, as we have seen, there is clear movement to be traced in individual texts, and also between texts.

Derrida in fact here invokes both 'death and birth' (Derrida 1979: 139) and refers to them in relation to 'the scene in which we are operating' (Derrida 1979: 139). The notion of textual operation can be seen to come from Mallarmé and also from Bataille. In this text, so many terms would 'slide' in their meaning. We must not decontextualise or think ourselves done with the question of style. This is feminism's problem, at least of a traditional sort ('gone the style') ['perd le style'] (Derrida 1979: 64/65). It is also the problem which Nietzsche faces in the *Nachlass* (Nietzsche 1990a) and there he shows its significance for political and cultural questions, on the grand scale. The connection between Nietzsche's *Nachlass* and Derrida's *Spurs* is to be seen most especially near the end of *Spurs*, where Derrida reiterates that the question of woman is not a regional question. At stake here would be the constant attempt to relegate the question of woman but also the question of style in this way. Both Nietzsche and Derrida resist this formulation, which is really a repression practiced by philosophy against its other.

In later texts, as we shall see, Derrida makes a similar accusation against Levinas, which repeats and in some ways intensifies his earlier criticisms of Levinas in 'Violence and Metaphysics' (Derrida 1997c). There, in 'At this moment' (Derrida 1997c), Derrida would accuse Levinas of seeking to bury the feminine under a neutral which is in effect, behind the scenes, still too masculine. This would be another way of saying à la Nietzsche that Levinas is trying to reduce the question of art, and of culture, to metaphysics. In another essay, 'Geschlecht: Différence Sexuelle, Différence Ontologique', Derrida's reading of Heideggerian 'Geschlecht' [Derrida 1997d] is similar but re oriented significantly from *Spurs*. Here, in *Spurs*, Heidegger would have skirted the question of woman and there too (in 'Geschlecht' [Derrida 1997d]), this accusation is repeated. But unlike Levinas, Heidegger would perhaps be seeking to neutralise not sexual difference, but 'sexual duality' (Derrida 1997d). I will return to these questions in Chapter 6. Insofar as sexual duality was neutralised, perhaps Heideggerian *Dasein* really does beckon towards the possibility of a new kind of sexual difference no longer dominated by binary opposition; the marriage of the couple, masculine-feminine; heterosexual/homosexual, etc. But here it is perhaps significant that Heidegger is also called in to complete the text of *Spurs*. Now, it is a question of forgetting. What Heidegger refers to as the 'forgetting of being' which he says has been treated as if it were like a question of a 'professor forgetting his umbrella' (quoted Derrida 1979: 142). Derrida, playing on a fragment here, refers to where Nietzsche precisely writes, 'I have forgotten my umbrella' (Derrida 1979: 135). This distinction between the ontological and the ontic highlights a certain elitism of truth of the 'destiny of being' in Heidegger. In seeking to make the 'I have forgotten my umbrella' equivalent to the 'forgetting of being', Derrida would once more be seeking to deconstruct a certain privileging of the high over the low, the hierarchical binary structure which has also subordinated the feminine to the masculine, man to woman, sex to asceticism, etc. 'Would the forgetting of a being (an umbrella, for example) be incommensurable with the forgetting of being? For which it would all the more be a bad *image*?' (Derrida 1979: 141) [Derrida's emphasis]. Once more, we are back within the structure of *mimesis*. The condescension towards the image would require subversion and *Spurs* would indeed have been another 'mimodrama' which sought to loosen the ties which bound *mimesis* and philosophy to the strict code of a Parmenides (or Heidegger) who 'neglects *mimesis*'. If the *Sophist* (Plato 1961) called for a parricide against Parmenides, perhaps we can read *Spurs* finally as a (double) parricide against parricide, directed primarily at Heidegger (and feminism of an essentialist sort). Like all doubles however, one wouldn't be able to read the meaning of such a sacrifice definitively or conclusively.

Chapter 6
On Derrida and Feminism

Introduction

In the last chapter, we looked at Derrida's opening up of the problematic of feminism in his key 1970s text *Spurs: Nietzsche's Styles* (Derrida 1979). This text has had a very significant influence on succeeding feminist thought, both initially in France (in the work of Irigaray, Cixous, Kristeva, Kofman, etc.) and more recently in Anglo-American feminism, although this latter has often been through the work of French-influenced American thinkers. Amongst other work, two main anthologies have been devoted to Derrida's work on feminism. Here, I will employ these significant texts and their diverse approaches to Derrida as a springboard into this complicated problematic.

As Ellen Feder, Mary Rawlinson and Emily Zakin make clear in their *Derrida and Feminism; Recasting the Question of Woman* (Feder et al. 1997a), the editors 'took a gamble' by focusing on Derrida. 'It was our gamble that Derrida had undecided all this and put woman into question again' (Feder et al. 1997a: 2). That is, what Jane Gallop called 'seventies feminism' (Gallop 1997) had been well and thoroughly usurped in its tendencies towards essentialism, not of course simply by Derrida. Nonetheless, it is significant how even feminist critics of Derrida see *Spurs* as a pivotal text in terms of its anti-essentialising influence. For these thinkers, Derrida's writing is a 'strategic science' which allows us to pinpoint the boundaries and margins of a discourse or a politics. And so Derrida's work has been precisely challenging to feminism, in this way, as a challenge to the self-made or self-defined boundaries and margins. Whether in agreement or not with Derrida on the nature of this challenge, however, I think it is clear that *Spurs* has been an extraordinarily productive text. It is in reality a very short intervention in the debate and although published in book form it is precisely only because is published in either bilingual or quadro-lingual versions that it actually reaches the limit of a book. It is in many respects an essay which resembles many of the essays in *Writing and Difference* (Derrida 1967c). So why the extraordinary effect of this essay? First, because as mentioned in the last chapter it is written at a time of extraordinary flowering of interest in the question of woman in France and beyond.

One important example here is Luce Irigaray's *Speculum*: *De l'autre femme* (*Speculum of the Other Woman*) [Irigaray 1985] published in France in 1974. This text caused immense furore in Lacanian circles and led to Irigaray being sacked from her post at Vincennes university. Margaret Whitford has described the text as 'Derridean-influenced' (Whitford 1991: 7) and this is undoubtedly true up to a point. Nonetheless, the Derrida-Irigaray encounter is emblematic of the affinities and disaffinities between Derrida and French feminist thinking during this period. In a later interview, entitled 'Questions', Irigaray is very critical of what she considers the 'discourse of mastery' at work in Derrida's equation of writing with the feminine principle (Whitford 1991: 7). We shall return to this question below.

But the importance of *Spurs* can also be seen as part of the great development of Theory, most especially in America and the growth of Cultural Studies as a discipline. Initially, this stemmed from the origins of the Cultural Studies movement in the Adult Education movement in Britain in the 1950s and 1960s. Figures such as Raymond Williams and Richard Hoggart explored the issue of 'culture and education' from the perspective of those groups or individuals who had been marginalised by the centralised education system and mainstream culture. Alternative versions of culture, especially working class culture, and education, especially adult education, were explored as a means of questioning the assumed principles of the centralised education system. Evolving out of this work in the 1970s, The Birmingham Cultural Studies Centre extended this new focus of attention to so-called 'youth culture' (Hall 1996). The importance of Cultural Studies can be seen as its refining of a Left Marxist perspective into the 1980s and 1990s, through a new emphasis on the interconnectedness of race, gender, sexuality and youth issues.

It is undoubtedly true that Derrida's work became very significant for this new culturalist approach within the academy, and most especially in its association with the much-vaunted Yale school of deconstruction in the USA. Second, it is also the case that *Spurs* should not be seen as a once-off text. It sets off a discourse on Derrida's work which has already been implicit around the issue of desire and sexual difference but which becomes more prominent from here. This evolves the 'writing of the body' thematic from Derrida's earlier work. We have already seen how Derrida's paradigm shift to an *avant-garde* thematics and away from phenomenology allows Derrida to foreground desire and the body and to self-implicate himself in these texts. Derrida continues to develop this work into the 1980s with 'Choreographies' (Derrida 1991c) and 'Geschlecht' (Derrida 1997d) and even up to the later work, such as the important *On Touching* (Derrida 2005) which we will return to in conclusion. It also connects with a broader political concern in Derrida's book which has always been present from the early work. For example, in the work on Artaud in *Writing and Difference*, Derrida is keen to stress the fact that the 'theatre of cruelty' is a political manifesto. He also links Artaud to the early Marx and he does the same with Bataille in 'From Restricted to General Economy' (Derrida 1967k). We will see in the next chapter how this will also develop into a dialogue with one of the main (neo)Marxist thinkers of the age, Jürgen Habermas (Habermas 1990).

It is interesting to think about the connection between the thematic of desire and sexual difference and its political dimension. Politics, we might argue, is always a matter of desire; perhaps we might go further and say that politics is through and through erotic. Of course, it is feminism which in many respects we can thank for this development. Feminism taught that 'the personal is the political'. Politics is not or should not be a matter of abstraction but of engaged passions (Hall 1994). This is precisely what Derrida means by challenging margins and boundaries. Derrida himself remarks that feminism has shaken the logic of identity and allowed a multiplication of possibilities within the field of sexual difference (Derrida 1997d). Derrida is thus also self-consciously indebted to feminism, both practical and theoretical. This, of course, is also an issue which goes beyond feminism itself to the whole nexus where the political meets the personal in changing times. Thus, we might mention queer theory here as another site of intervention, both theoretical and practical which has links to this sexualisation of the political space (Sullivan 2003). It would not simply be Derrida writing with the 'hand of a woman; and his inclusion within his text of explicitly female interlocutors who appear to write the text' (Feder et al. 1997a). We might say, in linking in with Derrida's attempt to think beyond the binaries of male/female (and heterosexual/homosexual), that genuinely 'queer' voices and traces can be recognised and heard within and without of Derrida's texts.

This enables some feminists to connect 'a discussion of performativity in [Judith] Butler and Derrida's work' (Salih 2003). Tina Chanter similarly uses the metaphor of *interruption* to thematise Derrida's and her own method (Chanter 1997). Chanter thus suggests disrupting an opposition which has been constructed between feminism and deconstruction, and indeed an opposition between queer theory and deconstruction. John Caputo (Caputo 1997) has relatedly talked about the possibility of a sexual difference which exceeds the number two. But this is very much a problematic of 'nineties feminism' (Gallop 1997), a feminism no longer seeking an essentialising identity, a feminism which seems to be very affirmative of deconstruction (if still harbouring some differences) but matters were not always thus. I will now turn to an analysis of the Feder et al. volume of essays on Derrida and feminism, so as to foreground the precise genealogy of this problematic of deconstruction and feminism. I will begin with reference to Jane Gallop's important essay on the differences between what she terms 'seventies feminism' and 'nineties feminism' (Gallop 1997).

On Feminism and Derrida

Jane Gallop has provided a fascinating and clear thinking genealogy of feminism which speaks of this transition between a so-called 'seventies feminism' and the move to a 'nineties feminism', with Derrida pictured as a key figure in this problematic. As Gallop observes (Gallop 1997: 9), 'seventies feminism envisioned a singular unity which could be collectivised under the name of woman'. This goes against the direction of Derrida's reading of Nietzsche in which 'woman in *Spurs* is figured as insistently plural' (Gallop 1997: 9). Derrida, as Gallop makes clear, through Nietzsche, criticises feminism's desire for a singular concept of woman. Gallop admits to having been awoken from her dogmatic slumbers by Derrida's reading. She is persuaded by his 'truth become female', as 'it becomes female' (quoted Gallop 1997: 11) and also by his interpretation of Heidegger: 'Heidegger skirts the woman' (quoted Gallop 1997: 11).

Derrida launches thus an 'attack on essentialising feminine fetishes' (Gallop 1997: 16). And to read Gallop is to realise that Derrida's impact was extraordinarily powerful, although we should not let him monopolise the debate. Rather, Derrida himself is keen already in 1972, to stress the importance of deconstructive movements. Rodolpe Gasché, for example, but also importantly Sarah Kofman, whose work on Derrida and Nietzsche has been significant in this respect, while also maintaining an intimate connection to feminism. It must be remembered, however, which side of the debate Gallop is on. One might argue that she is hardly representative of mainstream feminism – and we shouldn't thus underestimate the extent of criticism or distance with regard to Derrida from other feminists. We will come to these below. Perhaps it is best to say that there is no one feminism; like truth, feminism has become a pluralised phenomenon. So while it is true that Gallop is not a traditional feminist, she is certainly representative of a more *avant-garde* feminism which one might argue is quite Derridean in inclination. We will return to Gallop a little later in terms of her conception of the 'new woman', and how this relates for her to a reading of Klossowski, Bataille and also Sade (foremost in her text *Intersections* [Gallop 1981]).

For Gallop, then, 'Derrida spoke in and for the era that was 1972' (Gallop 1997: 16). But now Gallop assures us, feminism is more cognisant of context and relativity. 'Now in nineties feminism we try to attend to local differences...woman is defined differently in different circumstances' (Gallop 1997: 17). The whole notion of woman is now recognised as part of a 'sociolect' and this has led us to historicise the supposed essence of womanhood which was sought by the 'seventies feminism' (Gallop 1997: 9). Gallop acknowledges that she was shook up by the reading encounter 'which you could call Derrida' (Gallop 1997: 17) in the 1970s. That is, she affirms the centrality and importance of Derrida's original reading in *Spurs* (Derrida 1979). But now he seems suddenly 'out of it' (Gallop 1997: 18), Gallop states. When we read *Spurs* now, we are struck by how its own understandings are time bound. Even its critique of feminism seems 'stuck on a unified definition of sexual difference when we could see sexual differences all around'.

It is as if Derrida then 'believed that the only distinction that was sexual was the distinction male/female' (Gallop 1997: 18). Of course, Derrida's own thinking did not stand still after *Spurs* as we shall see. If we look to later texts such as 'Choreographies' (Derrida 1991c), 'Geschlecht' (Derrida 1997d) and, most especially, *On Touching* (Derrida 2005), we see a very different emphasis in Derrida's work, an emphasis on the 'plasticity' and the 'techne' of sex (Derrida 2005). As Gallop suggests, this is not really to criticise Derrida, he also seeks to date his *Spurs* text. His own thinking is constantly reiterating the importance of temporality and differences across space and time. Gallop is, she says, critiquing certain dependencies of Derrida's text in 1972, wanting to 'read rather than erase those marks' (Gallop 1997: 18). Gallop's essay is a fascinating genealogy of feminism since and through the debate with Derrida. It both highlights his importance for the debate but also shows how the debate has moved on and how we should not see *Spurs* (Derrida 1979) as a text with all the answers. But, of course, Derrida would never claim that it has, quite the contrary.

Departing from Derrida

Ellen Feder and Emily Zakin, in their essay 'Flirting with the Truth' (Feder and Zakin 1997) take a similarly ambiguous position in relation to *Spurs* (Derrida 1979). They first affirm its reading that identity cannot be fixed. They trace 'the interrogative metaphor – supposing truth to be a woman' (Feder and Zakin 1997: 22) to Nietzsche's text *Beyond Good and Evil* and they clarify how it is directed towards a critique of ontological dogmatism. For Feder and Zakin (Feder and Zakin 1997), 'philosophy is predicated upon a very real process of othering; that it regulates' (Feder and Zakin 1997: 22). This regulation of otherness is subverted by *Spurs* (Derrida 1979). Anyone wishing to read an essential truth off this text will also be disappointed however. 'Truth is a woman' is not a predicative statement of truth or essence. 'Nietzsche's metaphor collapses in on itself; woman has no truth and thus truth cannot be possessed' (Feder and Zakin 1997: 22).

Here, Derrida looks at how sexual difference is presented societally as 'nothing but the naturalised division of society into two sexes' (Feder and Zakin 1997: 22). Against this, Feder, Zakin and Derrida can agree that 'gender is an accomplishment…roles are designated and not natural' (Feder and Zakin 1997: 23). We can therefore understand that 'metaphysics is built on a lawless abyss' (Feder and Zakin 1997: 24), that there is an excessive 'dissonance' which exceeds all attempts to maintain order. Following this view, we might then understand sexual difference 'as Nietzsche understood subjectivity…as a grammatical structure' (Feder and Zakin 1997: 24), according to Feder and Zakin. So far, Feder and Zakin follow Gallop in affirming the significance and positivity of Derrida's reading in *Spurs*. But like her, they also depart from Derrida at a certain point.

In fact, their arguments against Derrida and against the complicity between deconstruction and feminism are stronger than those of Gallop (Gallop 1997). They recognise more of a distance from Derrida. They are more wary of the negative effects of deconstruction on the feminist project. In this, they are very interesting for our argument. One might also cite here Gayatri Chakravorty Spivak (Spivak 1997), who is a significant intellectual in her own right and also was Derrida's translator in *Of Grammatology* (Derrida 1974b). In her essay in Holland's collection, she makes clear her distance from Derrida, while recognising simultaneously a certain debt and admiration: 'the woman who is the model for deconstructive discourse is the woman generalised' (Spivak 1997: 43). In other words, we are not really getting at the specificity of woman in Derrida's texts, and this is in line with the criticisms which we saw from Feder and Zakin (Feder and Zakin 1997). Nonetheless, Spivak states that 'deconstruction is illuminating as a critique of phallocentrism. It is convincing in its warning to avoid another essentialising discourse' (Spivak 1997:

60). However, and this is key, deconstruction is not convincing as that alternative discourse itself; 'as a feminist discourse' (Spivak 1997: 60). In other words, Derrida is not a feminist; deconstruction is not feminism or even a version of feminism in use. 'It is caught on the other side of sexual difference' (Spivak 1997: 60).

For Feder and Zakin (Feder and Zakin 1997), despite all the affirmation, 'nonetheless *Spurs* betrays its masculine signature and the privilege which allows Derrida to ask the question of woman' (Feder and Zakin 1997: 24). Derrida is thus already a famous male philosopher and his political position is not without significance in the feminism debate. If it is a male philosopher who is 'asking the question of woman' and putting forward a critique of 1970s feminism, then this intervention is itself politically loaded. In effect, they are accusing Derrida of a certain disingenuousness in occluding this other dimension of the question. What is the danger? It is 'that the danger of asserting that there is no woman is to underestimate the significance of everyday political struggles for feminism' (Feder and Zakin 1997: 27–8). We can also, the writers suggest, take this beyond simply an issue of feminism and deconstruction. Rather, another aspect which is occluded here is what one might term the politics of sexuality, and most especially sexual orientation. 'Derrida's project remains libidinally heterosexual' (Feder and Zakin 1997: 28). Although they don't cite it explicitly here, one can identify this moment as a queer theory intervention in the debate which demonstrates that, at least in *Spurs*, Derrida certainly does not question this 'heterosexuality'. In his later texts, this unquestioning heterosexuality *is* put into question, most notably in 'Choreographies' (1991c). This is an important intervention as one might imagine that Derrida's work and queer theory are quite compatible. I will return to this question below but certainly at this point these 'queer' criticisms of Derrida seem well founded. For Feder and Zakin, 'If Derrida genuinely wants to destabilise the categories of sexual difference, this deconstruction "would require that it be aimed at the systematisation of heterosexuality as a norm"' (Feder and Zakin 1997: 28).

Moreover, this seems to be heterosexuality, at least on these terms, the terms of Feder and Zakin, which is very much one which subordinates the female heterosexual to the male. Derrida says as much at one point in *Spurs* (Derrida 1979), when he is talking about the 'distance' of woman or the distance one must keep from woman and he says that this could be 'advice from one man to another' (Derrida 1979), in the matter of seduction. This is also what Nietzsche seems to be warning men about: be careful lest you be seduced. What this occludes according to Feder and Zakin (Feder and Zakin 1997: 45) is the self-organisation of women, independent of men. This seems to have no place in *Spurs*, or in Derrida's thoughts. *Spurs* on these terms, does not allow women to discuss 'among-ourselves' (Feder and Zakin 1997: 46). It is an enclosed world of men and masculine privilege, however much Derrida seeks to present it as subversive. They speak of *Spurs* as involving a 'participation in patriarchal violence; mythologisation and alienation' (Feder and Zakin 1997: 45). Thus, for all they might learn from *Spurs*, 'feminist thinkers must 'resist the temptations of *Spurs*' (Feder and Zakin 1997: 46). We can see this as in line with more famous feminist critiques which are cited here, for example, Luce Irigaray's critique of Derrida and Rosi Bradiotti makes a similar criticism of Derrida (cited Feder and Zakin 1997: 48).

Reading Derrida Otherwise

Tina Chanter's (Chanter 1997) work can be seen as more in line with Derrida's although she takes her own enigmatic approach to *Spurs* and Derrida in her contribution to the volume, 'On not reading Derrida's texts' (Chanter 1997). She points to 'Derrida's own disavowal of misreadings which would decontextualise his work, ignoring the movement of 'on the one hand, on the other hand' (Chanter, 1997: 88). That is, many commentators, including feminist ones as Chanter acknowledges, tend to isolate an aspect of what Derrida says and forget to relate to it to the surrounding context. This decontextualisation leads to all sorts of interpretations of what Derrida is trying to do, often very confused. Again, this links back with Peggy Kamuf's (Kamuf 1991) reading of Derrida's work as coherent and developmental. One must respect the chronological and thematic development, even if this is not always linear. What Chanter seeks to do then is to avoid these decontextualised readings but also readings which would simply assume the worth of Derrida's project without any questioning, i.e. eulogistic or sycophantic interpretations. Rather, she wishes to 'read otherwise and not be captivated by either feminism or deconstruction' (Chanter 1997: 93). In looking at Derrida's reading of sexual difference, she asks 'what would it take to do justice to this reading?' (Chanter 1997: 93).

Chanter looks at Derrida's later reading of Levinas which she also mentions in relation to the 'Choreographies' (Derrida 1991c) interview with Christine McDonald, which we will look at below. In that interview, Derrida refers obliquely to the Levinas essay, 'En Ce Moment Même Dans Cet Ouvrage Me Voici' (Derrida 1997c) and McDonald provides a lengthy and clarifying footnote to explain the context of that essay's questioning of Levinas (Derrida 1991c). The questioning takes place in relation to a theme of sexual difference. Despite the supposed neutral dimension of the other, Derrida reads a masculine bias as against the feminine. The feminine voice is somehow buried under the hegemony of the masculinist paradigm. Against this, Chanter affirms Derrida's call to 'resexualise a philosophical discourse' (Chanter 1997: 94). But Chanter also mentions here Derrida's strategy of 'ingratitude' (Chanter 1997: 108) to properly respect another's discourse. This relates to Chanter's own conception of 'how not to read Derrida'. Sometimes, one must read *Bataille against Bataille* and *Derrida against Derrida*. Of course, this is already an option developed by Bataille himself in his notion of sovereignty which is always 'ungrateful' (Derrida 1967k).

When one reads a thinker against him or herself, one can certainly read this as a strategy. One must be careful, however, of seeing this as a formula or a method for deconstruction. Derrida has consistently reiterated that deconstruction is not a method. So, yes it is certainly true that Derrida reads Levinas against Levinas but this shouldn't hide the fact that he doesn't do this just for its own sake but because there are significant disagreements between Derrida and Levinas. His intervention at this moment can be read as a clear critique of certain aspects of Levinas' discourse (as well as respectful affirmation of others). In other words, Derrida's critique can be double, 'on the one hand, but on the other hand' (Chanter 1997: 88). But this shouldn't imply that his criticisms amount to nothing, where both sides would cancel each other out.

Chanter also explores a more positive sense of neutralisation than one gets in Levinas (Chanter 1997: 95). On first inspection, it is easy to see Heidegger's skirting of the woman question as Derrida mentions in *Spurs* (Derrida 1979) as leading to a similar masculinist neutralisation as the one practiced by Levinas. However, as Chanter shows, Derrida calls attention to a neutralisation which seeks to subvert, not sexual difference, but 'the sexual opposition between men and women' (quoted Chanter 1997: 95). This is a neutralisation of duality rather than difference which can be said to, in fact, allow the difference to disseminate. Certainly, in this essay and also in the later 'Geschlecht' (Derrida 1997d) essay, this seems to be the view which Derrida takes of Heidegger. That is, that we 'have the possibility through Heidegger of expanding the possibilities of sexual identity' (Derrida 1997d). This would seem to represent some kind of shift away from the more critical comments in *Spurs* on Heidegger and Nietzsche.

Chanter also wishes to apply a certain 'ingratitude' against Derrida so as to properly read him, that is to read him as honestly as possible. Here, she cites 'Teresa de Lauretis's three moments of feminism, including a third wave of feminism' (Chanter 1997: 100) where we might be able to position a more congruent relation between feminism and deconstruction. As Chanter clarifies, 'Geschlecht' also means 'race' (Chanter 1997: 99). Therefore, Chanter suggests, 'the logic of exclusion must not foreground sex to the detriment of other variables such as race or class' (Chanter 1997: 109). As we will see in the next chapter, the political dimension of Derrida's work develops his emphasis beyond sexuality to include 'class', amongst other variables. However, there would be disagreement here and some may see Derrida as overly emphasising what has come to be termed 'identity politics'. But despite my concerns about making deconstruction into a method of 'ingratitude', I think this last point also demonstrates the positive power of reading 'Derrida against Derrida', as Chanter does.

Dialectics of Desire

Another related site of interpretative conflict has been between deconstructive feminism and Lacanian or psychoanalytic feminism. Ziarek takes up this problematic in her 'From Euthanasia to the Other of Reason' (Ziarek 1997: 115). Here, Ziarek looks at a debate which has developed between Joan Copjec on one side, representing a neo-Lacanian view of feminism, a psychoanlalytic feminism, and Judith Butler who, simplifying here, might be seen as a deconstructive feminist. As Ziarek points out, Copjec's emphasis seems to be on epistemology and she accuses Derrida and the deconstructionists of 'a euthanasia of reason'

(Ziarek 1997: 116). In contrast, Butler criticises what she sees as the 'fixity' of the concept of the Real in Lacan, or at least in Copjec's Lacan. For Ziarek, Copjec has misunderstood the full potential of Derrida's work and thus of deconstructive feminism: 'Derrida rather opens the possibility of an ethics of sex difference' (Ziarek 1997: 115). In relation to the real, Ziarek points to how Butler tries to develop Derrida's work in a direction which can rethink the Lacanian Real as 'racial abject rather than as ahistorical' (Ziarek 1997: 129).

In other words, rather than the Real being somehow inaccessible and fixed at the same time (and thus outside the possibility of historical renewal or intervention), Butler proposes that we see the Lacanian concept of the Real as conditional upon certain power interests holding sway and maintaining their hegemony. As Ziarek puts it, 'Butler's emphasis on the historicity of exclusion removes the threat of psychosis and opens the borders of intelligibility to political contestation' (Ziarek 1997: 130). Of course, one can call into question Ziarek's reading of both Lacan and Copjec. The notion that the Real is completely 'ahistorical' is a notion which seems contestable. But it's the very setting up of a dialogue between deconstructive feminism and psychoanalytic feminism which I think is most interesting here. Rather than simply setting up an opposition in this context, Ziarek has a much more positive conception of where this debate might lead. She speaks of 'the invention of new alliances' (Ziarek 1997: 135), where Copjec and Butler, but also deconstruction and psychoanalysis, might be able to come to some dialogical insight or even rapprochement. In line with the openness of Derrida's own project, which is always stressing its own contingency, especially in *Spurs*, and also in line with Derrida's recent comments in interviews that the difference between him and his other contemporaries has perhaps been exaggerated, this possible rapprochement between, in this case Lacan and Derrida, seems very productive. But this would still be a rapprochement which would not erase distinctiveness and differences, somewhat like the Derrida-Habermas debate (Thomassen 2006).

The Derrida-Levinas encounter has already been mentioned in previous chapters and the next essay by John Caputo [Caputo 1997] (the only male contributor to the anthology) seeks to do justice to this relationship. Caputo speaks of Derrida's interpretation of sexual difference as a 'dreaming of the innumerable' (Caputo 1997: 141) referring also to Derrida's comments in 'Choreographies' (Derrida 1991c) concerning 'a sexuality without number'. In his contribution, Caputo says that he is 'interested in balancing this Nietzschean strain with a Levinasian emphasis on justice' (Caputo 1997: 141). This emphasis on Levinas is, he says, 'crucially important for correcting an overly Nietzschean reading of Derrida' (Caputo 1997: 145). He draws on Drucilla Cornell's distinction between two postmodernisms but suggests a certain reticence over her synonymity of deconstruction and the good. Nonetheless, he wishes to maintain a distinction between a more 'nihilistic' postmodernism and one which is more interested in justice and ethics. But, he argues, this must also be connected to a thinking and practice of 'the sexual otherwise' (Caputo 1997: 154). This would be constituted by 'the dream of a justice for a sexuality which is ontological, a polysexuality'

(Caputo 1997: 156) and, precisely in emphasising this, there would be in relation to Derrida's thought, a 'reorientation of his Nietzschean side by his Levinasian side' (Caputo 1997: 157). Caputo has always been an interesting and innovative reader of Derrida but here he overstresses the Levinasian case for Derrida.

Particularly when it comes to sexual difference, there would seem to be significant disagreement between Levinas and Derrida (as the essay 'At this Moment' makes clear) (Derrida 1997c), while the Nietzschean emphasis in *Spurs* delineates more of a congruence between Nietzsche and Derrida than Caputo would seem to like to admit (as he describes it as a reading of Derrida which is 'overly Nietzschean'). Finally, Drucilla Cornell returns to the Derrida-Lacan debate which has been opened up by Ziarek (Cornell 1997: 161). Cornell once again shows the tensions in the readings of desire and the feminine in the respective cases of Lacan and Derrida. There is a 'lost object of desire' (Cornell 1997: 197) in Lacan but for Cornell this, on Lacanian terms, requires a knowledge of what sex is. Lacan 'institutes a law of inertia', (Cornell 1997: 197) which also ties in with Butler's reading of the 'fixity of the real'. For Cornell, 'love is a possibility kept open in Derrida' (Cornell 1997: 197), 'a lack of knowledge which refuses lack' (Cornell 1997: 197). But this openness is refused on Cornell's terms in Lacan. One example she cites here is 'Derrida's innovative writing style as an openness to the other' (Cornell 1997: 197). Again this shows the inseparability of the form/content distinction, which has been separated in other commentaries on Derrida, such as in Dooley and Kavanagh (Dooley and Kavanagh 2008). But as with Ziarek, Cornell does not want to completely shut down the possibility of a dialogue between Lacan and Derrida, or more generally between deconstructive feminism and psychoanalytic feminism.

Cornell is also keen to stress the 'non-Hegelian' dimension of Lacan's understanding of the 'dialectic of desire' (Cornell 1997: 203–4). On Cornell's reading, Lacan speaks of the 'irreducible element in the instinct or the empty image which is what distinguishes Lacan on his own terms from Hegel's dialectic of desire' (Cornell 1997: 204) but Derrida, according to Cornell, is worried that Lacan reinstitutes the law of circularity of desire. Cornell also cites her disagreement with Slavoj Žižek's (Žižek 2006) attempt to give a Hegelian reading of Lacan. Again, these readings by Cornell are of course contestable but on a positive level, as with Ziarek (Ziarek 1997), what they demonstrate is the possibility of an affirmative relationship between deconstruction and psychoanalysis when it comes to feminism. This debate it would seem has now begun in earnest. This brings to a close the readings in Feder, Rawlinson and Zakin in their *Derrida and Feminism: Recasting the Question of Woman* (Feder et al. 1997). I now want to look at another, exactly contemporaneous, anthology of feminist writings on Derrida, *Feminist Interpretations of Jacques Derrida*, edited by Nancy Holland (Holland 1997).

In Holland's introduction to this collection, she speaks of the 'recognition that deconstruction can have properly feminist uses' (Holland 1997: 2). Holland also makes clear some of the possible tensions between deconstruction and feminism, 'the danger of essentialism in feminism' (Holland 1997: 7), in much of what Jane Gallop has referred to as 'seventies feminism' (Gallop 1997) but also 'the emphasis on the atomic subject' (Holland 1997: 7). Holland additionally makes a complicating point here; 'What is feminism?' This is a highly contested term, not simply in texts such as Derrida's *Spurs*, but also in intra-feminist argument. Holland clarifies that, in her text, feminism will be primarily given here a 'definition in use', that is, feminism will be defined in an ongoing way in terms of the way it is employed rather than in some kind of 'preformationism'.

Derrida and Queer Theory[1]

Elizabeth Grosz' essay on Derrida (Grosz 1997) is an important intervention in the debate, not least because Grosz is a respected and influential queer theorist and, as such, this brings us back to some of the earlier criticisms of Derrida from a queer theory perspective in the Feder and Zakin (Feder and Zakin 1997) essay. In her essay, 'Ontology and Equivocation' (Grosz 1997), Grosz is generally very affirmative of deconstruction in its relationship to feminism although she does also indicate some minor reservations. She seems to affirm Derrida's critique of 'reactive' feminism (Grosz 1997: 88–9) although, like Derrida, she is conscious of the way such criticism can be used in a negative way. She sees Derrida's work as a challenge to feminism which feminism is well capable of meeting because of the 'openness of feminism to change and revision' (Derrida 1997: 88/89). Here, she cites Deleuze and Lyotard as key thinkers also in this renewed debate around feminism, a postmodern feminism in effect. Nonetheless, she has one key problem with Derrida's account. In his vision of a polysexuality, Derrida she says 'distinguishes clearly between sexual opposition and sexual difference...but can we make such a clear distinction?' (Grosz 1997: 88). For Grosz, Derrida is eliding certain practical issues here in terms of embodiment and what she refers to as the 'sexed body'. The danger it seems of Derrida's approach she is suggesting is that because it exists at a very abstract or intra-theoretical level, it misses certain crucial empirical distinctions which may not be so easily negotiable.

This criticism of Derrida is reminiscent of the views put forward most famously by Braidotti (Braidotti 1991) and Irigaray (Irigaray 1985) that Derrida has missed the importance of woman's specific situation or in Sartrean or Beauvoirean terms, her 'facticity'. For Grosz, 'the question of the limits of each sexed body must be recognised' (Grosz 1997: 95). Here I think Grosz is right to point to a certain abstraction in Derrida's argument. Nonetheless, it is a little unclear what she is trying to posit as an alternative. When she speaks of 'recognising the 'limits of each sexed body', is she making an ontological claim about the sex of bodies? Or is she rather arguing that Derrida hasn't taken the full force of the social engineering

---

1   Noreen Giffney and Michael O'Rourke have published an edited text entitled *The Ashgate Research Companion to Queer Theory* (Ashgate 2009).

of bodies (their gendered construction) and the difficulty of overcoming this into account. Grosz herself has to be careful here lest she fall back into some kind of gender essentialism (however refined). As Peggy Kamuf argues in the same volume (Kamuf 1997), when we speak of the relation between feminism and deconstruction, we are above all speaking of a relationship that 'still has a future'. There is a danger that Grosz' reading is insufficiently open to that kind of possibility of futural transformation.

Interestingly, when one looks at the development of queer theory more recently (Sullivan 2003), it is clear that Grosz is precisely on the side of those who emphasise futural possibility and emancipation. Recent work in queer theory has seen a certain schism develop between those who would wish to adopt a more negative approach to queer studies, most notably through Lee Edelman's controversial text *No Future: Queer Theory and the Death Drive* (Edelman 2004), and those who would seek to develop a more 'emancipatory' approach to queer theory, such as Grosz and Judith Halberstam (Halberstam 1995). Derrida's work is strategically placed on the dividing line of these two discourses, but perhaps ultimately Derrida is more of a yeasayer than naysayer. Tavia Nyong'o (Nyong'o 2008), for example, has referred to a 'theoretical negativism' in certain aspects of queer theory, which in terms of its influence on queer theory has also been mediated through the work of Guy Hocquenghem and Leo Bersani.

Tvia Nyong'o has sought to provide a 'third way' out of this dilemma through a rapprochement between what he terms 'punk' and 'queer':

> by rethinking the grouping or networking expressed across the social figurations of punk and queer in a nonidentitarian way, we may be able to uncouple the *sinthome*-homosexual metonymy, which compels us to see social negativity in an unnecessarily limited frame…It is a politics of a very different sort than that which Edelman both rightly disparages and wrongly associates with politics as such (Nyong'o 2008: 113).

Grosz and Halberstam would also seem to come down on this more affirmative side of queer theory and I would argue that ultimately this is where Derrida's famous affirmative 'yes, yes' also situates itself. But, from a more critical perspective, the stress in an LGBT critique on what Gayle Rubin has termed the 'charmed circle' of sex in 'heteronormativity' has resonances with the criticism which Feder and Zakin (Feder and Zakin 1997) made of Derrida and his libidinal heterosexualism in *Spurs*. This thematic of 'heteronormativity' is also strongly present in Nikki Sullivan's influential text, *A Critical Introduction to Queer Theory* (Sullivan 2003).

Yet another movement in queer theory however, or counter-current, moves away from this exclusive focus on heteronormativity. In two main collections of essays, the Social Text collection from 2005, *What's Queer About Queer Studies Now?* (Halberstam 2005), and the 2008 Radical History Review collection, entitled *Queer Futures: The Homonormativity Issue* (Murphy 2008), one can see this paradigm shift as moving from a united queer movement against 'heteronormativity' to a more schismatic movement which pits a 'queer neo-liberalism' against a more radical queer politics, which rejects the supposed newly evolved complicity between queer liberalism and conservative society.

Here, the new target is what has been termed 'homonormativity'. As the queer activist Matthilda puts it in an interview with Jason Ruiz, entitled 'The Violence of Assimilation' (Ruiz 2008: 237ff.):

> in much the same way that *heterosexist* is really useful for thinking about homophobia, *homonormative* offers us the potential to see the violence that occurs when gays show unquestioning loyalty to many of the things that at this point are routinely challenged even within mainstream straight dominant cultures (Ruiz 2008: 239).

Again, it is interesting to think about how Derrida's work in *Spurs* might connect with such a thematic. In 'Choreographies' (Derrida 1991c), as we will see below, Derrida is critical of what he sees as the 'heterosexual/homosexual' binary, which on both sides really 'amounts to the same'. Whatever about the accuracy of such a formulation, it is clear that this view does connect Derrida to recent corrective criticisms of 'homonormativity'. Finally, with regard to queer theory in this context, it is worth mentioning an attempted escape route from the 'prisonhouse of straight male identity', Calvin Thomas' *Male Matters: Masculinity, Anxiety and the Male Body on the Line* (Thomas 1998), which although showing the influence of Bataille more explicitly can also be seen to have a strong Derridean resonance. This text is an extraordinary intervention in the discourse of sexuality and identity. Thomas stresses a new 'writing of the male body' (Thomas 1998) which can serve as an innovative model for developing strategies to articulate erotic and existential insights, beyond the strictures of more formalised academic language.

Indeed, although Thomas' primary focus is the topic of masculinity, his work bears interesting similarities to analogous attempts by female writers such as Cixous (Cixous 1994) to 'write the female body' and Alphonso Lingis's (Lingis 1985) enigmatic later texts. Ultimately, one can argue, this is a matter of *neither male nor female*. It also of course bears similarities to Derrida's own interpretation of Artaud (which we have been following throughout this book) when he speaks of a 'writing of the body' (Derrida 1967k). What is at stake is rather the very status of philosophy and criticism *vis-à-vis* their supposed 'objects', a question which in Thomas (as also in Cixous and Lingis's cases) leads to a blurring of the distinction between philosophy and literature/art. This, one can argue, culminates in a kind of *queer writing*. Derrida can in this context be seen as a queer theorist of a very singular kind.

A Way to Think Desire

To conclude this section, I would like to focus on Peg Birmingham's essay, 'Toward an Ethic of Desire: Derrida, Fiction and the Law of the Feminine' (Birmingham

1997), which is perhaps the most powerful of the essays in Holland's collection. Birmingham begins by referring to 'the indictment of Derrida [by a specific feminism], as offering nothing but a negative feminism' (Birmingham 1997: 125). We have already referred to Braidotti and Irigaray. On this reading, Derrida would be just another patriarch. For Birmingham, however, Derrida offers more than a negative feminism. He offers 'a way to think desire' (Birmingham 1997: 127). Birmingham interestingly and originally looks to the early readings of Husserl here: 'for Husserl, the productive act is constitutive and creative; this occupies Derrida throughout his work' (Birmingham 1997: 129).

In the *Introduction* to Husserl's *Origin of Geometry* (Derrida 1962), Derrida focuses on Husserl's attempt to dialecticise the Kantian Idea into a metaphysical truth which is intrinsic to the *lebenswelt* or world as such. In the particular context of geometry, Husserl puts forward strong criticisms of naive objectivism such as the system of Galileo, which posits geometrical truth as supra-temporal. According to Husserl, Galileo pays no attention to the 'origin' of geometry; he acts as if geometrical truth had simply fallen from the sky. In opposition to this vulgar objectivism, Husserl invokes the transcendentalism of Kant. In the first case, geometrical truth must have a subjective aspect, what he terms the Idea in the Kantian sense. Secondly, this aspect points to a specific kind of historical contingency – truth is not simply discovered as an extra-subjective object. It is also 'created' by the subjective geometer. Speaking of Derrida's early critique of phenomenology, Birmingham argues that 'Derrida is not offering an unfleshed nominalism, his reference to bound idealities connects the sense of history to that of embodiment, and to the social/historical effects of that embodiment' (Birmingham 1997: 135).

This is an original and important argument against those who would claim that deconstruction is a kind of textualism or idealism. Rather, much as Derrida argued for materialism in Mallarmé, so too Birmingham is arguing for a Derridean materialism; 'reconfigurations are materially located' (Birmingham 1997: 135). This is close to what Derrida has to say in *Dissemination* regarding Mallarmé and the 'materialisation of the idea'. Again, even more significantly, Birmingham reads *Irigaray against Irigaray* and argues that Irigaray's philosophy and Derrida's are much more compatible than might seem to be the case. Here, she refers specifically to Irigaray's concept of the 'sensible-transcendental', the 'irruption of the finite in the infinite' (Birmingham 1997: 135). On Birmingham's terms, Derrida's philosophy can be a help in this context.

Birmingham now goes on to look at Derrida's later essays on Blanchot, most especially 'The Law of Genre' (Derrida 1986a). She speaks of 'Derrida's understanding of the law in terms of the feminine silhouette, the law as an emergent erotic order' (Birmingham 1997: 138). Here, again, we see the importance of desire for Derrida, what he termed the need to 'resexualise' the discourse of philosophy, which we will look at more directly below in terms of a reading of 'Choreographies' (Derrida 1991c). For Birmingham, 'the imperative of desire is precisely what disallows anything like a teleology' (Birmingham 1997: 139). Linking Blanchot and Bataille to Derrida, Birmingham claims that 'the law procreates; rather than prohibits' (Birmingham 1997: 139). This brings us back to the earlier discussion in Chapter 2 of the relation between taboo and transgression or prohibition and transgression in Bataille. Rather than each of these elements being independent, there is a co-dependency, a mutual contamination.

Derrida here also, as in *Spurs*, foregrounds the principle of the feminine which he sees as fundamental to Blanchot's (Blanchot 1997) work. Analysing Blanchot's complex fictions or *récits*, which we have looked at a little in Chapter 4, Derrida argues that 'it is usually the feminine who says yes to…the opening of the event of the performance…to the uncertain contingencies…to the encounter' (quoted Birmingham 1997: 138/140). Here, we would seem to have an option of the encounter which derives from Blanchot rather than from Levinas. With the emphasis on the feminine, there still would be no possibility of a 'universal or essentialist notion of the feminine…the silhouette shuns essence' (quoted Birmingham 1997: 138). Much as in *Spurs*, Derrida disavows; 'he is not thinking the feminine as such, he is thinking sexual difference, "the madness of sexual difference"' (Birmingham 1997: 141).

What is original in this essay by Birmingham is her projected link between fiction per se, and the feminine. She speaks of 'an understanding of fiction as an engendering of sexual difference' (Birmingham 1997: 145). This is another way to understand Derrida's fascination with literature, or at least a certain kind of literature, rather than being some kind of levelling genre distinction as Habermas or Rorty claim (Habermas 1990). Derrida's interest in a specific literature would be in those literary texts which create a 'nonphilosophical space' where the dimunition of sexual difference (into a binaried sexual opposition which privileges the masculine) can be interrogated (Derrida 1986b). Blanchot's fictions would here in 'The Law of Genre' (Derrida 1986a) essay be cited as exemplary for Derrida in their opening of this problematic. Birmingham's essay seeks to foreground this very radicality (Birmingham 1997: 145). 'What I have shown is how this thinking of fiction allows one to understand the shadow of the feminine in Derrida's work as precisely "sexual difference"; that is, erotic generation' (Birmingham 1997: 145). In the next section, I want to look at how Derrida develops this thematic in two key essays from the 1980s which explicitly develop the theme of sexual difference and its relation to feminism; 'Choreographies' (Derrida 1991c) and 'Geschlecht' (Derrida 1997d).

Derrida in 'Choreographies' and 'Geschlecht'

In his important interview with Christine McDonald entitled 'Choreographies' (Derrida 1991c), Derrida returns to the complex relationship between Heidegger and sexual difference. We have already seen Derrida speak to this issue in *Spurs*, when he seemed to undermine the Heideggerian reading of Nietzsche, most especially insofar as Heidegger had repressed the 'question of woman' in Nietzsche. 'He had skirted the woman question.' There, in *Spurs*, Derrida also spoke of the crucial issue as being whether one could simply locate the issue of sexual difference in a larger question which would subsume it, such as the question of being or ontology. Or whether, on the contrary, the question of sexual difference was more than simply a 'regional' question. Now once again, he reiterates this as the central issue: 'at play in the Heidegger discussion is whether the question of sex difference is a question in a larger order…a regional question' (Derrida 1991c: 24). Already in *Spurs*, Derrida has acknowledged the key role played by the feminist movement both historically and theoretically in terms of a shaking up of old presuppositions and an opening up of new problematics. For Derrida, this is a question of 'liberation and reappropriation' (Derrida 1991c: 26).

An Anarchist Feminism

What Derrida seems to be suggesting here is that we must be careful lest what we think of as liberation becomes simply 'reappropriation'. Christine McDonald makes clear that the feminist movement has never been a unified monolith, a point we made above in terms of the increasing diversity of contemporary feminism. Gallop had made the distinction between a 'seventies feminism' and a 'nineties feminism' (Gallop 1997), the former being more conservative and essentialist, the latter being more eclectic and diverse. But McDonald makes an interesting point here in relation to an earlier version of feminism. By citing the example of Emma Goldman (Goldman 1924), McDonald foregrounds the complex relationship between reform or egalitarian feminism and more revolutionary feminism. From the very beginning, Goldman self-identifies as an anarchist and although Derrida doesn't take up this issue as he might, it is worth examining also the influence of Nietzsche on Goldman's work, as it creates an interesting caveat to Derrida's discussion of feminism in *Spurs*.

Goldman's essay, 'The Failure of the Russian Revolution' (Goldman 1924), captures both the radicality and refusal of dogmatism characteristic of anarchist thinking and is also instructive for our purposes in the measure to which it concludes with an affirmative reference to Nietzsche's key notion of a 'transvaluation of all values'. To begin, Goldman makes a stark contrast between the aims of the 'political party' and the 'revolution' (Goldman 1924: 155). Whereas the political party sought to maintain its power 'by all means at hand', the aims and tendencies of the revolution were diametrically opposed to those of the ruling political party: 'the revolution had an entirely different object; and in its very character it was the negation of authority and centralisation' (Goldman 1924: 155). In what Woodcock has referred to as a 'Nietzschean touch' (Woodcock 1977: 137), Goldman identifies the future of anarchism not with 'the replacement of one class with another' (Goldman 1924: 158) but with 'rather the fundamental transvaluation of values' (Goldman 1924: 158). Goldman is suggesting here a complete revolution in the way we think about life and morality. This is an implicit reference to Nietzsche's original notion of the 'transvaluation of values' which he introduces in the Preface to *The Genealogy of Morals* (Nietzsche 1967). The Nietzschean tonality is maintained in her development of this idea:

> revolution is the negation of the existing, a violent protest against man's inhumanity to man with all the thousand and one slaveries it involves…It is the herald of NEW VALUES…ushering in a transformation of the basic relations of man to man, and of man to society…It is first and foremost, the TRANSVALUATOR, the bearer of new values. It is the great TEACHER of the NEW ETHICS (Goldman 1924: 161; Goldman's emphasis).

This is, I think, very interesting for our purposes as it shows how the genealogy of feminism is a complex political history, and also that certain aspects of historical feminism were not at odds with Nietzsche, but in fact used specific concepts of his for their own purposes. By implication, Goldman's anarchism or anarchist feminism also has resonances with Derrida's version of feminism. Derrida's own thinking has interesting political affinities with anarchism and we will return to the question of Derrida's political thinking more generally in the next chapter with reference also to Artaud and Bataille's politics. In each of the latter cases, there is also a connection with a certain anarchism and also to the 'young Marx' – and the relation to Marxism has always been both positive and negative for anarchism (Bakunin's essay on the Russian revolution is a case in point) (Bakunin 1910). Indeed, one can also make the connection between Nietzsche and anarchism (Irwin 2010c). This leaves the issue of whether we can see the issue of sexual difference as a regional question not simply in a more general ontology (à la Heidegger) but also whether sexual difference can be contained in a wider politics or whether sexual difference is *the* political question, that is, the origin of the political. Derrida himself asks this question explicitly – do we think the question of being starting from sexual difference or do we think the problem of sexual difference starting from the study of being?

Derrida does briefly take up the Goldman reference in 'Choreographies' (Derrida 1991c). Derrida says that perhaps Goldman was referring to 'incalculable sexual differences' and inventing 'new sexual idioms', recognising both the specificity and the problematicity of interpreting what Goldman has said. Developing this notion of the quest for a freedom of woman, Derrida (following Goldman) states that 'I believe that I would not describe that place, there is no one place for woman' (Derrida 1991c: 27). It is this that lies at the basis in *Spurs* of his thinking of 'my truths' in the plural and the sense that woman evades essential definition. In many respects, 'Choreographies' and 'Geschlecht' can be seen as a working out more clearly and systematically of the philosophy of woman and embodiment (a 'writing of the body') which is implicit and suggestive in *Spurs*. It also shows the signs of Derrida having taken on board some of the criticisms of *Spurs* and its relation to feminism which we have also described with regard to the anthologies of feminist writings, already discussed. 'This idea is not feminist or anti-feminist' (Derrida 1991c: 27), Derrida tells us.

In line with Nietzsche's views and clarifying somewhat, Derrida says that there has always been 'a reactive feminism', but that nonetheless 'one should not combat it head on – other interests would be at stake in such a move' (Derrida 1991c: 27). This is an important reference to the way in which certain right-wing or reactive interests can sometimes manipulate one's intentions in these matters. Nonetheless, with regard to this 'egalitarian feminism' as Derrida describes it,[2] 'there should be a way of preventing it from occupying the entire terrain' (Derrida 1991c: 27). One should therefore be strategic with regard to this more traditional version of feminism. And this then leads into the deeper question of how one is to get at the more radical version of sexual difference and feminism. Where does this difference lie? What is it related to? What is the relation between difference per se and sexual difference? Must one think difference before sexual difference or starting off from it?

Although Derrida consistently disavows the notion that one can reduce deconstruction to a program or a set ideology, agenda or method, he nonetheless makes clear here a kind of provisional methodology. He says that there are 'two phases of deconstruction; a reversal of the terms followed by the invention of a new concept' (Derrida 1991c: 31/32). If we think of this in terms of what we have been discussing, we might say we have patriarchy or phallocentrism on one side and essentialist versions of feminism on the other. One must begin then by defending a certain feminism against patriarchy but one should not simply stay there. Rather there is needed the 'invention of a new concept'. Moreover, Derrida argues, we should not regard conceptuality itself as a structure without question: 'the concept of the concept should be undermined by sex difference' (Derrida 1991c: 33). Otherwise, there is a danger that when sexual difference is determined by opposition it goes back to Hegel's dialectic and the dominance of the masculine term, which just amounts to another version of 'phallocentrism' (Derrida 1991c: 34). This, it would seem, is precisely Derrida's argument against Levinas in 'At this Moment in the Work' (Derrida 1997c).

In this context, Derrida makes a distinction between his reading of Heidegger on sexual difference and his reading of Levinas. In the *Spurs* text, Heidegger seems to be criticised for 'skirting the woman question', but here Heidegger's notion of sexual difference seems to be given more credit or more potential for transformative power: 'the neutral of *Dasein* is not the absence of sexuality but the originary power' (Derrida 1991c: 35ff.) but this is always a sensitive operation and fraught with the dangers of falling back into essentialism and conservatism. Derrida cites his desire for a 'resexualising of the discourse' (Derrida 1991c: 37) and his reservations around the neutralisation of sex difference. In the latter case, there seems to be an important distinction made between the neutralisation of

---

2   One wonders as to whether this term describes what Derrida is intending to describe? Perhaps 'liberal feminism' would be a better description, to the extent that egalitarian feminism also includes in its ambit more revolutionary modes and emancipatory versions of feminist thinking.

sexual difference per se which he associates with Levinas and the neutralisation of a certain sexual duality or opposition which can paradoxically open the way for difference to flourish.

Derrida refers to his own strategies for invoking or affirming this sexual differentiation, one of which is captured in the title of the text itself, 'Choreographies' (Derrida 1991c). One's text must be 'polyvocal' (Derrida 1991c: 39). There is a need for the division of the voice; for a choreographic text with polysexual signatures. Of course, the foregrounding of a pluralised voice is also significant in terms of Derrida's supposed interest in phonocentrism. Once again, as I have tried to show in Chapters 3 and 4, Derrida is complexifying the idea of the voice. In a sense, he is radicalising the voice and showing that it can never be simply a question here of inverting the age old opposition between writing and the voice. It would not be a question as Derrida often makes clear of opposing a graphocentrism to a phonocentrism. This would be inversion of the most vulgar kind. Rather it is a question of the complexification of the relation between voice and writing, something that Plato was also doing and even Isocrates, as we have seen (the supposed univocal critique of phonocentrism is thus a not very accurate representation of Derrida's work) (Derrida 1972j).

Derrida develops this point in 'Choreographies' (Derrida 1991c) and its radicality is significant and, perhaps for some, surprising. Although it develops from *Spurs*, it seems as if Derrida is cutting through some of the interminable ambiguity of that text; 'I would like to believe in the multiplicity of sexually marked voices; a sexuality without number' (Derrida 1991c: 40). There is a consistency here with the earlier work but the emphasis on sexuality is more forceful than before. There is always 'dissymetry' in the sexual difference and the relation which he associates to the other. We are left wondering somewhat about which comes first, the difference, the other, or the sexual other. With regard to Derrida's implicit reference to Levinas here and the 'At this Moment' essay (Derrida 1997c), McDonald clarifies the context in the footnotes to the 'Choreographies' (Derrida 1991c) interview. Derrida is once again referring to 'the preeminence of man', however obscured this may be on the surface level of the text. 'The pre-differential is always marked by the masculine' (quoted Derrida 1991c: 41) and here Derrida would not simply be talking about Levinas, but also Heidegger and, perhaps even Plato's *khora*, amongst other attempts at marking the pre-differential. Derrida also notes here the importance of the fact that Levinas is commenting upon the text and not simply speaking in his own voice, he is commenting upon the Talmud although 'commentary' would never be innocent (quoted Derrida 1991c: 41).

Heidegger's Sexual Difference

Derrida takes up this thematic of sexual difference in another related and key essay, 'Geschlecht: Sexual Difference, Ontological Difference' (Derrida 1997d). In this context, he first of all makes clear that simply 'to remark the silence around sexual difference is somewhat facile' (Derrida 1991d: 380) and this is referring to Heidegger's discourse. But how might we nonetheless understand this? Certainly, Derrida thinks that we might see Heidegger's reticence in this regard almost as an issue of taste, as if he were saying 'there is too much obsession with sex'. We might see this as 'even haughty in relation to the babbling concerning sexuality in the present age; there has already been a lot of chatting about sexuality in the tradition' (Derrida 1991d: 382). Derrida here seems to go along with Heidegger to a degree; there has been enough chatting about sex, enough babbling, what Heidegger in *Being and Time* calls 'idle talk'. Nonetheless, there still might be said to be a structure of what is not said about sex, which could be interesting, 'but more generally what are the forms of the nonsaid of sexuality in the tradition?' (Derrida 1991d: 382). In analysing this question we must think about 'where one might expect a reference to sexuality, the sexual relation, sexual difference?' (Derrida 1991d: 382). That is, where would we in general expect to see such a reference to sex and is it there in Heidegger's text? There certainly seems to be a case of omission in Heidegger on this point: 'it (the analysis) would seek in vain in Heidegger for a discourse on desire and sexuality...and yet' (Derrida 1991d: 383). 'And yet', as Derrida makes clear elsewhere, is actually a favourite phrase of Heidegger's to redirect the discussion, to surprise the expectation. So what would be the 'and yet' in relation to Heidegger's thinking concerning sexuality and the status of *Dasein*?

As with Levinas' discussion of the other, there is, in *Dasein*, at least in principle, a 'neutrality, neither masculine nor feminine' (Derrida 1991d: 385). 'The neutrality of *Dasein* which means it is none of the two sexes' (Derrida 1991d: 385). Heidegger, then, has taken some care here to avoid patriarchal designations. He is thus, we might surmise, already concerned with issues of male and female relations, even if this is not immediately apparent. Feminism marks Heidegger's discourse, not explicitly, but in the decisions that are made in terms of how to describe *Dasein*. But, of course, there is more than simply feminism at issue, in this context. At stake is a broader critique of the human sciences, anthropology and psychology, which have tried to reduce philosophy and existence to an anthropomorphism. Derrida then proceeds to probe further into Heidegger's reasons for making *Dasein* neutral: 'ought one to think sexuality cannot be reduced to an anthropological theme?' (Derrida 1991d: 386). If this is the case, then Heidegger has put sexuality into reserve somewhat in his existential analytic. He has held it back lest it be 'reduced' or objectified, but we should also be careful to look at the exact meaning of 'asexual neutrality' in *Dasein*. A quick glance might lead us to believe that this is a matter once more, as it seemed to be with Levinas, of neutralising sexual difference, in the sense of excluding and marginalising it. Derrida begs to differ: 'a-sexual neutrality does not desexualise; on the contrary, its ontological negativity is not deployed with regard to sexuality itself, but with regard to sexual duality' (Derrida 1991d: 387). This is a crucial moment in Derrida's reading of Heidegger and does seem to mark a shift from his earlier comments in *Spurs*, although there everything was shrouded in ambiguity. Perhaps that is the key difference in 'Geschlecht' and indeed in 'Choreographies'. Derrida seems keen to speak more plainly, more directly (perhaps this is under the duress of previous feminist criticisms). But *Dasein* should not, he tells us, be interpreted as negating sex or woman. If there has been a 'skirting of the woman', this cannot be compared to a kind of essentialist masculinism which we might associate with the patriarchal tradition (for example, in Augustine or certainly in Aristotle). Rather, Derrida is suggesting that Heidegger's evasion (forgetting?) of sexual difference is strategic and considered and is meant to actually break with a certain sexual dualism which subordinates male to female. This is then what is neutralised, the male-female sexual duality, and what thus opens up is a more differentiated framework for understanding how male and female might relate to each other, or whether there even is any self-identity of gender, known as male and female. Heidegger's discourse suddenly takes on a completely different identity *vis-à-vis* feminism. That is, at least *vis-à-vis* 'nineties feminism' if not 'seventies feminism' (Gallop 1997) (where the latter's essentialist definitions of woman and feminine identity would have no commonality with Heidegger's discourse).

If *Dasein* is therefore neither male nor female, we can also say that *Dasein* is not 'das man' or the 'they': '*Dasein* is not just anyone whatever but the originary positivity and power of essence' (Derrida 1991d: 385). Usually, such talk of originarity would cause Derrida to be reticent but here it seems he wants to say something more affirmative. It is as if *Dasein* is the structure which allows male and female to be, but which is itself neither male nor female. Significantly and provocatively, Derrida associates this originary power with 'sexuality'; 'one must think of a predifferential and predual sexuality' (Derrida 1991d: 385). What Derrida seems to be suggesting here is that what we have being affirmed by Heidegger in *Dasein* is not sexual duality, male or female, not a sexed body essence, but rather a notion of sexuality which precedes the distinction between male or female genders or sexed bodies. What we have here, it seems, is some originary 'sexual power'.

This is significant in the measure to which it makes sexuality far more than simply a regional question; sex would be neither an ontic nor even a regional ontological question. In Heideggerean terms, sex would be fundamental, although understood here as sexual difference rather than any kind of sexual identity. This also of course brings Heidegger's discourse on sexuality and Derrida's very close together.[3] Derrida nonetheless makes clear Heidegger's own reticence with regard to naming sexuality: 'Heidegger is careful not to call this power sexuality; it is sexual difference and division which leads to negativity' (Derrida 1991d: 388). But this could simply be because Heidegger associates the term sexuality with all the ontic, anthropomorphic and psychological definitions he is so keen to avoid.

---

3   In the film *Derrida* (Derrida 2002), Derrida is asked what questions he would like to ask of philosophers and he says, mentioning Heidegger explicitly, 'I would like to ask them about their sex lives', as this is what is never explicit, never mentioned.

'*Dasein* deals with the power of the origin; the analytic of the origin does not deal with the existent itself' (Derrida 1991d: 389). The analysis of *Dasein* thus engages the question of 'what is an individual?', i.e. what makes an individual existent possible, not with the issue of this individual or that. Derrida returns to this problematic of *Dasein* and its originary power and continuing significance in the interview 'Eating Well' (Derrida 1995b). It has been argued that this seems to represent a move away of sorts away from an earlier critique of Heideggerean *Dasein* as 'nostalgic' in the *Margins* (Derrida 1982a) essays, such as 'Ends of Man' and 'Différance'. This issue has been taken up by Herman Rapaport and is important also for the *avant-garde*, as Rapaport relates it to Derrida's later work on Artaud (Rapaport 2002).

Derrida nonetheless wants to both invoke Heidegger here and radicalise his discourse on sexuality. It seems to be a matter of 'reading Heidegger against Heidegger'. 'What if the *da* of *Dasein* were already sexual? Perhaps another sex?' (Derrida 1991d: 390). This is certainly phrased in language which would never have been Heidegger's own and yet it follows from what has already been said. If we understand sexuality outside sexual opposition, then it is true that *Dasein* may be 'already sexual', although it is also true that Heidegger would never have put it like this (or never did). In moving beyond sexual duality, then, *Dasein* as 'asexually neutral', becomes precisely a matter of 'sexual difference'. *Dasein* opens the way for a very different kind of thinking of 'woman'; thinking otherwise about woman and sex. 'This opens up thinking to a sexual difference that would not be sexual duality; difference as dual. What the course neutralised was less sexuality itself than the generic mark of sexual difference, belonging to one of two sexes; hence, in leading back to dispersion and multiplication; the withdrawal of the dyad leads to the other sexual difference...' (Derrida 1991d: 401). Derrida's reading is no doubt provocative here, even polemical. It is certainly at odds with a certain reading in *Spurs* but if this is correct, it brings Heidegger much closer to Nietzsche than *Spurs* allowed. What is consistent between the two texts however and also in 'Choreographies' (Derrida 1991c) is Derrida's intent in opening up the question of sexual difference in the name of deconstruction. In *Spurs*, this remains more careful, more ambiguous, more abstract. In the two later texts, Derrida has become more committed to an affirmative sexual difference, still with ambiguity no doubt, but more directly expressed and less evasive (behind veils and sails). This move is also noticeable in Derrida's later text on Hélène Cixous (Derrida 2006b), and Cixous' own texts on Derrida (Cixous 2005/2007) are also highly significant in this regard.

Conclusion: Turning More Explicitly Political

This political dimension of Derrida's work has always been present. We saw it in the earlier avowals of Artaud and Bataille and the foregrounding of the political dimensions of both the *Theatre of Cruelty* and the general economy. There was also a political dimension to the reading of Plato, where the trial of Socrates and the critique of democracy by Plato was always in the background. In the discussion of *Spurs* and Nietzsche and the responses from feminism, we moved to a more explicitly political space – the politics of sex but also the way in which the politics of sex and desire interacts or engages with a whole other more formal space of politics. This is the politics of protest and the politics of parliamentary democracy, for example, in the discussion of feminist egalitarianism and the dangers both of advocating such an approach and the pitfalls politically of resisting it and allowing more reactive political forces to fill the vacuum. In terms of the specific Derridean discussion of *Dasein* and a sexual power and positivity before sexual opposition, we see a number of possibilities for rethinking the political. This is in line with the radical feminist 1990s critique of the political dominance of neo-liberalism and their evolution of the watchcry of 'the personal is the political'. In this chapter, we have already spoken about the possibilities of seeing connections between deconstructive feminism and psychoanalytical feminism.

Luce Irigaray's (Irigaray 1985) work has, as suggested earlier, strong connections with Derrida's work, despite her explicit criticism of the latter, as Margaret Whitford for example has pointed out (Whitford 1991: 7). Tina Chanter and Peg Birmingham have also pointed to possibilities of productive intersections between Derrida, Irigaray and Bataille. Three other significant feminist thinkers can also be especially mentioned here, Hélène Cixous (Cixous 1994), Julia Kristeva (Kristeva 1984) and Judith Butler (Butler 2003). Butler, firstly, exemplifies explicit connections between her work and that of Derrida. Her emphases on the 'opaque subject' and 'intersubjective bonds' (Salih 2003: 2) show Derridean inflections and we have already commented on her critique of the neo-Lacanian 'fixity' of the concept of the Real in a (psychoanalytic feminist) thinker such as Joan Copjec (Ziarek 1997). This latter critique would seem to be Derrida-inspired. But Butler's development of a discourse on gender and sexuality can be seen as radicalising Derrida's *Spurs* project and also as overcoming some of its limitations (as already pointed to by Gallop 1997). In particular, Butler's critique of 'hetero-normativity' shows the limits of a certain kind of heterosexist bias which we have seen in Derrida's earlier work, although perhaps this is less true of 'Geschlecht' and 'Choreographies'. Similarly, Julia Kristeva has always maintained close connections to Derrida's work from *Tel Quel* onwards and Kristeva stages one of the three interviews which make up the 1972 text *Positions* (Derrida 1972a). As Elizabeth Grosz has commented, in her text *Sexual Subversions* (Grosz 1989), Kristeva's employment of the 'maternal chora' is connected to Derrida's own employment of this term from Plato's texts (Grosz 1989: 49) but Kristeva is ultimately an original and eclectic thinker, who reinscribes Derrida's thinking in a very different context (Grosz 1989: 62). For Grosz, Irigaray and Kristeva employ Derrida for very different reasons. Kristeva employs Derrida's work so as to criticise feminist attempts to essentialise female identity while Irigaray employs Derrida's insights to clear a space in which women's own autonomous self-description can come into being.

'Whereas Kristeva uses it to designate the difference internal to each subject, Irigaray uses it to refer to the differences between one sex and another (Grosz 1989: 104).

Finally, with regard to our three feminist examples, one can say that the work of Hélène Cixous (Cixous 1994) is the closest of the three to Derrida. A close friend of Derrida since the 1960s, they share an Algerian background. There is a complex inter-textuality between Derrida and Cixous, especially from the late 1990s onwards, with both devoting significant texts to each other works. In an interview with Verena Conley in 1982, Cixous comments explicitly on *Spurs*. Before she does this, she foregrounds her important notion of 'écriture feminine', which very obviously bears a Derridean imprint. She describes it as follows; 'it is the inscription of something that carries in everyday language the determination of the provisional name of femininity, and which refers precisely to something that I would like to define in the way of an economy, of production, of bodily effects of which one can see a great number of traits' (Cixous 1991: 131). She then develops this point more explicitly in terms of *Spurs*. Asked by Conley to comment on Derrida's pronouncement concerning 'truth being a woman', Cixous says:

> in *Spurs*, Derrida deals with a femininity fantasised by Nietzsche. There are many relays which have to be taken into account. Besides, I do not deny that this capacity to read Nietzsche – who lets himself be fantasised, or one may say hallucinated, by a phantasm of femininity – does signify a proximity. There is proximity, true, but it is not an identity (Cixous 1991: 149).

This is fascinating but rather elusive; proximity to whom? Does she mean a proximity between her and Nietzsche, Nietzsche and Derrida or her and Derrida, or all three? She goes on:

> What about the phantasm itself? Derrida has very well defined the phantasm of femininity that haunted philosophical discourse, a phantasm, which among women, should provoke laughter. Unless of course, they take themselves for men (Cixous 1991: 149).

Again, one can read many things into this statement. But she seems to be suggesting that the best way to subvert patriarchy is not to take ourselves too seriously. In other words, to adopt the stance of a Derrida, a Bataille, or a Cixous, to subvert the Hegelian dialectic (the 'Hegelian-sexual-scene'), with laughter rather than with truth claims. Here, she seems to affirm the Derridean reading of Nietzsche in *Spurs*. Would this be feminist? Perhaps, we might say. If feminism is conducive to laughter, yes it would be feminist. If however, feminism is of the type where women seek to 'take themselves for men', then this would be an anti-Cixousian discourse. As with Gallop and many other female thinkers who have addressed *Spurs* since the 1970s, it would seem to be an issue of eschewing the limitations and biases of essentialist feminism. This, and not *Spurs*, would constitute the 'negative feminism' castigated by Braidotti, Irigaray and others.

In the next chapter, I will also make the connection with some of Derrida's later texts where he draws close to Habermas (and an interesting debate between Habermas and Derrida which leads to a kind of rapprochement), leading back to the 'early Marx' of the early 1960s texts. This will also lead us into the discourse of interculturalism, multiculturalism and what Charles Taylor calls the 'politics of recognition' (Taylor 1994). What I would like to stress in this context, however, is that if we take Derrida at his word in 'Geschlecht', in a sense all politics must start from sexuality or from what he terms sexual difference. Therefore, politics is always a matter of desire and sexuality, even when this is not made explicit. Here, we return to an age old theme, for example in surrealism, which sought to combine Marx and Rimbaud so powerfully (Trebitsch 1991). In the next chapter, I will also invoke what might be called Bataille's 'politics of the accursed share' and I will try to bring together some of the complex threads of this argument.

Chapter 7

Re-Politicising Deconstruction:
From 'The Old Mole' to Cosmopolitanism
to An-Economic Forgiveness

Introduction

In the last chapter, we looked at Derrida's complex encounter with feminism. Certainly, it is clear that this aspect of Derrida's work in the 1980s represented a clear move in a more explicit political direction. Nonetheless, the political dimension has been in Derrida's work from the very beginning, as I have stressed throughout this work. In his early concentration on the *avant-garde*, Derrida looked at the complex projects of such figures as Mallarmé, Artaud and Bataille. In each of these cases, the problematic of aesthetics was key but nonetheless Derrida stresses the political dimension of their aesthetic thinking. In this chapter, I want to look at this politics of the *avant-garde* in more detail, concentrating especially on Bataille, and also on Artaud and Blanchot. I then will look at how Derrida develops this into a discussion of the politics of difference, where he enters into dialogue with a number of political philosophers, such as Habermas.

Politicising the *Avant-Garde*: Writing the Social Body

In Mallarmé, the emphasis on a reconfiguration of the poetic and the emphasis on 'arts for arts sake' is accompanied by a clearly radical democratic agenda where Mallarmé sees his work as having very real material effects politically in the world (McCombie 2008). Moreover, his very attempt to move beyond the genre of a more traditionally defined literature is obviously a political move. His use of 'anecdote', for example, is symbolic here, as is his emphasis on the everyday as key theme.

We see this in Artaud also. In his two essays on Artaud in *Writing and Difference* (Derrida 1967h/j), Derrida connects Artaud's project of the theatre of cruelty to a political agenda: 'the theatre of cruelty is a political manifesto'. Also, Derrida speaks of the affinities between Artaud and the early Marx. On one level, this is because of the emphasis on the material element in Artaud, the 'physical language', the 'corps à corps', the stress on life and breath, a 'writing of the body', 'a theatre of the senses'. The political, especially understood in a materialist sense, can be seen to constitute a 'nonphilosophical' (Derrida 1986c) site, or one which stands both inside and outside traditional philosophy, but which gives an angle with which to question philosophy, and interrogate its limits. Derrida, in his later work on Artaud, develops and radicalises this political emphasis through the notion of the 'subjectile' (Derrida 1998a). Here, there is a clear connection to the surrealist movement which always sought to bring about a congruence between aesthetics and politics. Although Artaud could never be said to have belonged to any movement in an essentialist way, nonetheless we can speak accurately of Artaud (and Bataille) as 'dissident surrealists' (Ades 2006). This helps us to make sense of their political thinking; as connected to the surrealist project.

Here, we can cite André Breton's faith that Marxism and Surrealism can be adjoined: 'Marx said "Change the world", Rimbaud said "Change life"; for us, these two watchwords are one' (quoted Trebitsch 1991: xx). Artaud would have affirmed something similar to this in relation the *Theatre of Cruelty*. But politics must never lose sight of its basis in life and the relationship between art and the body: 'the art and body relation is transformed'. This is also true of Derrida, who takes up the surrealist mantle. We can see this in relation to Derrida's own self-implication in his texts which of course, amongst other things, is a political act (Derrida 1995a). In Derrida's return to Artaud in his later writing, we see that 'the body must be reborn' (Derrida 1998a). There is required a 'new bodily writing', a movement and a liberation; a 'force before form'.

From Blanchot to Pasolini

We can speak similarly of the politics of Maurice Blanchot (Blanchot 1997), another key *avant-garde* figure and a strong influence on Derrida. Or as Gerald Bruns notes in his important text on Blanchot, *Maurice Blanchot and the Refusal of Philosophy* (Bruns 2005), Blanchot is a 'radically antimessianic' thinker, and this highlights the political dimension of Blanchot's work, what Bruns sees as his 'dissidence' (Bruns 2005).

> Blanchot's dissidence is a philosophical anarchism that embraces both politics and poetry, anarchism seems more dystopian than utopian, an unavowable community. It is perhaps more defensible as an ethics or as a micropolitics than as a political philosophy writ large (Bruns 2005: 3).

The existential and political dimensions of Blanchot's work, then, should not be seen as contradictory. For Blanchot, there is a 'strangeness between man and man; a relation without common measure, an exorbitant relation' (Bruns 2005: 57). And this existential dimension consequently leads to an antimessianic politics: 'the disaster is nonapocalyptic; a nonmessianic theory of history...my response to the other must be "refusal, resistance, combat"' (Bruns 2005: 67). It is not difficult to trace the affinities with Derrida here, as Derrida has acknowledged (and we have discussed some of the political implications of Derrida's reading of Blanchot in relation to Peg Birmingham and 'The Law of Genre' essay in Chapter 6) (Birmingham 1997). Another important figure in this relation between literature and politics in France is, of course, the Marquis de Sade. Although not as often mentioned as the re-reading of Hegel, the French re-reading of Sade, through Pierre Klossowski (Klossowski 1991) most especially, is a key factor in later French thought. Interestingly, it is precisely this reading of Sade which Jane Gallop takes up in her seminal *Intersections* (Gallop 1981) book, and so it also relates to our thematic of Derrida and feminism.

There is a clear inheritance also in Blanchot's work from that of Sade. Pier Paulo Pasolini, the Italian filmmaker and poet, develops this affinity in his extraordinary film *Salò*. Several *avant-garde* writers are cited in *Salò* – Maurice Blanchot, Pierre Klossowski, Philippe Sollers and Roland Barthes (Pasolini 2007). The explicit unity between these authors can be described as their new reading of the work of Sade. *Salò* is an adaptation of Sade's *120 Days of Sodom* to Fascist Italy under Mussolini. But this film is also interesting as it shows how Blanchot's aesthetics and politics can be transposed to cinema, and there is a strong (and underrepresented) affinity between Blanchot and Pasolini, in terms of both aesthetics and politics. From an aesthetic point of view, Pasolini can be said to inherit a certain aesthetic modernism from Sade, but the mediation of Blanchot can be identified with regard to a more postmodern cinema aesthetic which Pasolini employs. That is, Pasolini refuses to present Nazi-Fascism in a 'realist' or 'neo-realist' perspective (Irwin 2004). Instead, we get a presentation in a radical form of the new cinema of the 'time-image', with its especial emphasis on formalism, mannerist detachment and camera consciousness (Irwin 2004).

This would then be the very Blanchotian inheritance which *Salò* proudly displays. Here, we can see a significant affinity between not simply Blanchot and Pasolini, but Blanchot and a certain revolutionary style in cinema aesthetics shared by a number of paradigmatic filmmakers. One can refer to several important stylistic procedures used by both himself and others such as Godard, Antonioni and Rohmer. These new styles also take Pasolini and the new cinema (as well as Blanchot) beyond a mere aesthetic definition of art, into a transvaluation of the 'morality' of art. If as one commentator has observed, neo-realism is more definable as a 'moral attitude' than as a semiotics, then it is also clear that Pasolini's cinema subverts such a morality or moralism, most especially in *Salò* (Irwin 2004). Here one sees how Pasolini's semiotics complements his more general philosophy and also how the affinities between Pasolini and Blanchot (made explicit by Pasolini in the credits to *Salò*) exemplify the politicisation of the aesthetic in Blanchot's writings. Once again, the connections to Derrida would be very significant.

A Radicalised Politics in Bataille

In 'From Restricted to General Economy' (Derrida 1967k), Derrida refers to the deep affinities between the work of Bataille and Blanchot. The political dimension of Blanchot's work is radicalised in Bataille. Bataille's work in both philosophy and literature provides an idiosyncratic and controversial perspective on the problem of political organisation and especially the sources of political power. If Derrida's early analysis of the *avant-garde* has foregrounded their 'writing of the body', we can see this as a certain *writing of the social body*. Beginning in the late 1920s and early 1930s, Bataille's writings confront directly the spectre of fascism and its challenge to the edifice of liberal democracy and a more rationalised politics, from what has been described as a position of 'left radicalism' (Habermas 1990: 212). In essays such as 'The "Old Mole" and the Prefix *Sur* in the Words *Surhomme* and Surrealist' (Bataille 1985b) and 'The Psychological Structure of Fascism' (Bataille 1985c) and novels such as *Blue of Noon* (Bataille 1986b), Bataille interrogates both the attractiveness of fascist politics for the masses but also the failures of liberalism to provide a successful alternative to this new, dangerous social movement.

His work can be said to be acutely prescient in terms of its anticipation of the hegemony to come of fascism in the later 1930s and 1940s. There is a significant issue in Bataille's work concerning the relation between the sacred and the political and parallels have been drawn by some commentators between Bataille's emphasis on the 'sacred' in the late 1930s and the contemporaneous emphasis on certain forms of 'enthusiasm' in fascism (Hollier 1997). However, Bataille was very much aware of these parallels and was precisely developing his interest in the 'sacred' for contrary reasons. His creation of and work for the group *Contre-Attaque* bears this out (Surya 2002: 218ff.). In re-invoking the religious and the sacred, Bataille is hoping the cultivate the very resources employed by fascism to combat the latter: 'We intend in our turn to use for our benefit the weapons created by fascism, which has been able to use humanity's fundamental aspirations for affective exaltation and fanaticism' (quoted Surya 2002: 221). Clearly, for Bataille, politics is not simply a cerebral matter but is caught within the problematics of embodiment, of a 'l'écriture du corps'. However, to this extent, Bataille's political writings also involve fundamental criticisms of the failure of liberal and egalitarian ideologies to engage with this very problematic and the consequent radicality of the fascist threat. Moreover, Bataille foregrounds here a constitutive erotic or libidinal dimension to politics which is often overlooked by the mainstream political tradition. We have referred to this in the last chapter on feminism.

From Foucault's point of view, Bataille's philosophy represents a re-opening of what Kant sought to close. Bataille's work introduces what Foucault refers to as a principle of 'contestation' (Foucault 1998: 61/62), a philosophical principle *par excellence* which Bataille defines in *Inner Experience* as 'having the power to implicate (and to question) everything without possible respite' (quoted Foucault 1998: 62). Bataille's thinking thus seeks not simply to provide an option within this (Kantian or liberal) political framework, but to question and contest the assumptions which fundamentally structure the Kantian anthropology and the political framework which follows from it. We will also see this anti-Kantian move repeated in Derrida. Bataille is also writing in an earlier period, in this instance in the 1930s in response to the rise of fascism (although his later work extends to the early 1960s).

The respective essays, 'The "Old Mole" and the Prefix *Sur* in the Words *Surhomme* and Surrealist' (Bataille 1985b) and 'The Psychological Structure of Fascism' (Bataille 1985c), exemplify the problematicity of the political and public sphere at a time of immense crisis. 'The Old Mole' essay is in many respects a typical Bataille piece, in its anti-bourgeois rhetoric and its lure of the destructive forces of excess, but it also unusual in that it includes Nietzsche amongst the targets of its criticism. In this essay at least, Bataille's referent is Marx whom he employs to found his conception of a 'base materialism' of *heterogeneous matter* (Bataille 1985b), where once more the conception of the 'body' of politics is to the fore. We can relate this Marxian dimension precisely to what Derrida has said about the affinities between Bataille and the early Marx in the 'From Restricted to General Economy' (Derrida 1967k) essay.

Indeed, the image of the title of the 'Old Mole' essay is taken from Marx himself who presents his own work as being like that of an 'old mole' burrowing down deep into the earth and opposing himself to the more 'Icarian' myths of those metaphysicians who would want to deny our earth-boundedness. Here, Nietzsche remains far too Icarian from Bataille's perspective, as is clarified by Bataille's explicit critique of the prefix 'sur' in Nietzsche's concept of 'sur-homme' (or his concept of 'über' in 'über-mensch'). Bataille wants to posit a 'materialism...a crude liberation of human life from the imprisonment and masked pathology of ethics...an appeal to all that is offensive, indestructible, and even despicable, to all that overthrows, perverts, and ridicules spirit...' (Bataille 1985b: 32).

Before Marx, for Bataille, there was never any revolutionary movement free of idealism (in the most vulgar sense of the word). He also refers affirmatively to a number of key 'decadent' poets; 'Baudelaire, Rimbaud, Huysmans and Lautréamont' (Bataille 1985b: 41). Once again, we see the key importance of the *avant-garde* for politics. The influence of this *avant-gardisation* of politics is significant on Derrida's own move towards the political in his later work and we have seen this influence appear crucially in *Writing and Difference* (1967c) and *Dissemination* (1972h). What is equally significant is the way that his has been downplayed to a great extent in favour of an emphasis on religious or ethical returns.

Although Bataille is keen to subvert any idealism in this essay and refers (in a Nietzschean vein) to the pathology of ethics, what is perhaps most striking about the essay is its attempt to harness the notion of 'materialism' to a politics. Unlike the idealisms which seek to posit a 'sur' element, materialism seeks rather to ground human projects and politics in the earth and in what Derrida calls a 'writing of the body'. Bataille's reading of the need for the 'elevation' of the human is here psycho-social: 'abused by a system that threatens to crush or domesticate them, individuals have put themselves, in practical terms, at the mercy of what appears to them, through blinding flashes and disheartening attacks of empty verbiage, to be above all the pitiful contingencies of their human existence, for example, spirit, surreal, absolute, etc.' (Bataille 1985b: 35). In contrast, the Marxist philosophy takes as its point of departure something else entirely:

> Marx's point of departure has nothing to do with the heavens, preferred station
> of the imperialist eagle as of Christian or revolutionary utopias. He begins in
> the bowels of the earth, as in the materialist bowels of proletarians... (Bataille
> 1985b: 35).

Although written several years earlier, the 'Old Mole' essay can be seen here as
providing the nucleus of the more elaborate and systematic reading of politics
and society in the 1933 essay 'The Psychological Structure of Fascism' (Bataille
1985c).

In the latter essay, Bataille foregrounds the structural problem of homogeneity
and heterogeneity. This essay will then elaborate the missing element in the
Marxist analysis, which is primarily its failure to provide an adequate theory of
the formation of political society, less from an economic standpoint (an analysis
which it does provide) but rather from an ideological perspective. The analysis
of society sets up a clear demarcation between two opposed principles, that first
more traditionally of homogeneity, and second, more radically, of heterogeneity
(Bataille 1985c: 140). While homogeneity may be the fundamental basis of any
society per se, it is not the only element. To the extent that this homogeneity is not
absolute or unconditional, the society finds itself in an unstable equilibrium: 'as a
rule, social homogeneity is a precarious form, at the mercy of violence and even of
internal dissent...the study of homogeneity and of the conditions of its existence
thus necessarily leads to the essential study of heterogeneity...' (Bataille 1985c:
140).

In this essay, Bataille is especially interested in how fascism developed an
acute connection to the heterogeneous elements in the society. He develops the
two main stages of the heterogeneous as follows. In the first case, he refers to the
relationship between the 'sacred' and the 'heterogeneous'; the sacred is in effect
a restricted form of the heterogeneous and Bataille here (following Durkheim and
Mauss) refers to the twin concepts of 'mana' and 'taboo' (Bataille 1985c: 141).
'Mana' refers to the 'mysterious or impersonal force possessed by individuals such
as kings and witch doctors', while taboo refers to 'the social prohibition of contact
pertaining, for example, to cadavers and menstruating women' (Bataille 1985c:
141). These elements constitute an 'otherness' to the social homogeneity which
structures everyday life. Second, Bataille refers to 'unproductive expenditure'
(Bataille 1985c: 142). Here, the category is wider and includes parts of the body,
eroticism, unconscious processes such as dreams and neuroses and the numerous
elements of social life which remain unassimilable to homogeneity, such as 'mobs,
aristocracy, impoverished classes, different kinds of violence, and those who refuse
homogeneity outright, such as "madmen, leaders, poets"' (Bataille 1985c: 142).

This is a category of the heterogeneous which is loaded with political
implications for the structuring of political organisation. Bataille goes on to look
briefly at the 'affective reactions' of such heterogeneous elements, which he says
can be either attractive or repulsive, but in terms of individuals or mobs who seek
to act on these elements or under the influence of these elements, the result is

a 'breaking of the laws of social homogeneity…heterogeneous reality is that of a force or shock' (Bataille 1985c: 143). Finally, he speaks of the heterogeneous as 'incommensurate…as something other' (Bataille 1985c: 143) and while the homogeneous may be evaluated and categorised by 'science…the knowledge of a heterogeneous reality as such is to be found in the mystical thinking of primitives and in dreams; it is identical to the structure of the unconscious' (Bataille 1985c: 143). This is a significant claim in that Bataille seems to be calling for a psychoanalysis of the heterogeneous as such, and to the extent that the heterogeneous is a political phenomenon par excellence, a *psychoanalysis of the political*. Here, the reference is to Freud, *Group Psychology and the Analysis of the Ego* (Freud 2009).

Having given his framework for understanding these heterogeneous elements in society, Bataille now focuses in on his specific object to analyse:

> if these suggestions are now brought to bear upon actual elements, the fascist leaders are incontestably part of heterogeneous existence. Opposed to democratic politicians, who represent in different countries the platitude inherent to homogenous society, Mussolini and Hitler immediately stand out as something *other* (Bataille 1985c: 143).

From the beginning then, and *de jure*, fascism is opposed to democracy and to homogeneity. Bataille refers to the 'platitude inherent to homogeneous society', suggesting that democratic society may not be all it claims to be. This has a clear Derridean ring to it. Bataille develops his argument in terms of the powerlessness of the homogeneous society in the face of the fascist lure:

> whatever emotions their actual existence as political agents of evolution provokes, it is impossible to ignore the force that disrupts the regular course of things, the peaceful but fastidious homogeneity powerless to maintain itself (the facts that laws are broken is only the most obvious sign of the transcendent, heterogeneous nature of fascist action) (Bataille 1985c: 143).

This aspect of the powerlessness of the edifice of liberal democracy in the face of the fascist threat is taken up most evocatively by Bataille in his novel (written in 1935–1936) *Blue of Noon* (Bataille 1986b), where the general 'faithlessness' (Self 2006: xi) of the liberal democratic citizens seems to allow the affective allure of fascism almost free rein (its is no coincidence that the name given the anti-hero of this novel is Troppmann, which as Will Self points out sounds like a 'Germanisation of "too much man"' (Self 2006: x). Here, in a more critical context, Bataille refers to the 'force' of the fascist leader as analogous to the effects of 'hypnosis' (Bataille 1985c: 143):

> The affective flow that unites him with his followers – which takes the form of a moral identification of the latter with the one they follow (and reciprocally) – is a function of the common consciousness of increasingly violent and excessive

energies and powers that accumulate in the person of the leader and through him become widely available (Bataille 1985c: 143).

To this extent, it is clear that fascism is very much part of the realm of the heterogeneous rather than the realm of homogeneity. However, what Bataille now wishes to claim is that there are two main opposed employments of the heterogeneous realm for political purposes; what he terms the 'imperative' and the 'subversive' (Bataille 1985c: 143ff.). The imperative in the first case involves an employment of the heterogeneous as authority (Bataille 1985c: 143), and specifically with regard to fascism, as the authority of a single leader:

> this concentration in a single person intervenes as an element that sets the fascist formation apart within the heterogeneous realm; by the very fact that affective effervescence leads to unity, it constitutes, as *authority*, an agency directed *against* men… (Bataille 1985c: 144) [Bataille's italics].

This is clearly a critique of the authoritarian aspects of fascism, which, although employing heterogeneous elements (which Bataille sees as crucial for political organisation), nonetheless turn these elements 'against men', and is distinct from an uprising which would be faithful to 'the men in revolt'. Clearly, Bataille is drawing a critical demarcation here between a more revolutionary employment of the heterogeneous which would be 'for men' and one which would be more authoritarian and fascist. This is a definite statement of political intent from Bataille (not without its own difficulties) but it gives the lie to those who would accuse Bataille of fascist sympathies. Unequivocally, 'The Psychological Structure of Fascism' (Bataille 1985c) critiques what amounts to a fascist distortion of the heterogeneous resources which remain essential to an authentic political project for Bataille.

But to the same extent, Bataille also seems to be outruling the communist or socialist alternatives. He concludes the essay as follows: 'unlike the situation during the period of utopian socialism, morality and idealism are no more questions today then they are in fascist forms: 'a vast compulsion opposes, not so much fascism to communism, but radical imperative forms to the deep subversion that continues to pursue the emancipation of human lives…' (Bataille 1985c: 159). Here we see the continuity between 'The Old Mole' essay and 'The Psychological Structure of Fascism', both opposing 'idealism' in favour of 'base materialism'. Bataille advocates a simultaneous critique of liberalism and socialism on the one side and fascism on the other. Nonetheless, he wishes to defend a politics of the heterogeneous which avoids the authoritarianism of each of these political ideologies and regimes, while seeking a fidelity to 'revolt' and an 'emancipation' of human lives.

What I have also claimed is that this represents a veritable *writing of the social body*. Derrida's 'l'écriture du corps', inherited from the *avant-garde*, is political through and through. I will argue below that Derrida's politics to come bear a significant influence from Bataille's earlier project.

Derrida's Re-Politicisation of Philosophy: Cosmopolitanism and Historical Genealogy

Derrida's revival of interest in the political connects with this strong *avant-garde* influence on the thinking of the political in France. As aforementioned, this comes through a re-reading of Sade which has been underplayed while the Kojèvian reading of Hegel has been arguably overplayed. Even with regard to the reading of Hegel, other mediators of the latter legacy such as surrealism and Marxism, in the years before Kojève, have been marginalised (Baugh 2005). And again, what these omissions share is an attempt to underplay the political dimension. Additionally, what they underplay is the embodied aspect of this politics, its 'base materialism' as a social 'l'écriture du corps'. In this section, I want to look at how Derrida focuses in specifically on political questions in two essays, 'Cosmopolites de Tous les Pays, Encore une Effort!' (Derrida 1997a) [hereafter 'On Cosmopolitanism' Derrida 2001c and 'On Forgiveness' Derrida 2001d].

Diogenes, Heraclitus and Beyond

As with so many of Derrida's themes, cosmopolitanism (although seemingly universalist) has had quite a marginalised history as an ideology. For if monoculturalism has a long and perhaps a rather hegemonic history of domination, its opposite philosophical perspective, cosmopolitanism, also derives from ancient sources while not sharing in the history of power to nearly the same degree. It is not insignificant in the Greek period that the two figures who one can most readily associate cosmopolitanism with are two rather marginal figures, even outcasts, Heraclitus and Diogenes the Cynic. Heraclitus' cosmopolitanism derives initially from his harsh criticisms of his own indigenous compatriots, the Ephesians. He says the Ephesians should be hung to a man for their treatment of superior individuals in their own society (Barnes 2005). It is not difficult to see the connection between Heraclitus and Nietzsche which is often made. In their attempt to standardise all, the Ephesians refuse the possibilities of difference and individuality.

Heraclitus wants no part of this monoculturalism and goes into voluntary exile. He is also on record as having criticised the strife between Greek peoples and he is the only early Greek thinker who is critical of the division between Greek and non-Greek, or Greek and barbarian (Barnes 2005). He seems, in his own enigmatic and oracular way, to argue not simply for a pan-Hellenism, as against the sectarianisms of the city states, but also for a pan-humanism which would finally undo the Greek/Barbarian dichotomy, which one still sees present in a later and supposedly more sophisticated thinker such as Aristotle.

If one is looking for a developer of this intercultural legacy within Greek thought, one shouldn't thus look to the giant systems of Platonism or Aristotelianism but rather to the minor philosophies such as Cynicism and Stoicism (of course, this was also the Greek philosophy which interested in different ways both Nietzsche and Marx). While Nietzsche concentrated on Pre-Platonic philosophy, Marx focuses on the Hellenistic schools. Heidegger's interest in the Presocratics is another important reference point here. The infamous Diogenes, founder of the Cynic movement and near contemporary of Socrates (referred to anecdotally as 'Socrates gone mad'), was said to have been the first to actually employ the concept of cosmopolitanism in his statement: 'The only true commonwealth is that which is as wide as the universe. I am a citizen of the world (cosmopolites)' (quoted Dudley and Griffin 1998).

This dictum has been interpreted by some commentators as having only a negative meaning. Thus Dudley claims that Diogenes merely meant 'I am not a citizen of any of your Greek cities', i.e. I am outside the law, an individual irreducible to conventional norms (Dudley and Griffin 1998). However, Dudley's dismissal of the significance of this statement misses the fact that even if it was intended as negative, its negation of sectarianism and monoculturalism still remains a significant precursor to later attempts to define cosmopolitanism more positively. This is because even positive definitions often evolved from a reaction to their more ethnocentric opposites. One should also note that the Cynic philosophy, as represented by Diogenes, was one of the first to stress an unashamed embodied dimension. Cynic politics always involved a 'writing of the body', social and individual.

The Tendency to Rhetorical Alibi

In his text 'On Cosmopolitanism' (Derrida 2001c), Derrida attempts to delineate, in broad outline, the genealogy of the concept of 'cosmopolitanism'. Leaving aside the early Greeks, Derrida rather focuses on the Stoics and their influence on the early Christians, particularly Pauline Christianity, and, on Derrida's interpretation, both of these can be seen as looking back to a specifically Hebraic tradition. What he locates in this tradition is an idea of cosmopolitanism which is analogous to the Heraclitean and Cynic conception but which is also more focused on a notion of a 'city of refuge':

> We shall recognise in the Hebraic tradition, on the one hand, those cities which would welcome and protect those innocents who sought refuge from what the texts of that time call 'bloody vengeance' (Derrida 2001c: 17).

For Derrida, this discourse on the city which provides protection to the most vulnerable outsiders first begins in the *Book of Numbers*, and constitutes, in a rather retrospective Derridean language, an 'urban right to immunity and to hospitality' (Derrida 2001c: 17). It is also to be found, Derrida tells us, in Joshua where it is stated of the 'resident alien or temporary settler': 'if they admit him into the city, they will grant him a place where he may live as one of themselves' (Derrida 2001c: 17). What appears to be at issue here is not some deconstructive hermeneutics of the Biblical unsaid but rather the very literalism of Biblical command: God ordered Moses to institute six cities of refuge.

The development of this radical intercultural and cosmopolitan logic can be seen in Hellenistic philosophy, particularly in Cicero's Stoic philosophy. What is at issue here for Derrida is an 'ethics of hospitality', although this cannot be just one ethic amongst others. Rather, the ethics of hospitality, of welcoming and making an irreducible place for the other, constitutes for Derrida the very ethics or ethos of ethics itself: 'insofar as it has to do with the ethos, that is, the residence, one's home, the familiar place of dwelling, inasmuch as it is a manner of being there, the manner in which we relate to ourselves and to others, to others as our own or as foreigners, *ethics is hospitality*' (Derrida 2001c: 17).

Significantly, the figure of St Paul, often regarded as the paradigmatic anti-philosopher, translates this philosophical and ethical cosmopolitanism, which has been very much marginalised at this time within the more mainstream Platonic-Aristotelian philosophies, into Christian thinking. As already mentioned, this thinking also has Hebraic antecedents. But it would be interesting to meditate upon a genealogy of cosmopolitical thinking which links St Paul with Heraclitus and Diogenes. For Derrida, Pauline Christianity radicalises the earlier germ of interculturalism into a co-citizenship of the world. As Paul writes in one of his letters to the Ephesians: 'you are no longer foreigners in a foreign land, but fellow-citizens with God's people, members of God's household' (Derrida 2001c: 19). Pauline Christianity thus seems to open its doors to those who are not nominally Christian, in the same way that in the Hebraic tradition a 'right to hospitality' is provided for those who would otherwise be viewed as 'alien' or 'temporary'.

To this point, then, for Derrida there has been a radicalisation of the original intercultural and cosmopolitan logic, most especially through the figure of St Paul, developing on an original Hebraic foundation. However, the further development of this cosmopolitanism through the Enlightenment and Kant and up to the present foregrounds for Derrida a more problematic situation. What he terms the 'secularisation' (Derrida 2001c: 20) of such Pauline cosmopolitanism, while it has attempted to maintain the insights of the intercultural tradition, has nonetheless placed limits on the original notion and these very limits are at the basis of much of the contested issues of interculturalism today. Derrida traces these limits carefully through an analysis of Kant's seminal text *Perpetual Peace: A Philosophical Essay* (Kant 1972). We spoke earlier of Bataille's 'contestation' of the Kantian paradigm.

Here, we see another link between Bataille and Derrida. Kant's cosmopolitical thinking in this essay initially seems to wholeheartedly echo the Pauline inclusiveness when Kant states that what he terms a 'right of visitation' exists for 'all mankind' (quoted Derrida 2001c). This right of visitation can be derived from what Kant terms 'our common right of possession on the surface of the earth' which implies *de jure* for all humankind when entering foreign territory that one should 'not be treated as an enemy' (quoted Derrida 2001c: 21). This is a direct corollary of Paul's conception of co-citizenship, although it seems to be already more negative: 'not an enemy'. It is also qualified by the sense that this situation can only be maintained as long as the foreigner 'conducts himself peaceably' and additionally the giver of hospitality still has the right to 'send [the foreigner] away' (Derrida 2001c: 22).

The transition from Pauline Christianity to Kantian ethics has thus seen a dimunition in the rights of the foreigner. Whereas the foreigner previously had a 'right of residence' with Paul, he or she now only has a 'right of visitation'. The right of residence may be instituted but it is made conditional by Kant on treaties between states whereas, for Paul, it was declared as unconditional, as an unconditional inheritance. This also then signifies a change in how one understands ethics, or what Derrida has previously referred to as the 'ethics of hospitality'. Whereas previously hospitality was something of a free or gratuitous gift, it now becomes 'dependent on and controlled by the law and the state police' (Derrida 2001c: 15). As Derrida also makes clear, in many instances, such state police operate as interpreters of the law with regard to refugees and asylum seekers, indeed as makers of the law. Invoking Walter Benjamin, Derrida refers to a 'police without borders, without determinable limit' (Derrida 2001c: 14), although he also cautions against a 'utopian suspicion of the function of the police' (Derrida 2001c: 14). What is being mooted here, however, is that the right of residence from Kant onwards becomes a conditional right and that while it is subject to law, in certain hyperbolic instances it can become subject to the whim of a police force acting beyond or below the law.

Derrida's discussion here moves between the realms of the ideal or abstract and the realm of the empirical. What his genealogical analysis makes clear is the philosophical contestation of a concept between various traditions which has been a formative influence on the evolution of immigration law and contemporary practice with regard to asylum seeking and refugee status. As Derrida observes:

> there is still a considerable gap separating the great and generous principles of the right to asylum inherited from the Enlightenment thinkers and from the French Revolution and, on the other hand, the historical reality or the effective implementation of these principles (Derrida 2001c: 11).

It is clear then that what Derrida refers to as a more 'mean-minded juridical tradition' (Derrida 2001c: 11) or, what in less moralistic language, we might refer to as a more 'economistic' juridical tradition, while laying claim to some form of cosmopolitanism, is little by little eroding the original ethical and philosophical meaning of that concept. For Derrida, this clearly represents an ethical deterioration. However, in his conclusion to the essay, he distances his own thinking from the apparent unconditionality of the cosmopolitanism evidenced, for example, in Pauline Christianity or even in Diogenes' earlier Cynic cosmopolitanism. It is this ethics which Derrida's own work is often associated with but here he marks a clear dissent. This kind of ethics he describes as an 'unconditional hospitality, offered *a priori* to every other, to all newcomers, whoever they may be' (Derrida 2001c: 22).

For Derrida, there is a certain danger in such an ethical purism. His remarks here remind one of his famous criticisms of Emmanuel Levinas' ethics, based on the absolute 'face to face relation' with the other who holds me responsible, criticisms which he puts forward in the early essay 'Violence and Metaphysics' (Derrida 1967f). What motivates Derrida's criticisms are the dangers inherent in an ideal concept, which is said to be beyond human law and human understanding. Idealism must be contested, for both Bataille and Derrida, with a corrective dimension of materialism. Such idealism remains too abstract for Derrida, disconnected from a 'writing of the body'. In 'The Old Mole' essay, Bataille had cautioned against the residues of the Icarian myth in politics. Similarly, the concept of a cosmopolitanism beyond all human nations and tribes and limitations, and also beyond the autonomy of state law, for Derrida, runs the 'risk of remaining a pious and irresponsible desire, without form and without potency, and of even being perverted at any moment' (Derrida 2001c: 23). The ideal of an ethics of hospitality therefore needs to be checked and balanced by the needs and responsibilities of individual states and citizenry.

At the same time, however, it is clear that a certain other kind of perversion can take place if all one is concerned with is sectional interest and state control. Indeed, for Derrida, this would seem to be a greater danger, a greater threat of perversion. It is in this context that the ideal of an ethics of hospitality, where 'unconditional hospitality, [is] offered *a priori* to every other, to all newcomers, whoever they may be' (Derrida 2001c: 22), needs to be maintained as an ideal and to intervene as a standard in policy and law making. Although much contemporary law on immigration, asylum and interculturalism often seems to nominally affirm this ideal, for Derrida 'the discourse on the refugee, asylum or hospitality, risks becoming nothing more than rhetorical alibis' (Derrida 2001c: 13).

For Derrida, then, the challenge of contemporary interculturalism is to transform and improve the empirical by drawing as intelligently and passionately as one can on the ideal. Through his exemplary genealogy of cosmopolitanism, Derrida has allowed us to see anew how the empirical dimension of cosmopolitanism has both, at times, faithfully translated this ideal and, as is increasingly the case, wilfully distorted it while invoking its ethical good name. In the next, concluding section, I want to look at how Derrida develops this analysis in a related essay, 'On Forgiveness' (Derrida 2001d), and also at how we might make sense of Derrida's cosmopolitanism in relation to his thinking on the political, more generally.

'On Forgiveness' and a Deconstructive Politics

We have seen, in our analysis of Derrida's concept of cosmopolitanism, that a conceptual genealogy foregrounds an irreducibly dual structure. There is, Derrida is claiming, a double or contradictory imperative in the concept of cosmopolitanism. On the one hand, there is an unconditional hospitality but, on the other, it is conditional. There is an ideal dimension but this must constantly be brought down to earth. Here, once more, we see the continuity with Derrida's earlier readings of Nietzsche feminism and the *avant-garde*. There has, therefore, in practical terms, to be some limitation on rights of residence and our (necessary) idealism must be tempered with negotiation and context-specific pragmatism.

For Derrida, this emblematises a contradictory logic, but nonetheless a 'necessary' (or unavoidable) logic. This text foregrounds a political emphasis (and concern) in Derrida's work, which has not always been as immediately apparent. The view of Derrida, put forward for example in Habermas' text *The Philosophical Discourse of Modernity* (Habermas 1990), has been more paradigmatic. Habermas there sees Derrida as a relativist who either aestheticises or completely occludes questions of political relevance. Although I do not subscribe to the notion that either Derrida's early or late work is apolitical in this Habermasian sense, nonetheless it is clear that it is an accusation which is easier to make against his earlier work, which avoids explicit political thematics (however implicitly, and radically, political the early works may nonetheless be). Indeed, even Habermas, who is perhaps Derrida's most vehement (and eloquent) critic on political issues, achieves more of a rapprochement with the later Derrida. I will return to this late 'compromise agreement' between Derrida and Habermas below, as it is significant for our theme (Thomassen 2006). First, however, I will look at an essay which is written a few years later than 'On Cosmopolitanism', and which is also explicitly political, Derrida's text 'On Forgiveness' (Derrida 2001d).

The Doubling Structure of Forgiveness

As with cosmopolitanism, so too with the concept and political process of forgiveness, argues Derrida. Once again, it is a question of a 'double structure', but, if anything, matters are even more fraught in the context of forgiveness than in the case of the cosmopolitical. More appears to be at stake here, at least with regard to the inter-personal dimension of the political. Derrida has always returned to the motif of the 'double', which he introduced most powerfully in his discussion of French poetics (Derrida 1972h) in the text *Dissemination*, and which we discussed in Chapters 3 and 4. There, Derrida's theme was literature, but as always with Derrida (and against the standard reading of his early work) such aesthetic interpretations are shot through with political significance. Here, in the later essay (written thirty years later) 'On Forgiveness' (Derrida 2001d), Derrida is interrogating the political significance of this doubling phenomenon. Forgiveness, Derrida argues, also has a double structure which testifies to an equivocation within the Western heritage.

It is, once more, a question of a negotiation between the conditional and the unconditional, between the absolute and the relative. Looked at in a theological setting, for example, forgiveness can be understood in either of two ways. If forgiveness is given by God, or 'inspired by divine prescription', it must be a 'gracious gift...without exchange and without condition' (Derrida 2001d: 44). However, there is also an equivocal understanding of divine forgiveness in the very same tradition, a 'contradictory logic'. 'Sometimes it requires, as its minimal condition, the repentance and transformation of the sinner' (Derrida 2001d: 35). For

Derrida, this tension at the heart of the original idea of forgiveness is paradigmatic for more intra-human notions of forgiveness. One must make a distinction, Derrida tells us, between the 'infinite, aneconomic forgiveness…granted to the guilty as guilty…even to those who do not repent or ask forgiveness' (Derrida 2001d: 34) and, on the other side, 'a conditional forgiveness proportionate to the recognition of the fault, to repentance, to the transformation of the sinner who then explicitly asks forgiveness' (Derrida 2001d: 34).

Between these two poles of conceptual understanding, Derrida argues, there is a relation of contradiction, where they remain irreducible to one another but also indissociable. According to Derrida, here, responsible political action consists in the negotiation of these two irreconcilable yet indissociable demands. Therefore, responsible political action has to be related to a moment of unconditionality. Just as with the concept of cosmopolitanism, the concept of forgiveness has an enigmatic structure. Derrida argues that:

> if one is only prepared to forgive what appears forgivable…then the very idea of forgiveness would disappear…From which comes the aporia, which can be described in its dry and implacable formality, without mercy: forgiveness forgives only the unforgivable (Derrida 2001d: 32ff.).

This is where the tension arises between more orthodox political discourse and Derrida's work. The discourse of forgiveness is not reducible to a binary logic. 'One cannot, or should not, forgive; there is only forgiveness, if there is any, where there is the unforgivable' (Derrida 2001d: 33). What is significant in this discussion, in intercultural terms, relates to how Derrida is distinguishing two ethical or political processes which can take place between protagonists involved in intercultural conflict. Derrida seems to be saying that, in political terms, this kind of interculturalism may seek a 'reconciliation' for past wrongs in terms of a recognition of a fault, and a consequent 'repentance' on the part of the wrongdoing party, who then ask forgiveness from those who have been victimised or oppressed against. One thinks of the Truth and Reconciliation process in South Africa, for example. However, Derrida is arguing here that we must make a distinction between 'forgiveness' and 'reconciliation'. Whereas the latter is indeed conditional on admission of guilt, repentance, some form of reparation or punishment, etc., the former concept is less 'economic'. That is, for Derrida, authentic 'forgiveness' is not reducible to a process of reconciliation, but is rather 'an-archic', or in Derrida's phrase, 'mad' (Derrida 2001d: 39). It would be 'forgiveness' then, and not 'reconciliation', which would evolve Derrida's 'l'écriture du corps'. Here, we see the strong connection back to Bataille's discussion of the political and an excessive heterogeneity.

Another example here that Derrida cites is the 'crime against the Jews under Vichy' (Derrida 2001d). This crime, according to Derrida, is 'inexpiable', that is, there is no punishment which could be proportionate to the crime. However, Derrida disagrees that this means that there can be no forgiveness. Certainly, understood in terms of a more binary logic, if there is no adequate reparation, there can be no forgiveness. But Derrida's 'double' concept of forgiveness works in a more contradictory way. On his terms, it is precisely the 'unforgivable' which can be forgiven, or which opens itself to the possibility of a forgiveness, which lies beyond any possible exchange or reparation. To invoke the previous analogy which Derrida has used in terms of theological forgiveness, Derrida is suggesting that humans too (like God) can forgive where there is no reason to forgive, who can forgive gracefully, arbitrarily and freely.

For Derrida, this so-called 'madness' is not to be understood in a negative sense. It can, rather, have very significant (and positive) political effects. On Derrida's terms, this kind of forgiveness is revolutionary.

> It is even, perhaps, the only thing that arrives, that surprises, like a revolution, the ordinary course of history, politics, and law. Because that means that it remains heterogeneous to the order of politics or of the juridical as they are ordinarily understood (Derrida 2001d: 39).

One can also derive the correlative conclusion regarding the dynamics of punishment and forgiveness through reparation only. If graceful forgiveness is revolutionary, then a more economic forgiveness is always in danger of being reactionary.

This analysis reminds one of Nietzsche's discussion of the real basis of supposed moral altruism in *On the Genealogy of Morals* (Nietzsche 1967). For Nietzsche, traditional ethics hides a will-to-power, altruism most often finds its source in what he terms 'ressentiment', or reactiveness. There are also clear connections here to Bataille's analysis of the heterogeneous (aneconomic) and homogeneous (economic) elements in society, and his discussion of their political significance (Bataille 1985c). Finally, the 'nineties feminism' (Gallop 1997) critique of essentialist identity also has strong affinities with this approach.

Although Derrida doesn't draw out the connections between this text and 'On Cosmopolitanism' (Derrida 2001c), it is clear that Derrida is here seeking to distinguish his version of cosmopolitics from that which would seek a rationalist universalism, as in the case of Kant. Here, Derrida (true to form) is designating an aspect of the an-economic, of the an-archic, which remains irreducible within the political sphere. The connections back to the an-archism of those original cosmopolitical thinkers, Diogenes and Heraclitus, is evident. There must always be space for 'dissensus', but also for the unpredictable. Politics must not, indeed in principle for Derrida cannot, become formulaic. Interculturalism or cosmopolitanism cannot, therefore ever become a finished object; they always project towards a future, what Derrida refers to as a 'democracy to come'. In the concluding section, I want to look at how this view of interculturalism draws Derrida close to Charles Taylor and Habermas, but how it ultimately also clearly demarcates his political thinking from theirs.

Conclusion: Derrida, Habermas, Taylor on Intercultural Politics

Charles Taylor, in his essay 'The Politics of Recognition' (Taylor 1994) provides a stirring genealogy of the development of the discourse of interculturalism, of rights and recognition, and its relation to the evolution of modern liberal thought, foregrounding both its strengths and its interminable tensions and strains. Taylor, although ultimately defending a particular version of liberalism, presents a subtle and nuanced picture of the acute tensions which exist not simply between liberalism and the discourse of interculturalism, but also within liberalism itself between those who would wish to defend a 'difference-blind' liberalism and those who would outline a more 'difference-sensitive' liberalism (Taylor 1994). Derrida's arguments in relation to both cosmopolitanism and forgiveness can be described as 'difference-sensitive', but they would not seem to be compatible even with a more nuanced (Taylorean) version of liberalism. Indeed, Taylor is vehemently critical of Derrida in this essay, putting him into the pejorative category of 'neo-Nietzscheanism', which seems to be synonymous with 'nihilism' (Taylor 1994). If Derrida's arguments in regard to difference seem hyberbolic at times, it still seems unfair (and hyperbolic in itself) to regard him as a nihilist.

While hardly an uncritical advocate of modernity (he is critical of its excesses), Taylor is nonetheless keen to defend the positive potential of the modern project in philosophy and values. He is also eager to distinguish the affirmative dimension of modernity from the aspects of the postmodern era which he considers to be 'nihilistic' (singling out here Nietzsche and the 'neo-Nietzscheans' Derrida and Michel Foucault for especial ire). Taylor's argument with regard to the discourse of recognition and rights can thus be read as a microcosm of the debate between neo-modernity and postmodernity, most especially as it has implications for the political realm. A relevant Derrida text in this debate is his 'Hostipitality' (Derrida 2006a) essay, where he argues that 'we do not know what hospitality is' and where he speaks of the 'double bind' of hospitality: 'the troubling analogy in their common origin between *hospis* as host and *hostis* as enemy, between hospitality and hostility' (Derrida 2006a: 223). Taylor's analysis, on my interpretation, is at its least convincing when it addresses the work of Derrida and the neo-Nietzscheans, where he seems to jettison his usual subtlety and resorts to caricature. Derrida's work, in particular amongst this sub-group, seems constructive in its engaging with both the responsibilities and acute tensions of the intercultural problematic.

A subtle critic of Taylor who is more Derridean in this respect (but still eminently constructive rather than nihilistic), is K. Anthony Appiah. Appiah, for example, in his essay 'Identity, Authenticity, Survival: Multicultural Societies and Social Reproduction' (Appiah 1994) claims that there is an underestimation of the individual self in Taylor's discussion of the politics of recognition. Appiah points to two main issues here. First, that Taylor underplays oppositional aspects of individualised authenticity, which he associates with Lionel Trilling's classic discussion *The Opposing Self: Nine Essays in Criticism* (Trilling 1955). Second, that even if one sees such oppositional notions of the self as too subjectivist, nonetheless, our collective identities do not have to be as essentialist as Taylor claims. As Appiah observes, 'a politics of identity can be counted on to transform the identities on whose behalf it ostensibly labors' (Appiah 1994: 163). This, we might say, is an *existentialist (or deconstructive) politics of identity* as opposed to an essentialist one. It is certainly nuanced in relation to unpredictability and ambiguity, but it is hardly nihilistic. It points towards the horizon of a more political (Derridean) 'l'écriture du corps'. What Appiah also brings out here is a (paradoxical) possible rapprochement between Taylor and Derrida. The differences here do not seem fundamental but rather relate most especially to Taylor's rather polemical reading of Derrida's political thinking. By the same token, it might be argued that Derrida's insistent emphasis on undecidability also has an irreducibly polemical dimension.

One significant example of how such polemic can occlude real philosophical and political affinities can be seen in the context of the Derrida-Habermas encounter (Thomassen 2006). As already mentioned, Habermas (most especially in *The Philosophical Discourse of Modernity*, Habermas 1990) had painted Derrida as a 'relativist'. In return, Derrida had written several polemical asides about 'exclusion of otherness' in Habermas' work. However, a chance meeting at a party at Northwestern University led the two thinkers to put aside such antagonism and to focus instead on philosophical and political affinities. The results are perhaps surprising but also full of hope for those who seek to overcome what often appear to be insurmountable barriers in political and social thinking and practice. As Habermas observes, 'Derrida, like only Foucault, stirred the spirit of an entire generation' (quoted Thomassen 2006). But the rapprochement between the two thinkers goes beyond mere mutual respect. In his later encounter with Derrida, Habermas seems to recognise that Derrida's emphasis on difference (which we have looked at in this essay through the themes of 'cosmopolitanism' and 'forgiveness') is more than simply a question of aesthetics. If there are aesthetic issues involved here, we might say that they can only be understood in Walter Benjamin's terms as a 'politicisation of the aesthetic'. On Taylor's terms, we can say that Habermas begins to understand that Derrida is concerned with issues (amongst others) of 'nonrecognition' or 'misrecognition', a problematic which is also crucial to both Habermas and Taylor (Taylor 1994).

Nonrecognition or misrecognition can, as all three thinkers understand, inflict harm, can be a form of oppression, thus imprisoning someone in a false, distorted and reduced mode of being. One form of common misrecognition can be what might be termed *a patronising recognition*, which really amounts to another form of nonrecognition or misrecognition. Habermas is especially sensitive to this problem. He deals interestingly with this issue of 'patronising benevolence' in his essay 'Religious Tolerance: The Pacemaker for Cultural Rights' (Habermas 2006). Habermas argues that only a 'network of relationships of reciprocal recognition' can overcome this problem. 'It requires that integration of all citizens – and their mutual recognition across cultural divisions as citizens – within the framework of a shared political culture' (Habermas 2006: 205). What is most significant about this essay is that Habermas rejects the assumed political neutrality of the secularist state, and instead points out that 'political neutrality can be violated just as easily by the secular or laical side as by the religious camp' (Habermas 2006: 203). What constitutes political neutrality in a democracy is thus an ongoing *project* and cannot be predefined by, for example, secular assumptions.

While not without a certain difference in emphasis and tone, Habermas' reference to an ongoing 'project' of democracy has affinities with Derrida's invocation of a 'democracy-to-come'. It also bears comparison to Taylor's conception of a 'fusion of horizons' (Taylor 1994) which would involve opening up to the other's perspective (which he distinguishes from more ethnocentric approaches). While wishing to avoid a dialectical predeterminism which would underestimate disagreements between the three thinkers, nonetheless it seems legitimate to speak of the possibility of an 'interculturalism-to-come', which would involve the work of Habermas, Taylor and Derrida in mutual dialogue. Each of these thinkers, in their own idiosyncratic way, have participated and contributed to the furtherance of the processes of democratisation, which involve as much disagreement as agreement. It is precisely in the context of this notion of a challenging politics, perhaps an idiosyncratic or polemical politics, that I think we can best understand Derrida's contribution to the debate surrounding cosmopolitanism, interculturalism and their wider social, political and philosophical implications. And once more, it is clear that this politics has a lineage which extends from Derrida back through Bataille and Artaud to Nietzsche (and Marx).

Conclusion

To conclude, I would like to foreground one of Derrida's late texts (at least in its final most developed version). Derrida had certainly been working on the thought of Jean-Luc Nancy for perhaps ten years but it wasn't until 2000 that *Le Toucher – Jean-Luc Nancy* was published in French. Here, I want to look at some of its key and provocative insights. The themes of this text bring our own thematic of Derrida, embodiment and the *avant-garde*, from the *Theatre of Cruelty* to Platonism to 'sexual difference', into sharper relief. As with much of Derrida's work, we start with the Greeks. Derrida refers to 'the aporia of the tangible in Aristotle' (Derrida 2000: 15, Derrida 2005: 5). Again, as with so many of Derrida's texts there is also a connection between this thematic of the Greeks and the relation to Christianity. Derrida refers to Nancy's project of a 'deconstruction of Christianity' ['déconstruction du Christianisme'] (Derrida 2000: 74, 2005: 60). We have already looked at the consistent thematic of Platonism in Derrida's work which explores how, in dialogues such as the *Phaedrus* (Plato 1961), the whole notion of the theory of Forms is complicated and any supposed dualism is undone, so that the bodily and the sensible become re-affirmed.

As with our insistent theme, Derrida returns to the *avant-garde* in *On Touching – Jean-Luc Nancy* (Derrida 2005). We have seen this in other late works such as his later essays on Artaud (Derrida 1998a). Here, it is, on one level, because Nancy's own work has been imbued, similarly to Derrida's own, with an *avant-garde* influence. Thus, we see the figure of Bataille most especially prominent in Nancy's work. But, second, it is because it was the *avant-garde* who first opened up this most radical questioning of the body. Certainly, Nietzsche radicalised the earlier thinking but we have also seen how the *avant-garde* brought this Nietzschean thinking into the twentieth century and applied it to specific contemporary problems, most notably in terms of the contemporary politics of the world wars and fascism, as we saw in the last chapter.

Derrida first invokes Artaud, citing his project of the 'proper body' and referring to Artaud's conception of 'nerve-scales' or 'nerve-meters' ['Pèse-nerfs'] (Derrida 2000: 75, Derrida 2005: 61). There would, nonetheless, need to be a certain ambivalence here, Derrida warns, towards any notion of a 'body proper'. We have seen in the Artaud essays in *Writing and Difference* that Derrida also sounds a note of caution with regard to a certain kind of residual metaphysics in Artaud, despite the fact that Artaud is said to resist clinical and critical exegeses 'like no one before' (Derrida 1967h). Similarly, in the case of Bataille, in 'From Restricted to General Economy' (Derrida 1967k), Derrida points to the caution with which one must undertake any attempted opposition to classical philosophy, most especaily in its Hegelian guise. Otherwise, one risks falling back into the very categories one was attempting to break free from. This, according to Derrida, is Bataille's greatest insight, his ability to take Hegel (and philosophy) seriously but not too seriously.

Derrida introduces Nancy's discourse in *On Touching* with this proviso: there will also be a deconstruction at work here, an interminable deconstruction. Derrida refers to this as 'Nancy's turning point, an implacable deconstruction of modern philosophies of the body proper and the flesh' ['implacable deconstruction des philosophies modernes du corps proper ou de la "chair"'] (Derrida 2000: 77, Derrida 2005: 63). One must be careful, then, lest we confuse Derrida's subtle thinking regarding desire and embodiment with the much vaunted return of the 'the body in academe (cultural studies, etc.)' ['l'académie américaines'] (Derrida 2000: 79, Derrida 2005: 64), which itself would be different in kind from the renewed emphasis on the 'flesh' ('chair'), most notably in France through phenomenology (and which refers back most especially to Merleau-Ponty's work). This foregrounding of such a complex problematic marks *On Touching* out as a central work in Derrida's *oeuvre*. He has rarely, except perhaps in interviews, been so forthcoming regarding his relation to his contemporaries in France (e.g. Derrida 2005: 77ff., 117ff., 123ff., 184ff., 191ff.), for example, Deleuze, Merleau-Ponty, Lacan and Levinas, and it is not coincidental that it is in a book 'on touching' that this emphasis becomes foregrounded. There is something very direct about Derrida's approach in this text. As we have also clarified, the reference to the *avant-garde* is insistent throughout this text. In these respects, we can say that *On Touching* (Derrida 2005) is exemplary for our purposes. Moreover, as a later work, it shows how there is a consistency in Derrida's work, giving the lie to those who would see deconstruction as either arbitrarily developing and being divided into an earlier (more deconstructive/*avant-garde* phase) and a later (more ethical or religious phase). Rather, deconstruction remains atheological and, in many respects, anethical throughout Derrida's work and additionally the references to the *avant-garde* are there, early to late.

Beginning with Levinas, it is significant that the reference here is again quite negative (Derrida 2000: 92). Derrida is concerned with Levinas' conception of the 'caress' ['la caress'] (Derrida 2005: 77) which is described as a 'contact beyond contact' ['comme contact au-delà du contact'] (Derrida 2005: 77). In a text which is focused on the dynamisms of touch and embodiment, Levinas' notion of 'contact beyond contact' has the resonance of the kind of phraseology used by negative theology. As we know, Derrida is quite critical of this approach elsewhere, most notably in 'Comment ne pas parler: Dénégations' (Derrida 1997f). The danger of such disavowals of contact is that they succeed first, in disavowing the embodied and material, and second, that they often reserve a hyperessentialism beyond the here and now. Derrida is here then distancing Levinas' approach from a more affirmative approach which he is going to locate in the work of Nancy. A few pages later, he refers to 'Levinas' masculine signature' (Derrida 2005: 80) which, of course, relates back to Derrida's earlier work on Levinas (Derrida 1997c).

He also refers significantly regarding Levinas here to 'Levinas' mistrust of the tactile' (Derrida 2005: 329) which is akin to Merleau-Ponty's thematics of the 'untouchable' (Derrida 2005: 77). Derrida observes that Levinas is against a certain 'living within the flesh': 'as if he were...wanting to efface the symmetry...and above all the "concupiscence", that is the concupiscent desire for what Christian language calls the flesh – but not the erotic' (Derrida 2005: 333).

On Touching (Derrida 2005) seems to mark the culmination of Derrida's critique of Levinas, beginning with 'Violence and Metaphysics' (Derrida 1967f), 'At this Moment' (Derrida 1997c) and evolving in *On Touching* (Derrida 2005). It is difficult to understand how these readings can give rise to conceptions of Derrida and Levinas as somehow thinkers of great affinity. On my reading at least, there has always been a significant disagreement marking these two discourses. As we will see below, Derrida also takes the chance here to mark his distinction from Merleau-Ponty's discourse of the flesh. He refers in passing to 'Merleau-Ponty and a certain untouchability of the other' (Derrida 2005: 77). Again, this concept of 'untouchability' leads to caution on Derrida's part in regard to the danger of asserting a beyond of the touch, which reduces the touch to something lesser or in Heidegger's terms, something 'ontic'. In contrast, it is clear that Derrida feels himself close to the discourse of Jean-Luc Nancy. And, once more, the figure of Bataille seems to mark a crucial affinity with deconstruction (as it did, more or less, *contra* Levinas in 'At this Moment', Derrida 1997c). In a later footnote, for example, Derrida refers to 'the insignificance of death; laughing; the end is endless' (Derrida 2005: 377), a very Bataillean phraseology. Similarly, he quotes from Nancy speaking of it not being 'a question of rejoining an intact matter; we are not opposing immanence to transcendence' (quoted Derrida 2005: 373). This discussion of Nancy's text is strongly Bataillean, not opposing immanence to transcendence but searching for 'the between' ('l'entre'), which is also Platonic, amongst other references.

Derrida points to the fact that 'Nancy is thinking "with" Bataille' (Derrida 2005: 117), in a specific context, but also, we might argue, more generally. Nancy would be developing a certain legacy of Bataille (as would Derrida). This is a legacy, Derrida says, 'between loss and appropriation' (Derrida 2005: 118). It is this 'between' which we have already foregrounded playing such a crucial part in the texts of *Dissemination*, the 'hymen between Plato and Mallarmé, inter Plato and Mallarmé?' (Derrida 1972k). On Bataille's terms, it seems to relate back to the notion of a relation between 'meaning and the absence of meaning' (Derrida 1967k), or what Barbara Johnson calls 'the gap between desire and fulfillment' (Johnson 1981).

Here, then, close to the body but being wary of a body proper which would be too metaphysical, and also wary of the 'contact beyond contact' of the Levinasian caress or the 'untouchability' of Merleau-Ponty's emphasis on 'flesh', we have what Derrida refers to as 'the quasi-transcendental privilege of the tactile' (Derrida 2005: 119). This would be Nancy's affirmation, but also, we might say, that of Derrida too. Derrida would be following Nancy here although one could also argue that Nancy's discourse has developed out of an encounter with Derrida's early work. Here is where Derrida would come to pay respects to a thinker who, to go back to *Spurs* (Derrida 1979), has developed the deconstructive discourse in his own way. Once again, there is a reference back to the Greeks, to Plato's *Phaedo* (Plato 1961) and the extraordinary disavowal there of the tactile and the senses, of the body per se *vis-à-vis* the soul. This is all the more extraordinary given what we looked at in Chapters 3 and 4 concerning Plato's avowals of the body and eros in the *Phaedrus*, *Symposium* and the *Sophist*. But, in Plato's *Phaedo*, we have a clear reading that 'Plato dismissed the senses' (Derrida 2005: 120). There is there also 'the prefiguring of touch' (Derrida 2005: 120) by which Derrida means the construction of a prefigured or preformed discourse which would subordinate touch first within the hierarchy of senses (to vision most especially but also to hearing). This will then be exacerbated by a hierarchy of sense subordinated to the intelligible or the rational. Derrida thus presents Plato here (or at least this singular version of Plato's textuality) via Nancy as 'anti-tactile' (Derrida 2005: 120).

Derrida then introduces a fascinating schema concerning some of his contemporaries which will lead, a little later, to a whole disavowal of a certain 'French phenomenology of the flesh' (Derrida 2005: 13ff.). Here, we encounter Hélène Cixous, Gilles Deleuze and there is an important reference back to Artaud's notion of the 'body without organs' (so influential on Deleuze and Guattari's *Anti-Oedipus*) [Deleuze and Guattari 2004]. Derrida's relation to Cixous is perhaps his closest to any of the French feminist philosophers of his generation. His late text *H.C. For Life: That is to Say* (Derrida 2006b) is an affirmation of her work and she has written several late texts on Derrida (*Insister of Jacques Derrida*, *Portrait of a Young Jewish Saint*, etc.) (Cixous 2005/2007). Cixous' work is also concerned with embodiment, desire and sexual difference, and here we can see how Derrida sees her work as on a similar trajectory to that of Nancy (and indeed that of his own work). His Foreword to the *Cixous Reader* (Cixous 1994) asserts her intepretation of a multiplied sexual difference as paradigmatic (Derrida 1994).

With Gilles Deleuze, matters would be more complex. However, Derrida does cite Deleuze in *Spurs* and Deleuze's text *Nietzsche and Philosophy* (Deleuze 1963) was a key intervention, in terms of a rereading of Nietzsche in France, which paved the way for Klossowski's later text (Klossowski 1997) and Derrida's own (Derrida 1979). Deleuze was also at the Cerisy-la-Salle conference where Derrida originally delivered *Spurs* as a text. During the 1970s, Deleuze (with Felix Guattari) also published *Anti-Oedipus* (Deleuze and Guattari 2004), one of the most important texts on the erotic and sexuality in the 1970s, and like Derrida, Deleuze offers a critique of the dominance of a Lacanian reading of desire and embodiment. In a recent interview, Derrida has spoken of how often his relationship to his contemporaries was misunderstood (for example, to Deleuze), as more negative or indifferent than it actually was. In fact, the relation for all the differences nonetheless had something shared in common. In *On Touching*, Derrida seems to want to mark this connection with Deleuze's thematic, while also marking a disagreement. In the first case, he mentions Artaud's 'the body without organs'. This notion which tried to deconstruct the whole 'organisation' of the body, is centrally important for Deleuze in *Anti-Oedipus*. We know from Chapter 1 that Derrida is also a keen advocate of many aspects of Artaud's discourse. Certainly, with regard to our *avant-garde* thematic, it is clear that both Derrida and Deleuze share a significant influence of the *avant-garde* in their work.

Here, in *On Touching* (Derrida 2005), Derrida, while recognising the shared Artaudian inheritance and also the thematics of desire, nonetheless offers a critique of Deleuze's concept of 'smooth space' (Derrida 2005: 126). This is contrasted with Deleuze's concept of 'straited space' and seems to involve a notion of complete liberation of desire from the shackles of repression. For Derrida, however, there is a real danger here of simply inverting the metaphysical opposition and privileging the previously subordinated term. Going back to the earlier analysis of Bataille, it is clear that, for Derrida, this is too simplistic. Bataille had undertaken a subtle and rigorous interrogation of Hegel's work and his dialectics of desire. In contrast, Deleuze seems to want to simply project himself 'completely outside' (Derrida 2005: 126). This also brings one back to Derrida's discussion in 'The Ends of Man' (Derrida 1982d) of the various strategies which one can employ to engage with the metaphysical tradition. Rather than simply thinking that one can move outside in a single step, Derrida is suggesting that this move is philosophically naïve. Of course, Derrida's own discourse constantly runs this risk and one is never assured, as again Derrida says of Bataille's discourse (Derrida 1967k). If one is assured or certain, then one falls back into a 'restricted economy' of philosophy, which refuses to acknowledge that which is irreducible to meaning. So Derrida is foregrounding an emphasis on 'sense' through Jean-Luc Nancy (which also reminds one of Artaud's 'theatre of the senses'), but the metaphysical danger would loom large. Therefore it must be, as it is for Bataille and Nancy, 'sense without an ontology of presence' (Derrida 2005: 130).

Another tradition which we saw foregrounded in Derrida's early work but which recedes somewhat after that is the movement of phenomenology. Derrida's early texts on Husserl demonstrate his indebtedness to a certain kind of phenomenological rigor but, as Derrida has often claimed (Derrida 1986b), he tries to leave behind the phenomenological method. Here, there is an attempt to move towards a philosophical approach more akin to Nietzsche's genealogical method or the *avant-gardist* approach which I spoke about above. Nonetheless, most especially with Merleau-Ponty's 'phenomenology of perception' (Merleau-Ponty 2002) and the later Merleau-Ponty's work on the 'flesh' and on the 'visible and the invisible', one might argue that there are clear connections between the two thinkers. Significantly, Derrida does reinvoke phenomenology in *On Touching* (Derrida 2005), but the text is perhaps surprisingly strong in its criticisms of Merleau-Ponty, most especially.

This indicates what Derrida refers to as a 'distancing from French phenomenology of the flesh' (Derrida 2005: 184). This distancing takes place in both Derrida and Nancy's discourse, and Derrida is most intent here on distinguishing between Nancy's discourse and that of phenomeonology, most particularly that of Merleau-Ponty who superficially could be seen to have a lot in common with Nancy. Significantly, Derrida cites Husserl here as an authority in criticism of Merleau-Ponty, insofar as Merleau-Ponty in speaking so much of the other and the 'mit-sein', runs the risk of reducing the other and especially the other's body. Whereas Husserl, according to Derrida, had more precautions set up to prevent this taking place (Derrida 2005: 200ff.). Nonetheless, in the final analysis, Derrida 'still recognises that Merleau-Ponty has made a radical displacement', 'at once both infinitesimal and radical' ['un déplacement à la fois infime et radical'] (Derrida 2000: 230, 2005: 203). One of the difficulties with the phenomenological approach to the body, however, as Derrida clarifies here from a deconstructive perspective, is that it reaches a certain 'anthropological limit of phenomenology' ['d'un coup au-delà des limites anthropologique'] (Derrida 2000: 249, 2005: 220). This brings us back to the 'The Ends of Man' (Derrida 1982d) essay. Phenomenology would still be too humanistic. For Derrida, at least, Jean-Luc Nancy takes us beyond this anthropological limit. There is an interesting connection here between what Derrida affirms in this context of *On Touching* (Derrida 2005) and what he says about Nancy in '"Eating Well" or the Calculation of the Subject' (Derrida 1995b). There, he had sought to redraw the boundaries of the subject in relation to Heidegger's *Dasein* and the Cartesian *Cogito*. Here, he foregrounds a different but related problematic of 'plasticity and technicity' ['en compte de la plasticité et de la technicité'] (Derrida 2000: 249, 2005: 220).

Derrida seems to be arguing against the notion that one can draw the boundaries of touch at the organic limits of bodies. Rather we now have to consider a whole new dimension of 'touch' and 'sense', which has evolved from 'the intertwining of techne and the body [verflectung]' (Derrida 2005: 237). The term 'verflectung' is a Merleau-Pontyian term from the *Visible and the Invisible* (originally Husserlian,) but here Derrida is using it precisely and explicitly to extend beyond the limits of what he sees as an anthropological boundary in phenomenology. We should also note that this 'intertwining' ('verflectung') looks back to Derrida's discussion of the 'between' ('l'entre') in *Dissemination* [Derrida 1972h] (the French here is '*l'entre*lacement'). 'L'écriture du corps', the writing of the body, would also be a kind of 'l'entrelacement', of intertwining. If we are going to talk of 'intertwining' with Jean-Luc Nancy we need to engage the philosophical significance of the virtual, or techne, of plasticity and technicity, of 'machine-bodies' ('ce corps-machine', Derrida 2000: 266, 2005: 237). This also connects us to the discourse and the art of Deena Des Rioux, whose 'Robot Fashionista' work exemplifies this problematic perfectly.[1]

Nancy's discourse, according to Derrida, seems attuned to this new 'virtual' realm in a way which other discourses are not. One might have thought that Deleuze's engagement with the virtual would have Derrida's approval here but Derrida remains critical of Deleuze for what he regards as a rather naïve

---

1   Deena Des Rioux.

philosophical dimension. Nancy, on the other hand, is affirmed as a more nuanced thinker, who develops, through this emphasis on the virtual, a concept of 'self-incompatibility' ['l'incompatible avec soi-même'] (Derrida 2000: 335, 2005: 299). This relates back to Derrida's discussion with Nancy in the '"Eating Well", or the Calculation of the Subject' (Derrida 1995b) interview but now it also has a stronger emphasis on the virtual element (there are approximately six years separating these Derrida-Nancy encounters). Derrida speaks of 'amorous bodies, wrestling in the sheets of the internet's webs' ['corps amoureux dans les draps du Web'] (Derrida 2000: 338, 2005: 301) and the whole image of virtual sexuality (or what Luciana Parisi has called 'abstract sex' [Parisi 2004]) looms large. This revolutionises what we mean by touching, beyond an anthropological limit: 'the sense of touch is the sense of the electronic age' ['le sense de l'âge électronique'] (Derrida 2000: 227, 2005: 354). This is 'distance touching' ['toucher à distance érogène'] (Derrida 2000: 338, 2005: 301).

Derrida additionally refers to the fact that Nancy has had a heart transplant operation. Nancy doesn't know who his heart belongs to but we also of course have the sense here of the way in which the body's integrity is both extended and compromised by modern medical and entertainment technologies. With regard to sexual difference, this could be a woman's heart which Nancy now has, involving the 'transplantation of another sex' (Derrida 2005: 306). Here, we reach the 'limit of sense' ['la limite du sens'] (Derrida 2000: 396, 2005: 308). Referring back to Artaud's 'nerve scales', his whole discourse of the 'body without organs', Derrida clarifies that such a discourse (at least in Nancy) 'does not belong to an immediacy' (Derrida 2000: 396, 2005: 308). This separates it out from Hegelianism, and brings it close to Bataille and Nietzsche. Had Derrida not already employed Nietzsche to speak about the 'distance' of the artist-philosopher in *Spurs* (Derrida 1979)?

Our senses would now become 'spaced out' into an 'areality': 'sight becomes distended' ['la vue elle-même s'y distend'] (Derrida 2000: 347), and this would be something to affirm for Derrida: 'the oui that jouit' ['le oui qui jouit'] (Derrida 2000: 347). This is a reference to the 'yes that plays' in Cixous' discourse (Cixous 1994: xviii) and it would all come back to the deconstructed I: 'as in je/jeu' (Cixous 1994: xviii). This is the 'I' that plays or the self which is also a 'game', or 'in the game', 'en jeu', in Artaud's sense of 'on stage'. One can see here how Derrida's emphasis links the problematic of sexual difference to playfulness but also a politics. There would be a 'betting' involved here or a need for betting. 'I think of Nancy as a thinker of the bet and a player' (Derrida 2005: 309). Derrida admits however that this is not obvious in the explicit discourse of Nancy. This 'would not be Nancy's thing' Derrida says (it would be more Bataille's) and if there is a difference between Derrida and Nancy, it would be located here in 'a Christian style' ['le style de Christianisme'] (Derrida 2000: 347, 2005: 309) which is more Nancy's than Derrida's. In Nancy's obituary for Derrida in *Le Monde*, Nancy spoke of a 'salutation renouncing salvation' (Nancy 2005 in Derrida 2005: 310). Could this also be what Derrida is getting at here, an idea he has come back to, particularly in his later work on negative theology (Derrida 1997f) but which is insistent from the early work onwards: deconstruction is atheological (yet another Bataillean resonance from the latter's projected but never completed *La Somme Athéologique*)? Nancy goes on: '*salut* to the vision that did not cling to forms or ideas, but let itself be touched by forces' (Nancy 2005 in Derrida 2005: 310). Here, again, we see how central the whole *avant-garde* project of Artaudian 'force before form' has been for Derrida, as recognised by Nancy. And there would be a 'touching' here, and a being-touched, but beyond anthropology and with a certain post-modern virtuality. This would not lead to any greater sense but to a 'clarity that only obscurity possesses…the manifest secret of life and death' (Nancy 2005: 310). Like Bataille, Nancy would be recognising, through Derrida, the ultimate aporia of life and death, the gaping chasms between desire and fulfilment. And yet also this would be a joyous recognition of fundamental aporia, 'the oui that jouit' as in 'je/jeu' (Cixous 1994: xviii). This joyous (and somewhat raucous) element in deconstruction also reminds one of Foucault. There is, it seems to me, a strong affinity in the spirit of their work, if not always in the exact letter. Significantly, in his 'A Preface to Transgression' essay on Bataille (Foucault 1998), Foucault also returns in conclusion to the thematics of touch. Again, it is a matter of transgression, of a transgressive act, and here Foucault is referring to Bataille's infamous novel *L'Histoire de L'Oeil*: 'the act that crosses the limit *touches* absence itself' (Foucault 1998: 86, my emphasis). It has been the journey of this book to explore how Derrida has developed and extended this legacy of touch in such innovative and insightful ways, precisely through a radically singular and uncompromising 'l'écriture du corps' or 'writing of the body'.

Bibliography

I. Derrida – Primary Sources in French

Derrida, J. 1962. Introduction à *L'Origine de la géométrie* par Edmund Husserl. Paris, Presses Universitaires de France.

Derrida, J. 1967a. *De la Grammatologie*. Paris, Éditions de Minuit.

Derrida, J. 1967b. *La Voix et le Phénomène*. Paris, Presses Universitaires de France.

Derrida, J. 1967c. *L'Écriture et la Différence*. Paris, Éditions du Seuil.

Derrida, J. 1967d. 'Force et Signification', in *L'Écriture et la Difference*. Paris, Éditions du Seuil, 9–49.

Derrida, J. 1967e. 'Edmond Jabès et la question du livre', in *L'Écriture et la Difference*. Paris, Éditions du Seuil, 99–116.

Derrida, J. 1967f. 'Violence et Métaphysique: Essai Sur La Pensée D'Emmanuel Levinas', in *L'Écriture et la Difference*. Paris, Éditions du Seuil, 117–228.

Derrida, J. 1967g. 'Genèse et Structure et la Phénoménologie', in *L'Écriture et la Difference*. Paris, Éditions du Seuil, 229–51.

Derrida, J. 1967h. 'La Parole Soufflée', in *L'Écriture et la Difference*. Paris, Éditions du Seuil, 253–92.

Derrida, J. 1967i. 'Freud et La Scène de L'Écriture', in *L'Écriture et la Difference*. Paris, Éditions du Seuil, 293–340.

Derrida, J. 1967j. 'Le Théatre de la Cruauté et La Clôture de la Représentation', in *L'Écriture et la Difference*. Paris, Éditions du Seuil, 341–68.

Derrida, J. 1967k. 'De L'Économie Restreinte À L'Économie Générale: Un Hegelianisme Sans Réserve', in *L'Écriture et la Difference*. Paris, Éditions du Seuil, 369–407.

Derrida, J. 1967l. 'La Structure, Le Signe et Le Jeu Dans Le Discours Des Sciences Humaines', in *L'Écriture et la Difference*. Paris, Éditions du Seuil, 409–28.

Derrida, J. 1967m. 'Ellipse', in *L'Écriture et la Difference*. Paris, Éditions du Seuil, 429–36.

Derrida, J. 1972a. *Positions*. Paris, Les Éditions de Minuit.

Derrida, J. 1972b. *Marges De La Philosophie.* Paris, Les Éditions de Minuit.

Derrida, J. 1972c. 'Tympan', in *Marges De La Philosophie.* Paris, Les Éditions de Minuit, i–xxv.

Derrida, J. 1972d. 'La Différance', in *Marges De La Philosophie.* Paris, Les Éditions de Minuit, 1–29.

Derrida, J. 1972e. 'Les Fins de l'Homme', in *Marges De La Philosophie.* Paris, Les Éditions de Minuit, 129–64.

Derrida, J. 1972f. 'La Mythologie Blanche: La Métaphore dans le Texte Philosophique', in *Marges De La Philosophie*. Paris, Les Éditions de Minuit, 247–324.

Derrida, J. 1972g. 'Qual Quelle: Les Sources de Valéry', in *Marges De La Philosophie*. Paris, Les Éditions de Minuit, 325–63.

Derrida, J. 1972h. *La Dissémination*. Paris, Éditions de Seuil.

Derrida, J. 1972i. 'Hors Livre: Préfaces', in *La Dissémination*. Paris, Éditions de Seuil, 9–67.

Derrida, J. 1972j. 'La Pharmacie de Platon', in *La Dissémination*. Paris, Éditions de Seuil, 71–197.

Derrida, J. 1972k. 'La Double Séance', in *La Dissémination*. Paris, Éditions de Seuil, 199–318.

Derrida, J. 1972l. 'La Dissémination', in *La Dissémination*. Paris, Éditions de Seuil, 319–407.

Derrida, J. 1974a. *Glas*. Paris, Éditions Galilée.

Derrida, J. 1979. *Éperons. Les Styles de Nietzsche/Spurs: Nietzsche's Styles*. Bilingual Edition French/English with English translation by Barbara Harlow. Chicago, Chicago University Press.

Derrida, J. 1986a. *Parages*. Paris, Editions Galilée.

Derrida, J. 1988. *Signéponge*. Paris, Éditions du Seuil.

Derrida, J. 1991a. *Donner le Temps*. Paris, Editions Galilée.

Derrida, J. 1992a. *Points de Suspension*. Paris, Éditions Galilée.

Derrida, J. 1992b. 'Choréographies', in *Points de Suspension*. Paris, Éditions Galilée, 89–109.

Derrida, J. 1997a. *Cosmopolites de Tous les Pays, Encore une Effort!* Paris, Éditions Galilée.

Derrida, J. 1997b. *Psyché: Inventions de l'autre*. Paris, Éditions Galilée.

Derrida, J. 1997c. 'En Ce Moment Même Dans Cet Ouvrage Me Voici', in *Psyché: Inventions de l'Autre*. Paris, Éditions Galilée.

Derrida, J. 1997d. 'Geschlecht: Différence Sexuelle, Différence Ontologique', in *Psyché: Inventions de l'Autre*. Paris, Éditions Galilée.

Derrida, J. 1997e. 'La Main de Heidegger' (Geschlecht II), in *Psyché: Inventions de l'Autre*. Paris, Éditions Galilée.

Derrida, J. 1997f. 'Comment Ne Pas Parler. Dénégations', in *Psyché: Inventions de l'Autre*. Paris, Éditions Galilée.

Derrida, J. 2000. *Le Toucher, Jean-Luc Nancy*. Paris, Éditions Galilée.

Derrida, J. 2002a. *Artaud le Mômo*. Paris, Galilée.

II. Derrida – Primary Sources in English Translation

Derrida, J. 1973. *Speech and Phenomena and Other Essays on Husserl's Theory of Signs*. Edited and translated with an introduction by David B. Allison. Evanston, Northwestern University Press.

Derrida, J. 1974b. *Of Grammatology*. Translated by Gayatri Chakavorty Spivak. Baltimore, John Hopkins University Press.

Derrida, J. 1978a. *Writing and Difference*. Translated by Alan Bass. Chicago, University of Chicago Press.

Derrida, J. 1978b. 'Force and Signification', in *Writing and Difference*. Chicago, University of Chicago Press, 3–30.

Derrida, J. 1978c. 'Edmond Jabès and the Question of the Book', in *Writing and Difference*. Chicago, University of Chicago Press, 64–78.

Derrida, J. 1978d. 'Violence and Metaphysics: An Essay on the Thought of Emmanuel Levinas', in *Writing and Difference*. Chicago, University of Chicago Press, 79–153.

Derrida, J. 1978e. '"Genesis and Structure" and Phenomenology', in *Writing and Difference*. Chicago, University of Chicago Press, 154–68.

Derrida, J. 1978f. 'La Parole Soufflée', in *Writing and Difference*. Chicago, University of Chicago Press, 169–95.

Derrida, J. 1978g. 'Freud and the Scene of Writing', in *Writing and Difference*. Chicago, University of Chicago Press, 196–231.

Derrida, J. 1978h. 'The Theatre of Cruelty and the Closure of Representation', in *Writing and Difference*. Chicago, University of Chicago Press, 232–50.

Derrida, J. 1978i. 'From Restricted to General Economy: A Hegelianism Without Reserve', in *Writing and Difference*. Chicago, University of Chicago Press, 251–77.

Derrida, J. 1978j. 'Structure, Sign and Play in the Discourse of the Human Sciences', in *Writing and Difference*. Chicago, University of Chicago Press, 278–93.

Derrida, J. 1978k. 'Ellipsis', in *Writing and Difference*. Chicago, University of Chicago Press, 294–300.

Derrida, J. 1979. *Éperons: Les Styles de Nietzsche/Spurs: Nietzsche's Styles*. Bilingual Edition French/English with English translation by Barbara Harlow. Chicago. Chicago University Press.

Derrida, J. 1981a. *Dissemination*. Translated with an introduction by Barbara Johnson. Chicago, University of Chicago Press.

Derrida, J. 1981b. 'Outwork, prefacing', in *Dissemination*. Translated with an introduction by Barbara Johnson. Chicago, University of Chicago Press, 3–59.

Derrida, J. 1981c. 'Plato's Pharmacy', in *Dissemination*. Translated with an introduction by Barbara Johnson. Chicago, University of Chicago Press, 61–172.

Derrida, J. 1981d. 'The Double Session', in *Dissemination*. Translated with an introduction by Barbara Johnson. Chicago, University of Chicago Press, 173–286.

Derrida, J. 1981e. 'Dissemination', in *Dissemination*. Translated with an introduction by Barbara Johnson. Chicago, University of Chicago Press, 287–366.

Derrida, J. 1981f. *Positions*. Translated by Alan Bass. Chicago, University of Chicago Press.

Derrida, J. 1982a. *Margins of Philosophy*. Translated by Alan Bass. Chicago, University of Chicago Press.

Derrida, J. 1982b. 'Tympan', in *Margins of Philosophy*. Chicago, University of Chicago Press, ix–xxix.

Derrida, J. 1982c. 'Différance', in *Margins of Philosophy*. Chicago, University of Chicago Press, 3–27.

Derrida, J. 1982d. 'The Ends of Man', in *Margins of Philosophy*. Chicago, University of Chicago Press, 109–36.

Derrida, J. 1982e. 'White Mythology: Metaphor in the Text of Philosophy', in *Margins of Philosophy*. Chicago, University of Chicago Press, 207–72.

Derrida, J. 1982f. 'Qual Quelle: Valéry's Sources', in *Margins of Philosophy*. Chicago, University of Chicago Press, 273–306.

Derrida, J. 1982g. 'Choreographies: An Interview with Jacques Derrida'. Edited and translated by Christie V. McDonald, *Diacritics*, vol. 12, no. 2, 66–76.

Derrida, J. 1986b. *Glas*. Translated by John P. Leavey Jr. and Richard Rand. Lincoln, University of Nebraska Press.

Derrida, J. 1986c. 'Interview', in R. Kearney, *Dialogues with Contemporary Continental Thinkers*. Manchester, Manchester University Press, 105–27.

Derrida, J. 1989. *Edmund Husserl's 'Origin of Geometry': An Introduction*. Translated with an Introduction by John P. Leavey Jr. Lincoln, University of Nebraska Press.

Derrida, J. 1991b. *A Derrida Reader: Between the Blinds*. Edited by Peggy Kamuf. Hemel Hempstead, Harvester Wheatsheaf.

Derrida, J. 1991c. 'Choreographies: An Interview with Jacques Derrida', in *A Derrida Reader: Between the Blinds*. Edited by Peggy Kamuf. Hemel Hempstead, Harvester Wheatsheaf.

Derrida, J. 1991d. 'Geschlecht: Sexual Difference, Ontological Difference', in *A Derrida Reader: Between the Blinds*. Edited by Peggy Kamuf. Hemel Hempstead, Harvester Wheatsheaf.

Derrida, J. 1992c. 'How to Avoid Speaking: Denials', in *Derrida and Negative Theology*. Edited by H. Coward and T. Foshay. New York, State University of New York Press, 73–143.

Derrida, J. 1992d. *Given Time*. Chicago, University of Chicago Press.

Derrida, J. 1992e. *Acts of Literature*. Edited by Derek Attridge. London, Routledge.

Derrida, J. 1994. 'Foreword', in Cixous, H. 1994. *The Hélène Cixous Reader*. Edited by Susan Sellars. London, Routledge, vii–xii.

Derrida, J. 1994a. 'At This Very Moment in This Work Here I Am', in *Re-Reading Levinas*. Translated by Ruben Berezdivin. Edited by Robert Bernasconi and Simon Critchley. London, Routledge, 11–51.

Derrida, J. 1995a. 'Between Brackets I', in *Points…Interviews, 1974–1994*. Edited by Elisabeth Weber. Stanford, Stanford University Press, 5–29.

Derrida, J. 1995b. '"Eating Well" or the Calculation of the Subject', in *Points… Interviews, 1974–1994*. Edited by Elisabeth Weber. Stanford. Stanford University Press, 255–88.

Derrida, J. 1998a. 'To Unsense the Subjectile', in Derrida, J. and Thévenin, P. 1998. *The Secret Art of Antonin Artaud*. Translated by Mary Ann Caws. Cambridge, MIT Press, 59–157.

Derrida, J. 1998b. *Right of Inspection*. Translated by David Wills (photographs by Marie-Francoise Plissart). London, Monacelli Press.

Derrida, J. 1999. *Circumfession*. Chicago, Chicago University Press.

Derrida, J. 2001a. (with Maurizio Ferraris) *A Taste for the Secret*. London, Polity.

Derrida, J. 2001b. *Cosmopolitanism and Forgiveness*. London, Routledge.

Derrida, J. 2001c. 'On Cosmopolitanism'. Translated by Mark Dooley. In J. Derrida, *Cosmopolitanism and Forgiveness*. London, Routledge, 1–24.

Derrida, J. 2001d. 'On Forgiveness'. Translated by Michael Hughes. In Derrida, J. *Cosmopolitanism and Forgiveness*. London, Routledge, 25–75.

Derrida, J. 2002. *Derrida* (film). New York, Drakes Avenue Pictures.

Derrida, J. 2005a. *On Touching – Jean-Luc Nancy*. Stanford, Stanford University Press.

Derrida, J. 2006a. 'Hostipitality', in *The Derrida-Habermas Reader*, ed. Lasse Thomassen. Edinburgh, Edinburgh University Press.

Derrida, J. 2006b. *H.C. for Life: That is to Say*. Stanford, Stanford University Press.

Derrida, J. and Thévenin, P. 1998. *The Secret Art of Antonin Artaud*. Translated by Mary Ann Caws. Cambridge, MIT Press.

III.   Selected Secondary Texts

Ades, D., Baker, S., Hancock, C. and Hollier, D. 2006. *Undercover Surrealism: Georges Bataille and Documents*. London. Hayward Gallery.

Agosti, S. 1979. 'Coup upon Coup: An Introduction to *Spurs*', in J. Derrida *Spurs: Nietzsche's Styles*. Chicago. Chicago University Press, 1–25.

Appiah, K.A. 1994. 'Identity, Authenticity, Survival: Multicultural Societies and Social Reproduction', in *Multiculturalism*. Edited by A. Gutmann. Princeton, Princeton University Press, 149–65.

Aristotle. 2004. *The Metaphysics*. London, Penguin.

Artaud, A. 1968a. *Collected Works: Volume One*. London, Calder.

Artaud, A. 1968b. 'Umbilical Limbo', in *Collected Works: Volume One*. London, Calder, 5–15.

Artaud, A. 1968c. 'Nerve Scales', in *Collected Works: Volume One*. London, Calder, 16–27.

Artaud, A. 1970. *The Theatre and its Double*. Translated by Victor Corti. London, Calder.

Ashbery, J. 1960. 'Antonin Artaud: Poet, Actor, Director, Playwright', in *John Ashbery: Selected Prose*. Edited by E. Richie. Manchester, Carcanet, 24–33.

Augustine. 1961. *Confessions*. Translated by R.S. Pine-Coffin. London, Penguin.

Augustine. 1972. *City of God*. Translated by Henry Bettenson. London, Penguin.

Auster, P. 1982. *The Random House Book of Twentieth-Century French Poetry*. Edited by Paul Auster. New York, Random House.

Badiou, A. 2001. *Ethics*. London, Verso.

Badiou, A. 2003. *Saint Paul: The Foundation of Universalism*. Translated by Ray Brassier. Stanford, Stanford University Press.

Barber, S. 2004. *Jean Genet*, with an introduction by Edmund White. London, Reaktion.

Barnes, J. 1990. *Early Greek Philosophy*. London, Penguin.

Barnes, J. 2005. *Early Greek Philosophy*. London, Penguin.

Bass, A. 1978. 'Translator's Introduction', in Derrida, J., *Writing and Difference*. Chicago, University of Chicago Press, ix–xiv.

Bataille, G. 1970–88. *Oeuvres Complètes*. Paris, Gallimard.

Bataille, G. 1985a. *Visions of Excess: Selected Writings 1927–1939*. Edited by Allan Stoekl. Minneapolis, University of Minnesota Press.

Bataille, G. 1985b. 'The "Old Mole" and the Prefix *Sur* in the Words *Surhomme* [Superman] and Surrealist', in *Visions of Excess: Selected Writings 1927–1939*. Edited by Allan Stoekl. Minneapolis, University of Minnesota Press, 32–45.

Bataille, G. 1985c. 'The Psychological Structure of Fascism', in *Visions of Excess: Selected Writings 1927–1939*. Edited by Allan Stoekl. Minneapolis, University of Minnesota Press, 137–61.

Bataille, G. 1986a. *My Mother/Madame Edwarda/The Dead Man*. Translated by Austryn Wainhouse. London, Marion Boyars.

Bataille, G. 1986b. *Blue of Noon*. New York, Marion Boyars.

Bataille, G. 1988. 'De l'existentialisme au primat de l'économie', in Vol. 11 of *Oeuvres Complètes 1970–88*. Paris, Gallimard, 515–26.

Bataille, G. 1988a. *Inner Experience*. Translated with an introduction by Leslie Anne Boldt. New York, University of New York Press.

Bataille, G. 1988b. *Guilty*. San Francisco, Lapis.

Bataille, G. 1988c. 'Letter to Blank, Instructor of a Class on Hegel', in *Guilty*. San Francisco, Lapis, 123–5.

Bataille, G. 1990. *Theory of Religion*. Translated by Robert Hurley. New York, Zone.

Bataille, G. 1991. *The Accursed Share*. Zone Books, New York

Bataille, G. 2001a. *Eroticism*. London, Penguin.

Bataille, G. 2001b. *The Unfinished System of Nonknowledge*. Edited with an introduction by Stuart Kendall. Minnesota, University of Minnesota Press.

Bataille, G. 2001c. *Story of the Eye*. Translated by Joachim Neugroschal. London. Penguin.

Bataille, G. 2004. *Divine Filth*. Translated by Mark Spitzer. London, Creation.

Baudelaire, C. 1998. *Complete Poems.* Translated by Walter Martin. Manchester, Carcanet.

Baudrillard, J. 1994. *Simulacra and Simulation.* Chicago, University of Michigan Press.

Baugh, B. 2005. *French Hegel: From Surrealism to Postmodernism.* London, Routledge.

Bersani, L. 1996. *Homos.* Harvard, Harvard University Press, 1996.

Birmingham, P. 1997. 'Toward an Ethic of Desire: Derrida, Fiction and the Law of the Feminine', in *Feminist Interpretations of Jacques Derrida.* Edited by N. Holland. Pennsylvania, Pennsylvania University Press, 125–46.

Blanchot, M. 1997. *Awaiting Oblivion.* Lincoln, University of Nebraska Press.

Blanchot, M. 2004. *Lautréamont and Sade.* Stanford, Stanford University Press

Blond, P. 1997. *Post-secular Philosophy: Between Philosophy and Theology.* London, Routledge.

Braidotti, R. 1991. *Patterns of Dissonance: Study of Women and Contemporary Philosophy.* London, Polity Press.

Brannigan, J., Wolfreys, J. and Robbins, R. (eds) 1999a. *The French Connections of Jacques Derrida.* New York, State University of New York Press.

Brannigan, J. 1999b. 'We have Nothing to Do with Literature: Derrida and Surrealist Writing', in *The French Connections of Jacques Derrida.* Edited by J. Brannigan et al. New York, State University of New York Press, 53–71.

Breillat, C. 2000. *Romance* (film). London, Blue Light.

Breillat, C. 2005. *Anatomy of Hell* (film). London, Tartan.

Breton, A. 1982. 'No Prosecution', in *The Random House Book of Twentieth-Century French Poetry: With Translations by American and British Poets.* Edited by Paul Auster. New York, Random House, 186–7.

Bruns, G. 2005. *Maurice Blanchot:The Refusal of Philosophy.* Baltimore, John Hopkins.

Buchanan, I. 2008. *Deleuze and Guattari's Anti-Oedipus.* London, Continuum.

Butler, J. 2003. *The Judith Butler Reader*. Oxford, Blackwell.

Caillois, R. 2001. *Man and the Sacred.* Chicago, University of Illinois Press.

Caputo, J.D. 1997a. 'Dreaming of the Innumerable: Derrida, Drucilla Cornell, and the Dance of Gender', in *Derrida and Feminism: Recasting the Question of Woman.* Edited by E.K. Feder, M.C. Rawlinson and E. Zakin. New York, Routledge, 141–61.

Caputo, J.D. 1997b. *The Prayers and Tears of Jacques Derrida: Religion without Religion.* Bloomington, Indiana University Press.

Caws, M.A. 1998. 'Preface: Derrida's Maddening Text: AR-TAU', in J. Derrida and P. Thévenin, *The Secret Art of Antonin Artaud.* Translated by Mary Ann Caws. Cambridge, MIT Press, xi–xiv.

Chanter,T. 1997. 'On Not Reading Derrida's Texts: Mistaking Hermeneutics, Misreading Sexual Difference, and Neutralising Narration' in *Derrida and Feminism: Recasting the Question of Woman.* Edited by E.K. Feder, M.C. Rawlinson and E. Zakin. New York, Routledge, 87–115.

Cioran, E.M. 1995. *Tears and Saints.* Translated by I.Z. Johnston. Chicago, University of Chicago Press.

Cixous, H. 1991. 'Interview', in V. Conley, V. *Hélène Cixous: Writing the Feminine.* Lincoln, University of Nebraska Press.

Cixous, H. 1994. *The Hélène Cixous Reader.* Edited by Susan Sellars. London, Routledge.

Cixous, H. 2005. *Portrait of Jacques Derrida as a Young Jewish Saint.* New York, Columbia University Press.

Cixous, H. 2007. *Insister of Jacques Derrida.* Edinburgh, Edinburgh University Press.

Conley, V. 1991. *Hélène Cixous: Writing the Feminine.* Lincoln, University of Nebraska Press.

Cornell, D. 1997. 'Where Love Begins: Sexual Difference and the Limits of the Masculine Symbolic', in *Derrida and Feminism: Recasting the Question of Woman.* Edited by E.K. Feder, M.C. Rawlinson and E. Zakin. New York, Routledge, 161–207.

Coxon, A.H. 1986. *The Fragments of Parmenides: A Critical Commentary and Translation.* Assen, Van Gorcum.

Critchley, S. 1999. *The Ethics of Deconstruction.* Edinburgh, Edinburgh University Press,

De Beauvoir, S. 1997. *The Second Sex.* London, Vintage.

Deleuze, G. 1986. *Nietzsche and Philosophy.* London, Methuen.

Deleuze, G. and Guattari, F. 2004. *Anti-Oedipus.* London, Continuum.

Des Rioux, D. 2006. *Robotic Erotica* (artworks). New York.

Despentes, V. and Trinh Thi, C. 2006. *Baise Moi* (film). Paris, Universal.

Dooley, M. 2001. *The Politics of Exodus*: *Søren Kierkegaard and the Ethics of Responsibility.* New York, Fordham University Press.

Dooley, M. and Kavanagh, M. 2008. *Derrida.* London, Acumen.

Downing, L. and Nobus, D. (eds) 2006. *Perversion: Psychoanalytic Perspectives, Perspectives on Psychoanalysis.* London, Karnac.

Drolet, M.(ed.). 2003. *The Postmodernism Reader.* London, Routledge.

Dudley, D. and Griffin, M. 1998. *History of Cynicism.* Bristol, Classical Press.

Edelman, L. 2004. *No Future: Queer Theory and the Death Drive.* Durham, Duke University Press.

Eshleman, C. and Bador, B. (eds) 1995. *Antonin Artaud Watchfiends and Rack Screams: Works From The Final Period.* Boston, Exact Change.

Feder, E.K. and Zakin, E. 1997. 'Flirting with the Truth: Derrida's Discourse with "Woman" and Wenches', in *Derrida and Feminism: Recasting the Question of Woman.* Edited by E.K. Feder, M.C. Rawlinson and E. Zakin. New York, Routledge, 21–53.

Feder, E.K., Rawlinson, M.C. and Zakin, E. (eds) 1997a. *Derrida and Feminism: Recasting the Question of Woman.* New York, Routledge.

Feder, E.K., Rawlinson, M.C. and Zakin, E. (eds) 1997b. 'Introduction', in *Derrida and Feminism: Recasting the Question of Woman*. Edited by E.K. Feder, M.C. Rawlinson and E. Zakin. New York, Routledge, 1–7.

Ferrari, G.R.F. 1983. *Listening to the Cicadas: A Study of Plato's Phaedrus*. Cambridge, Cambridge University Press.

Ferrari, G.R.F. 1992. 'Platonic Love', in *The Cambridge Companion to Plato*. Edited by Richard Kraut. Cambridge, Cambridge University Press.

Fink, E. 2003. *Nietzsche's Philosophy*. London, Continuum.

Foucault, M. 1997. *The History of Sexuality: The Will to Knowledge v. 1*. London, Penguin.

Foucault, M. 1998. 'A Preface to Transgression', in *Aesthetics – Essential Works of Foucault 1954–1984 Volume 2*. Edited by James D. Faubion. London, Penguin, 69–89.

Foucault, M. 1999. *Religion and Culture*. Selected and Edited by Jeremy R. Carrette. Manchester, Manchester University Press.

Foucault, M. 2004. 'Foreword', to Deleuze G. and Guattari, F. 2004. *Anti-Oedipus*. London, Continuum, xi–xll.

Freud, S. 2009. *Group Psychology and the Analysis of the Ego*. London, Books LLC.

Frutiger, P. 1930. *Les Mythes de Platon*. Paris, Alcon.

Gallop, J. 1981. *Intersections: A Reading of Sade with Bataille, Blanchot and Klossowski*. Lincoln, University of Nebraska Press.

Gallop, J. 1997. '"Women" in *Spurs* and Nineties Feminism', in *Derrida and Feminism: Recasting the Question of Woman*. Edited by E.K. Feder, M.C. Rawlinson and E. Zakin. New York, Routledge, 7–21.

Giffney, N. and O'Rourke, M. (eds) 2009. *The Ashgate Research Companion to Queer Theory*. Farnham, Ashgate.

Girard, R. 2004. *Oedipus Unbound: Selected Writings on Rivalry and Desire*. Stanford, Stanford University Press.

Goldman, E. 1924 (1977). 'The Failure of the Russian Revolution', in *The Anarchist Reader*. Edited by G. Woodcock. Glasgow, Fontana, 155–161.

Grosz, E. 1989. *Sexual Subversions: Three French Feminists*. London, Allen and Unwin.

Grosz, E. 1995. *Space, Time and Perversion: Essays on the Politics of Bodies*. New York, Routledge.

Grosz, E. 1997. 'Ontology and Equivocation: Derrida's Politics of Sexual Difference', in *Feminist Interpretations of Jacques Derrida*. Edited by N. Holland. Pennsylvania, Pennsylvania University Press, 88–109.

Guthrie, W.K.C. 1956. *The Protagoras and the Meno*. London, Penguin.

Guthrie, W.K.C. 1967. *The Greek Philosophers: From Thales to Aristotle*. New York, Methuen.

Guyotat, P. 1995. *Eden Eden Eden*. Translated by Graham Fox. London, Creation Books.

Guyotat, P. 2003. *Tomb for 500,000 Soldiers.* Translated by Romain Slocombe. London, Creation Books.

Habermas, J. 1990. *The Philosophical Discourse of Modernity.* London, Polity.

Habermas, J. 2006. 'Religious Tolerance: The Pacemaker for Cultural Rights', in *The Derrida-Habermas Reader.* Edited by L. Thomassen. Edinburgh, Edinburgh University Press, 195–208.

Hackforth, R. 1952. *Plato's Phaedrus.* Cambridge, Cambridge University Press.

Halberstam, J. and Livingston, I. (eds) 1995. *Posthuman Bodies.* Bloomington, Indiana University Press.

Halberstam, J., Eng, D.L. and Munoz, J.E. 2005. *What's Queer about Queer Studies Now? Social Text* Special Issue Fall/Winter 2005.

Hall, S. 1996. 'Cultural Studies and its Theoretical Legacies', in *Stuart Hall: Critical Dialogues in Cultural Studies.* Edited by David Morley and Kuan-Hsing Chen. London, Routledge, 262–276.

Hegel, G.W.F. 1979. *Phenomenology of Spirit.* Translated by A.V. Miller. Oxford, Oxford University Press.

Heidegger, M. 1978. *Being and Time.* Oxford, Blackwell.

Heidegger, M. 1991. *Nietzsche: The Will to Power as Art v. 1.* Translated by David Farrell Krell. New York, Harper Collins.

Holland, N. (ed.) 1997. *Feminist Interpretations of Jacques Derrida.* Pennsylvania, Pennsylvania University Press.

Hollier, D. 1997. *Absent Without Leave: French Literature Under the Threat of War.* Translated by Catherine Porter. Harvard, Harvard University Press.

Honoré, C. 2005. *Ma Mère* (film). London, Revolver.

Irigaray, L. 1985. *Speculum of the Other Woman.* New York, Cornell University Press.

Irigaray, L. 1985. *This Sex Which is Not One.* Translated by Catherine Porter. New York, Cornell University Press.

Irwin, J. 1998. 'Reviving an Ancient-Modern Quarrel: A Critique of Derrida's Reading of Plato and Platonism', unpublished PhD thesis, University of Warwick, supervisors Martin Warner and Cyril Barrett.

Irwin, J. 2003a. 'On Prohibition and Transgression: Georges Bataille and the Possibility of Affirming Evil', in *This Thing of Darkness: Perspectives on Evil.* Edited by Margaret Sönser Breen and Richard Hamilton. London/Amsterdam, Rodopi, 131–47.

Irwin, J. 2003b. 'Deconstructing God: Defending Derrida Against Radical Orthodoxy', in *Explorations in Contemporary Continental Philosophy of Religion.* Edited by Patrick Maxwell and Peter Deane-Baker. Amsterdam/New York, Rodopi, 55–76.

Irwin, J. 2004. 'The Problem Not The Theorem of War: On Pasolini's Salò', in *War and Virtual War: The Challenges to Communities.* Edited by Jones Irwin, Amsterdam, Rodopi.

Irwin, J. 2010a (in press). 'Diogenes, St. Paul, Habermas and Beyond – Derrida on Cosmopolitanism', in *Interculturalism – Between Culture and Politics*. Edited by J. Irwin and N. Billias. Amsterdam, Rodopi.

Irwin, J. 2010b (in press). 'Philosophy as a "Theatre of Cruelty" – Making Derrida Perform Through Artaud', in *Ethical Encounters: Boundaries of Theatre, Performance and Philosophy*. Edited by D. Watt and D. Meyer-Dinkgrafe. Amsterdam, Rodopi.

Irwin, J. 2010c (in press). 'A Well-Being Out of Nihilism? On The Affinities Between Nietzsche and Anarchist Thought', in *Anarchism and Moral Philosophy*. Edited by Benjamin Frank. London, Palgrave.

Johnson, B. 1981. 'Translator's Introduction' in *Dissemination*. Chicago, University of Chicago Press.

Kamuf, P. 1991. 'Preface', in *A Derrida Reader: Between the Blinds*. Edited by Peggy Kamuf. Hemel Hempstead, Harvester Wheatsheaf, vii–xii.

Kamuf, P. 1997. 'Deconstruction and Feminism: A Repetition', in *Feminist Interpretations of Jacques Derrida*. Edited by N. Holland. Pennsylvania, Pennsylvania University Press, 143–56.

Kant, I. 1972. *Perpetual Peace: A Philosophical Essay*. New York, Garland.

Kearney, R. 1986. *Modern Movements in European Philosophy*. Manchester, Manchester University Press.

Kearney, R. 1988. *The Wake of the Imagination*. London, Routledge.

Kerr, F. 1998. 'Reviews: *Word Made Strange; The Liturgical Consummation of Philosophy; Post-Secular Philosophy*'. *New Blackfriars* 79, 351–356.

Klossowski, P. 1989. *Roberte Ce Soir/Revocation of Nantes*, translated by Austryn Wainhouse. London, Marion Boyars.

Klossowski, P. 1991. *Sade, My Neighbour.* Translated by Alphonso Lingis. Chicago, Northwestern University Press.

Klossowski, P. 1997. *Nietzsche and the Vicious Circle.* Translated by Daniel W. Smith. London, Athlone.

Klossowski, P. 1998. *The Baphomet.* Translated by Sophie Hawkins and Stephen Sartarelli. New York, Marsilio.

Kojève, A. 1980. *Introduction to the Reading of Hegel: Lectures on the Phenomenology of Spirit.* New York, Cornell University Press.

Kristeva, J. 1984. *Powers of Horror: An Essay on Abjection.* New York, Columbia University Press.

Lautréamont, Comte de 1978. *Maldoror and Poems*. London, Penguin.

Lawlor, L. 2002. *Derrida and Husserl: The Basic Problem of Phenomenology*. Bloomington, Indiana University Press.

Levinas, E. 1981. *Otherwise Than Being or Beyond Essence.* Translated by Alphonso Lingis. The Hague, Nijhoff.

Lingis, A. 1985. *Libido: The French Existential Theories*. Bloomington, Indiana University Press.

Lyotard, J.F. 2004. *Libidinal Economy*. London, Continuum.

Macksey, R. 2007. *The Structuralist Controversy: The Languages of Criticism and the Sciences of Man*. Baltimore, John Hopkins University Press.

Mallarmé, S. 2008. *Collected Poems and Other Verse*. Oxford, Oxford University Press.

Marion, J.-L. 1998. *Reduction and Givenness: Investigations of Husserl, Heidegger and Phenomenology*. Translated by Thomas Carlson. Evanston, Northwestern University Press.

McCabe, C. 2001. 'Introduction', to G. Bataille, *Eroticism*. London, Penguin, i–viii.

McCombie, E. 2008. 'Introduction', to S. Mallarmé, *Collected Poems and Other Verse*. Oxford, Oxford University Press, ii–viii.

Merleau-Ponty, M. 2002. *Phenomenology of Perception*. London, Routledge.

Michelfielder, D. and Palmer, R. 1989. *Dialogue and Deconstruction: Gadamer-Derrida Encounter*. New York, State University of New York Press.

Millar, M.H. 1986. *Plato's Parmenides: The Conversion of the Soul*. Princeton, Princeton University Press.

Mishima, Y. 1986. 'Georges Bataille and Divinus Deus', in *My Mother/Madame Edwarda/The Dead Man*. G. Bataille. Translated by Austryn Wainhouse. London, Marion Boyars, 11–21.

Mundy, J. (ed.) 2006. *Surrealism Unbound*. London, Tate.

Murphy, K., Ruiz, J. and Serlin, D. (eds) 2008. *Queer Futures: The Homonormativity Issue. Radical History Review*. Winter 2008.

Nancy, J.-L. 2005. 'Salut to You, Salut to the Blind We Become', in Derrida, J. *On Touching – Jean Luc Nancy*. Stanford, Stanford University Press, 313–17.

Nietzsche, F. 1967a. *On the Genealogy of Morals*. Translated by Walter Kaufmann and R.J. Hollingdale. London, Vintage.

Nietzsche, F. 1967b. *The Birth of Tragedy*. Translated by Walter Kaufmann. London, Random House.

Nietzsche, F. 1979. *Ecce Homo*. Translated by R.J. Hollingdale. London, Penguin.

Nietzsche, F. 1986. *Human All Too Human*. Translated by R.J. Hollingdale. Cambridge, Cambridge University Press.

Nietzsche, F. 1987. *Thus Spake Zarathustra*. London, Penguin

Nietzsche, F. 1990. *Beyond Good and Evil*. Translated by R.J. Hollingdale. London, Penguin.

Nietzsche, F. 1990a. *Philosophy and Truth: Selections from Nietzsche's Notebooks of the Early 1870s*. Edited by Daniel Breazeale. New York, Humanities Paperback Library.

Nietzsche, F. 1990b. 'The Last Philosopher. The Philosopher. Reflections on the Struggle between Art and Knowledge', in F. Nietzsche, *Philosophy and Truth: Selections from Nietzsche's Notebooks of the Early 1870s*. Edited by Daniel Breazeale. New York, Humanities Paperback Library, 3–61.

Nietzsche, F. 1990c. 'The Philosopher as Cultural Physician', in F. Nietzsche, *Philosophy and Truth: Selections from Nietzsche's Notebooks of the Early*

1870s. Edited by Daniel Breazeale. New York, Humanities Paperback Library, 69–79.

Nietzsche, F. 1997. *Untimely Meditations*. Translated by R.J. Hollingdale. Cambridge, Cambridge University Press.

Norris, C. 1987. *Derrida*. London, Fontana.

Nyong'o, T. 2005. 'Punk'd Theory', in *What's Queer about Queer Studies Now?* Edited by J. Halberstam et al. *Social Text* Special Issue Fall/Winter 2005, 113–127.

Oliver, K. 1997. 'The Maternal Operation: Circumscribing the Alliance', in *Derrida and Feminism: Recasting the Question of Woman*. Edited by E.K. Feder, M.C. Rawlinson and E. Zakin. New York, Routledge, 53–69.

Parisi, L. 2004. *Abstract Sex*. London, Continuum.

Pasolini, P.P. 2007. *Salò* (film). London, British Film Institute.

Pickstock, C. 1998. *After Writing: On The Liturgical Consummation of Philosophy*. Oxford, Blackwell.

Plato. 1900-1907. *Platonis Opera*. Edited by J. Burnet. 5 Volumes. Oxford, Clarendon Press.

Plato. 1953. *The Dialogues of Plato*. Edited by B. Jowett. Oxford, Clarendon Press.

Plato. 1961. *The Collected Dialogues of Plato*. Edited by E. Hamilton and H. Cairns. New York, Pantheon.

Raeder, H. 1905. *Platons Philosophische Entwickelung*. Leipzig, B.G. Teubner.

Rapaport, H. 2002. *Later Derrida: Reading the Recent Work*. London, Routledge.

Rawlinson, M.C. 1997. 'Levers, Signatures and Secrets: Derrida's Use of Woman', in *Derrida and Feminism: Recasting the Question of Woman*. Edited by E.K. Feder, M.C. Rawlinson and E. Zakin. New York, Routledge, 69–87.

Rayment-Pickard, H. 2003. *Impossible God: Derrida's Theology*. Aldershot, Ashgate.

Reed, J. 2005. *Jean Genet: Born to Lose*. London, Creation.

Richardson, M. 2006. 'Introduction', to G. Bataille, *Absence of Myth: Writings on Surrealism*. London, Verso, 1–28.

Rimbaud, A. 1962. *Collected Poems*. London, Penguin.

Robbins, R. and Wolfreys, J. 1999. 'In the Wake of ...: Baudelaire, Valéry, Derrida', in *The French Connections of Jacques Derrida*. Edited by J. Brannigan et al. New York, State University of New York Press, 23–53.

Robin, L. 1964. *La Theorie Platonicienne de l'Amour*. Paris, Presses Universitaires de France.

Rowe, S. 1986. *Phaedrus,* with translation and commentary. Warminster, Aris and Philips.

Rubin, A. 1984. *André Masson*. New York, Centre for Contemporary Arts.

Ruiz, J. 2008. 'The Violence of Assimilation: An Interview with Matthilda aka Matt Bernstein Sycamore', in *Queer Futures: The Homonormativity Issue*. Edited by K. Murphy et al. *Radical History Review* Winter 2008, 237–49.

Salih, S. 2003. 'Introduction', to *The Judith Butler Reader*. Oxford, Blackwell, 1–15.

Sartre, J.P. 1947. *Situations I*. Paris, Gallimard.

Sartre, J.P. 1980. *Existentialism and Humanism*. London, Methuen.

Sayre, K. 1983. *Plato's Late Ontology*. Princeton, Princeton University Press.

Scheer, E. 2000. *100 Years of Cruelty: Essays on Artaud*. Sydney, Power Institute.

Scheer, E. 2004. *Antonin Artaud: A Critical Reader*. London, Routledge.

Self, W. 2006. 'Introduction', to G. Bataille, *Blue of Noon*. London, Penguin, vii–xiv.

Soble, A. (ed.) 2002. *The Philosophy of Sex: Contemporary Readings*. Oxford, Rowman and Littlefield.

Sontag, S. 1994. 'Marat/Sade/Artaud', in *Against Interpretation*. London, Vintage.

Sontag, S. 2001. 'The Pornographic Imagination', in *Story of the Eye*. G. Bataille. Translated by Joachim Neugroschal. London. Penguin, 95–110.

Spivak, G.C. 1974. 'Translator's Preface', in J. Derrida, *Of Grammatology*. Baltimore, John Hopkins University Press, 1–55.

Spivak, G.C. 1997. 'Displacement and the Discourse of Woman', in *Feminist Interpretations of Jacques Derrida*. Edited by N. Holland. Pennsylvania, Pennsylvania University Press, 40–65.

Sullivan, N. 2003. *A Critical Introduction to Queer Theory*. New York, New York University Press.

Surya, M. 2002. *Georges Bataille: An Intellectual Biography*. London, Verso.

Taylor, C. 1994. 'The Politics of Recognition', in *Multiculturalism: A Critical Reader*. Edited by D. Goldberg. London, Blackwell, 75–107.

Taylor, C. 2007. *A Secular Age*. Harvard, Harvard University Press.

Temple, M. 1999. 'Mallarmé, par Jacques Derrida', in *The French Connections of Jacques Derrida*. Edited by J. Brannigan et al. New York, State University of New York Press, 1–23.

Thévenin, P. 1998. 'The Search for a Lost World', in J. Derrida and P. Thévenin, *The Secret Art of Antonin Artaud*. Translated by Mary Ann Caws. Cambridge, MIT Press, 1–59.

Thomas, C. 1998. *Male Matters: Masculinity, Anxiety and the Male Body on the Line*. Chicago, University of Illinois Press.

Thomassen, L. (ed.) 2006. *The Derrida-Habermas Reader*. Edinburgh, Edinburgh University Press.

Trebitsch, M. 1991. 'Preface', to Lefebvre, H., *Critique of Everyday Life*, Volume 1. London, Verso, vii–xxviii.

Trilling, L. 1955. *The Opposing Self: Nine Essays in Criticism*. New York, Viking Press.

Tufail, B. 1999. 'Oupilian Grammatology: La règle du jeu', in *The French Connections of Jacques Derrida*. Edited by J. Brannigan et al. New York, State University of New York Press, 119–35.

Voegelin, E. 1982. *Order and History*. London, Methuen.

Whitford, M. 1991. 'Introduction', to *Irigaray Reader*. Oxford, Blackwell, 1–15.

Woodcock, G. 1977. 'Anarchism: A Historical Introduction', in *The Anarchist Reader*. Edited by G. Woodcock, Glasgow, Fontana, 11–57.

Zeller, E. 1980. *Outlines of the History of Greek Philosophy*. New York, Dover.

Ziarek, E.W. 1997. 'From Euthanasia to the Other of Reason: Performativity and the Deconstruction of Sexual Difference', in *Derrida and Feminism: Recasting the Question of Woman*. Edited by E.K. Feder, M.C. Rawlinson and E. Zakin. New York, Routledge, 115–41.

Žižek, S. (ed.) 1994. *Mapping Ideology*. London, Verso.

Žižek, S. 1994a. 'Introduction: The Spectre of Ideology', in *Mapping Ideology*. London, Verso, 5–31.

Žižek, S. 1997. *The Plague of Fantasies*. London, Verso.

Žižek, S. 2006. *Lacan*. London, Granta.

Index